Shakespeare's Folly

This study contends that folly is of fundamental importance to the implicit philosophical vision of Shakespeare's drama. The discourse of folly's word-play, jubilant ironies, and vertiginous paradoxes furnish Shakespeare with a way of understanding that lays bare the hypocrisies and absurdities of the serious world. Like Erasmus, More, and Montaigne before him, Shakespeare employs folly as a mode of understanding that does not arrogantly insist upon the veracity of its own claims – a fool's truth, after all, is spoken by a fool. Yet, as this study demonstrates, Shakespearean folly is not the sole preserve of professional jesters and garrulous clowns, for it is also apparent on a thematic, conceptual, and formal level in virtually all of his plays. Examining canonical histories, comedies, and tragedies, this study is the first to either contextualise Shakespearean folly within European humanist thought or to argue that Shakespeare's philosophy of folly is part of a strand of Western philosophy, which itself reflects upon the folly of the wise. This strand runs from the philosopher-fool Socrates through to Montaigne and on to Nietzsche, but finds its most sustained expression in the Critical Theory of the mid to late twentieth-century, when the self-destructive potential latent in rationality became an historical reality. This book makes a substantial contribution to the fields of Shakespeare, Renaissance humanism, Critical Theory, and Literature and Philosophy. It illustrates, moreover, how rediscovering the philosophical potential of folly may enable us to resist the growing dominance of instrumental thought in the cultural sphere.

Sam Gilchrist Hall is a teacher of English at the British Council, Hungary, and a Visiting Instructor at the Department of British Studies, University of Debrecen.

Routledge Studies in Shakespeare

For a full list of titles in this series, please visit www.routledge.com.

7 **Retheorizing Shakespeare through Presentist Readings**
James O'Rourke

8 **Memory in Shakespeare's Histories**
Stages of Forgetting in Early Modern England
Jonathan Baldo

9 **Reading Shakespeare through Philosophy**
Peter Kishore Saval

10 **Embodied Cognition and Shakespeare's Theatre**
The Early Modern Body-Mind
Edited by Laurie Johnson, John Sutton, and Evelyn Tribble

11 **Mary Wroth and Shakespeare**
Edited by Paul Salzman and Marion Wynne-Davies

12 **Disability, Health, and Happiness in the Shakespearean Body**
Edited by Sujata Iyengar

13 **Skepticism and Belonging in Shakespeare's Comedy**
Derek Gottlieb

14 **Shakespeare, *Romeo* and *Juliet*, and Civic Life**
The Boundaries of Civic Space
Edited by Silvia Bigliazzi and Lisanna Calvi

15 **Shakespeare in Hate**
Emotions, Passions, Selfhood
Peter Kishore Saval

16 **Shakespeare and Hospitality**
Ethics, Politics, and Exchange
Edited by David B. Goldstein and Julia Reinhard Lupton

17 **Shakespeare, Cinema, Counter-Culture**
Appropriation and Inversion
Ailsa Grant Ferguson

18 **Shakespeare's Folly**
Philosophy, Humanism, Critical Theory
Sam Gilchrist Hall

Shakespeare's Folly

Philosophy, Humanism, Critical Theory

Sam Gilchrist Hall

Routledge
Taylor & Francis Group
LONDON AND NEW YORK

First published 2017
by Routledge

2 Park Square, Milton Park, Abingdon, Oxfordshire OX14 4RN
52 Vanderbilt Avenue, New York, NY 10017

Routledge is an imprint of the Taylor & Francis Group, an informa business

First issued in paperback 2019

Library of Congress Cataloging-in-Publication Data

Names: Hall, Sam, 1988–, author.
Title: Shakespeare's folly: philosophy, humanism, critical theory / by Sam Hall.
Description: First edition. | New York: Routledge, 2016. | Series: Routledge studies in Shakespeare; 18 | Includes bibliographical references and index.
Identifiers: LCCN 2016007637
Subjects: LCSH: Shakespeare, William, 1564–1616—Criticism and interpretation. | Shakespeare, William, 1564–1616—Philosophy. | Folly in literature. | Wisdom in literature. | Paradox in literature. | Truth in literature. | Humanism in literature.
Classification: LCC PR3001 .H35 2016 | DDC 822.3/3—dc23
LC record available at https://lccn.loc.gov/2016007637

ISBN: 978-1-138-65522-5 (hbk)
ISBN: 978-0-367-87791-0 (pbk)

Typeset in Sabon
by codeMantra

Contents

Preface

> And I gave my heart to know wisdom, and to know madness and folly: I perceived that this also is vexation of spirit.
>
> (*KJV*, Ecclesiastes, 1. 17)

Shakespeare's fascination with folly runs throughout his career and is as apparent in his histories and tragedies as it is in his comedies. And since it can be discerned on a thematic, conceptual and formal level in virtually every play, folly is not the sole preserve of professional jesters, such as Touchstone. Rather, the paradoxical wisdom of folly is central to the elusive philosophical vision of Shakespearean drama. Indeed, folly proves to be an essential component of Shakespeare's fabled 'Negative Capability' – the way in which his plays, according to Keats, inculcate a way of thinking that 'capable of being in uncertainties without any irritable reaching after fact and reason'.[1]

Shakespeare's Folly is the first study of its kind to read Shakespeare's interest in folly in the light of some of the seminal works of European humanism – Erasmus's *Praise of Folly* (1511), More's *Utopia* (1516) and Montaigne's *Essays* (1580). Situating Shakespearean folly in the intellectual fervent of Renaissance humanism, I suggest, enables us to perceive more presciently the ways in which folly provides a critical space in which the contradictions – and dangers – of reason can be assayed. In fact, as Chapter 3 shows, the idea that folly provides a space for critical reflection is already apparent in Plato's *Symposium*, in which Alcibiades's image of the Silenus figurine expresses the wisdom of the outwardly foolish Socrates. I map the development of this idea from classical antiquity through to Erasmus and Montaigne and on to Shakespeare, who, in *The Merchant of Venice*, dramatises an outwardly unpromising casket with a beautiful image inside it; ultimately, this study suggests, the Casket Test implies that wonder can be experienced through reflection on aesthetic semblance alone.

However, as the interpretations of selected histories, comedies and tragedies, with which the second half of this study is concerned, make clear, Shakespeare was no blithe aesthete, and it is primarily through the discourse of folly that he stages the problematic relation of literature to reality. This can be discerned in Shakespeare's critique of historiography in the Second

Tetralogy, which is analysed in Chapter 4. Here, the manifestly mendacious discourse of folly works to expose the misapprehensions and falsehoods that warp the accounts of the past peddled by his sources. But it is also clear in Shakespeare's comic techniques of ironic estrangement in *As You Like It*, *Twelfth Night* and *The Winter's Tale*, with which Chapter 5 is concerned; employing the kind of Socratic irony described by Friedrich Schlegel as 'playful and serious, guilelessly open and deeply hidden',[2] Shakespearean comedy uses folly to express a scepticism about the serious world more radical than even Nicholas of Cusa's *docta ignorntia*. Building on the critique of stultifying poetic commonplaces and musty narrative tropes apparent in the comedies, this study concludes with an analysis of *Hamlet* and *King Lear*; in these plays, folly takes centre stage and underpins Shakespeare's aesthetics of disfigurement and derangement – an aesthetics that refuses to forget art's complicity in perpetuating real suffering.

Although this attempt to fathom Shakespeare's folly has undoubtedly been a 'vexation of spirit', it has not, I hope, been entirely a fool's errand, since to understand the wisdom of folly takes us a little closer to understanding how Shakespeare's plays comprehend their world and art's place within it.

Notes

1. 'To George and Tom Keats, 21 Dec. 1817', in *The Selected Letters of John Keats*, ed. by Grant F. Scott (cambridge: Harvard University Press, 1959; repr. 1983), pp. 59–61 (p. 60).
2. *Philosophical Fragments*, trans. by Peter Firchow (Minneapolis and London: University of Minnesota Press, 1991), p. 13.

Acknowledgements

Over the past five years, countless individuals and several institutions have aided and abetted my quest for folly. The Arts and Humanities Research Council provided me with a full scholarship, which made this project possible in the first place, and generously supported my archival research in Berlin. Michael Schwartz of the Akademie der Künste, Berlin, proved an invaluable and generous guide through some of Adorno's manuscripts – my sincere thanks to him and his colleagues at the Walter Benjamin Archive.

My PhD supervisor, Professor Kiernan Ryan, was indefatigable in his support of this project. It has been an immense privilege to work with him. My advisor, Dr Deana Rankin, was also an invaluable source of advice and encouragement. Timo Uotinen was consistently wise and kind and Preti Taneja was enthusiastic about the project from the outset. My father, mother and stepfather were a source of patient moral support throughout my PhD and Masters degrees. But special thanks must be given to Natalie Leeder, to whom this book is dedicated. Without her love (and proof reading), it would never have been completed.

An earlier version of 'Deformity and Degeneracy in *Richard II*' appeared in *The Discourses of Folly, Onstage and Off*, ed. by Richard Hillman, Theta - Tudor Theatre, vol. XI (online publication, Tours: Centre d'Études Supérieures de la Renaissance, 2014; <http://umr6576.cesr.univ-tours.fr/publications/Theta11/>). It is republished here by permission.

My thanks also to De Gruyter who gave me permission to reproduce and translate lines from Nietzsche.

A Note on References

All quotations from Shakespeare are from *The Norton Shakespeare*, ed. by Stephen Greenblatt and others, first edition (New York: Norton, 1997) and are cited, as per the MHRA handbook, in the body of the text and in following manner: *Cymbeline*, V. 5. 238–41. The references to *Hamlet* and *King Lear* are to the Arden Third Series.

When the available translation is adequate, quotations from Adorno are cited in the following manner: *MM*, p. 192, with the italicised abbreviation referring to the English version. Where the available translation is inadequate or misleading, I retranslate (or modify the existing translation), citing the German text first with the English version in square brackets thus: (MM, p. 218; [*MM*, 192]). The German edition of Adorno's works used is his *Gesammelte Schriften*, ed. by Rolf Tiedemann and others, 20 vols (Frankfurt: Suhrkamp, 2003).

Unless otherwise stated, quotations from German books and articles are my own; German literature is quoted in the original and a translation is given in a footnote

Abbreviations

Primary Sources

CWE: the *Collected Works of Erasmus*, trans. and ed. by various, 89 Vols (Toronto: University of Toronto Press, 1972–). The title of the work discussed, volume number and page number are given in the text. Since this edition provides references to the major Latin editions on every page, it would be otiose to include references to the Latin.

CWM: The Complete Works of St. Thomas More, trans. and ed. by various, 15 vols (London: Yale University Press, 1976–1997). The title of the work discussed, volume number and page number are given in the text.

E: *Essays vvritten in French by Michael Lord of Montaigne, Knight of the Order of S. Michael, gentleman of the French Kings chamber: done into English, according to the last French edition, by Iohn Florio reader of the Italian tongue vnto the Soueraigne Maiestie of Anna, Queene of England, Scotland, France and Ireland, &c. And one of the gentlemen of hir royall priuie chamber*, trans. by John Florio (London: Melch. Bradwood, 1613). This text is preferred, unless I am referring to the 'C-Text' of the *Essays* or if Florio's translation is unclear. The book, chapter and page numbers are given in the text.

F: *The Essays of Montaigne*, trans. by Donald M. Frame (London: Everyman, 2003). The book, chapter and page numbers are given in the text.

Geneva The Byble that is to say all the holy Scripture: in whych are co[n] tayned the Olde and New Testamente, truly [and] purely tra[n]slated into English, [and] nowe lately with greate industry [and] dilige[n]ce recognised, trans. by William Tyndale and others (London: S. Mierdman, 1549). Book, chapter, and verse are cited. This edition is used in discussions of Shakespeare's biblical references.

GP: Gargantua and Pantagruel, trans. by Sir Thomas Urquhart and Pierre Le Motteux (London: Everyman, 1994). The book, chapter and page numbers are given in the text.

KJV: The Bible: Authorized King James Version with Apocrypha, ed. by Robert Carroll and Stephen Prickett (Oxford: Oxford University Press, 1997). Book, chapter and verse are cited.

NDSS: The Narrative and Dramatic Sources of Shakespeare, ed. by Geoffrey Bullough, 8 vols (London: Routledge, 1957–75). The volume number and page number are given in the text.

PF: The Praise of Folie, trans. by Sir Thomas Chaloner, ed. by Clarence H. Miller, Early English Text Society, 257 (London: Oxford University Press, 1965). The page number is provided in the text.

U: Utopia: With Erasmus' The Sileni of Alcibiades, ed. and trans. by David Wootton (Cambridge: Hackett, 1999). The book and page numbers are given in the text.

Vulgate Biblia Sacra Vulgata: Holy Bible in Latin, ed. by Rodger Gryson and others, 4th rev. edn (Peabody, MA: Hendrickson, 1994). Book, chapter and verse are cited.

Secondary Sources

Adorno

AT: *Aesthetic Theory*, ed. by Gretel Adorno and Rolf Tiedemann, trans. by Robert Hullot-Kentor (London: Continuum, 2004; repr. 2012).

DA: Max Horkheimer and Theodor W. Adorno, *Dialektik der Aufklärung: Philosophische Fragmente* (Frankfurt: Fischer, 1969; repr. 2010).

DE: Dialectic of Enlightenment: Philosophical Fragments, ed. by Gunzelin Schmid Noerr, trans. by Edmund Jephcott (Stanford CA: Stanford University Press, 2002).

LHF: History and Freedom: Lectures 1964–1965 ed. by Rolf Tiedemann, trans by. Rodney Livingstone (Maldon: Polity, 2008).

LND: Lectures on Negative Dialectics, ed. by Rolf Tiedemann, trans. by Rodney Livingstone (Cambridge: Polity, 2008).

M: Metaphysics: Concept and Problems, ed. by Rolf Tiedemann, trans. by Edmund Jephcott (Oxford: Blackwell, 2000).

MM: Minima Moralia: Reflections on a Damaged Life, trans. by Edmund Jephcott (London: Verso, 2005).

ND: Negative Dialectics, trans. by E. B. Ashton (London: Continuum, 1973; repr. 2007).

NL: Notes to Literature, ed. by Rolf Tiedemann, trans. by Shierry Weber Nicholson, 2 Vols (Chichester: Columbia University Press, 1991).
TEF: 'The Essay as Form', trans. by Robert Hullot-Kentor and Frederic Will, *New German Critique*, 32 (1984), 151–171.

Foucault

A: Abnormal: Lectures at the Collège de France, ed. by Valerio Marchetti and Antonella Salomoni, trans. by Graham Burchell (London: Verso, 2003).
GSO: The Government of Self and Others: Lectures at the Collège de France, 1982–3, ed. by François Edward and Alessandro Fontana, trans. by Graham Burchell (Basingstoke: Palgrave, 2010).
HM: The History of Madness, trans. and ed. by Jean Khalfa and Jonathan Murphy (Basingstoke: Routledge, 2006).
SD: "Society Must Be Defended": Lectures at the Collège de France, 1975–1976, ed. by Mauro Bertani and Alessandro Fontana, trans. by David Macey (London: Verso, 2003).

1 Towards a Philosophy of Folly

1.1 Introduction

> Nur Narr, Nur Dichter!
> Nur Buntes redend.
> Aus Narrenlarven blunt herausredend.
> Herumsteigend auf lügnerischen Wortbrücken.
> Auf Lügen-Regenbogen
> zwischen falschen Himmeln
> herumschweifend, herumschleichend—
> *nur* Narr! *Nur* Dichter!
>
> —Friedrich Nietzsche, 'Dionysos-Dithyramben'[1]

Since he 'nothing affirms and therefore never lieth',[2] the fool is akin to the poet. Liberated from telling the truth in a straightforward manner, fools and poets alike revel in the possibilities that the counterfactual realm affords them to expose the absurdities of the serious world, for both writing fiction and donning a jester's cap enable one to critique prevalent ways of understanding, without dogmatically asserting the veracity of one's own claims. This idea finds implicit expression in the late Romance *Cymbeline*, when, baffled by Jupiter's riddling prophecy, Posthumous refers to it as:

> [...] still a dream, or else such stuff as madmen
> Tongue, and brain not; either both, or nothing,
> Or senseless speaking, or a speaking such
> As sense cannot untie.
>
> (V. 5. 238–41)

'Or senseless speaking, or a speaking such | As sense cannot untie': this study takes as its basis the paradox that finds compressed expression in these remarkable lines: namely, that sense and nonsense are locked in a mutually defining relationship. Although 'senseless' utterance cannot be neatly categorised and incorporated into reason's domain, it could not come into being without reason's classification of it as something peculiar, something beyond its remit, a 'speaking such as sense cannot untie'.

Indeed, as Walter Kaiser writes in his seminal comparative interpretation of folly in Erasmus, Rabelais, Shakespeare and Cervantes: 'The ability of reason to question itself and yet emerge with wisdom is key for these great Renaissance writers'.[3] Thus perceiving the limitations of 'sense' is itself an act of reason, an act of reason that is embodied in much of the most significant literature of the early modern period, from *Praise of Folly* to *Don Quixote*. In Shakespeare's drama – as in the works of Rabelais, More, Erasmus and Cervantes – folly does not offer blithe relief from the tyranny of good sense. Rather, many of Shakespeare's most profound philosophical ideas stem from the discourse of folly's critique of dominant modes of reason. The wordplay, jubilant ironies and vertiginous paradoxes intrinsic to this discourse offer alternatives to the instrumental ways of understanding that continue to dominate and dogmatise serious philosophy.

While the paradoxical wisdom of Shakespearean folly has been examined in individual essays and articles,[4] extended studies have all but ignored folly's philosophical potential, despite the fool's manifestly critical function within the plays. For instance, although it provides a detailed taxonomy of Shakespeare's gulls, melancholics, lunatics, lovers, verbose clowns and fully paid-up wise fools,[5] Robert Bell's recent study, *Shakespeare's Great Stage of Fools*, is content to assert that folly can constitute a sort of wisdom, without elucidating *why* this is the case. He contends that the 'postmodern decentring project has reconstructed our sense of folly as wisdom',[6] but neither establishes how exactly postmodernism achieves this, nor what exactly this 'decentring project' is in the first place.

Shakespeare's Folly: Philosophy, Humanism, Critical Theory redefines the paradoxical wisdom of folly in Shakespeare's drama: folly, it argues, is of key structural, aesthetic and philosophical importance to the plays. And it is for this reason that fools cannot be analysed in isolation from the plays that they inhabit – as is the case in the studies of Enid Welsford, William Willeford,[7] Kaiser, Bell, Dimiter Daphinoff, Frederick Warde,[8] and Robert Goldsmith, who wrote the only study solely devoted to Shakespeare's professional jesters.[9] Because there are numerous fine studies that consider the socio-historical formation of the fool,[10] I do not examine closely the social function of early modern fools and clowns. Nor do I propose to augment the fine work of C. L. Barber,[11] Robert Weimann,[12] Françoise Laroque,[13] Sandra Billington,[14] Phoebe Jenson[15] and Michael Bristol,[16] all of whom analyse the role of fools and jesters in early modern drama in connection with the transmission of popular customs.

Robert Hornback's 2009 study, *The English Clown Tradition*, however, is remarkable in its subtle reconstruction of how Shakespeare's plays *transformed* existing modes of foolery.[17] Furthermore, Hornback elsewhere demonstrates how Shakespeare exploits emblems of natural folly and the assumptions that underlie the blackface theatrical tradition in *Othello*; this association of blackness with irrationality contributed to the pseudo-scientific theories of race of the nineteenth century:[18] strikingly, the pseudo-scientific discourse of eugenics, which held sway in the world of reason for nearly a century, borrows its basic assumptions from medieval and early modern *fictions*.

Yet with the notable exceptions of Hornback and Billington, these studies ultimately argue that, in Barber's famous formulation, 'a Saturnalian reversal of social roles need not threaten the social structure, but can serve instead to consolidate it'.[19] On the face of it, it may seem that the emphasis this book places on the critical function of folly in Shakespeare's drama is an extended endorsement of the idea that there is indeed 'slander', subversive potential, in the raillery of an 'allowed fool' (*Twelfth Night*, I. 5. 80) – despite Olivia's suggestion to the contrary. However, I seek to overcome the staid dichotomy between those who consider folly in particular – and comedy more generally – to offer a meaningful subversion of the *status quo* and those who argue, with Barber, for the subversion and containment theory. Rather than subverting the powers that be, the paradoxical wisdom of folly offers, I suggest, a determinate negation of them. In other words, while folly offers an alternative to instrumental ways of behaving, thinking and arguing, it nonetheless takes the prevalence of existing modes of reasoning into account. Besides, as we have seen, for the paradoxical wisdom of folly to appear wise in the first place, it requires an ostensibly reasonable order of things, from which to dissent.

After clarifying the scope and aims of this study, I justify its theoretical position: Shakespeare, I suggest, shares an intellectual affinity with a strand of western philosophy that is formed by the works of Socrates, Montaigne, Nietzsche, Foucault and Adorno. Throughout this study, I employ these thinkers, all of whom are deeply sceptical both about the efficacy of man's theories and about their own sceptical take on the power and utility of theoretical knowledge to throw into relief the epistemic implications of Shakespearean foolery. This chapter then offers a critical conspectus of Shakespeare's wise fools, clowns and witty servants, which establishes the structural, thematic and poetic integrity of these fascinating characters.

Shakespeare's Folly: Philosophy, Humanism, Critical Theory is the first study of its kind to read Shakespeare's folly in the context of and as informed by contemporary humanism – in particular, Erasmus's *Praise of Folly* and Montaigne's *Essays*. While the question of the exact nature of Erasmus's and Montaigne's influence on the plays is far from inconsequential, this study is less concerned with ascertaining the direct influence of these humanists on Shakespearean drama as with illustrating their shared tendency to think about – and, more importantly, *through* – folly. It is, in fact, in the figure of Montaigne, a self-professed 'unpremeditated and accidental philosopher' (*F*, Book 2, Chapter 7, p. 487), that, as Chapter 2 shows, the theoretical standpoint of the study and the historical context of Shakespeare's plays coincide: in particular, Montaigne's anti-methodological form, the essay, and his understanding of the playful essence of thought had a considerable influence on Adorno.

Through close readings of *Praise of Folly*, Thomas More's *Utopia* and Montaigne's *Essays*, Chapter 2 establishes both the significance of wise folly within the intellectual milieu from which Shakespeare sprang and the shared philosophical preoccupations of Erasmus, More, Montaigne and Shakespeare. These include a suspicion of the dogma that arises from sincerely held convictions; an awareness of the power of custom to blind people to their better natures; and a critique of man's tendency to create nature in his own image. Chapter 2 concludes by illustrating the parallels between Adorno's critique of 'identity-thinking' (*ND*, p. 149 *et passim*) and Montaigne's sceptical estimation of the capacity of man's theories to get to the bottom of things, which reaches its zenith in his Pyrrhonist essay, 'An Apologie of *Raymond Sebond*'.

It is important to stress, however, that the intention of *Shakespeare's Folly: Philosophy, Humanism, Critical Theory* is neither to *apply* theory to early modern texts, nor to imply that twentieth century critical theory "got it all" from Renaissance humanism. Rather, I establish that certain speculative correspondences between these historically and culturally disparate thinkers enable an analysis of the central concepts and problems inherent in Shakespearean folly, an analysis that does not attempt to petrify this essentially ephemeral phenomenon under the medusan gaze of analytical classification. Whereas Chapter 2 is concerned with the shared philosophical preoccupations of Shakespeare and his humanist contemporaries, the study as a whole is more interested in the *modes* of speculation shared by Shakespeare, the Renaissance Humanists and the twentieth-century critical theorists, whose ideas help me to elucidate what the philosophical import of Shakespearean foolery is today. The valuable work of Andy Mousley,[20] Hugh Grady[21] and Gerhard Schweppenhäuser,[22]on which I hope this study will build, has already illustrated several speculative correspondences between Critical Theory and Renaissance Humanism. And while it lies beyond the scope of this study to provide full accounts of Critical Theory's varying conceptions of the purpose of the aesthetic, I do hope to show the ways in which Shakespeare's drama *stages* some of the key tensions in Adorno's aesthetics and how Shakespeare's plays presage Foucault's theories of political power.

Chapter 3 moves away from considering the themes shared by Erasmus, Montaigne and Shakespeare. Instead, it illustrates the different ways in which these writers engage with the concept of the 'Sileni of Alcibiades', which hails from Plato's *Symposium,* where it is used the contrast between the philosopher-fool Socrates's ridiculous appearance and his beautiful mind. Because it encapsulates the disjunction between appearance and essence, between the Father and the Son, for Erasmus, the philosophical implications of this image are enormous. Montaigne, in contrast, develops a self-effacing Silenic register: his essays offer profound philosophical insights in everyday language. And such a register is crucial for Montaigne's philosophical project because he finds the extraordinary in the ordinary. Chapter 3 concludes with a re-reading of the casket plot of *The Merchant of Venice*; when Shakespeare dramatises the consequences of choosing the outwardly unpromising lead casket with the beautiful picture of Portia inside it, he evokes the idea of the Silenus figurine, an outwardly grotesque case that contained a beautiful gold statuette. Rather than using reason in a quixotic attempt to get to the essence of things and establish certainties, in *The Merchant of Venice* Shakespeare implies that it is through reflection on aesthetic semblance alone that philosophical wonder may be experienced.

With the theoretical position and historical context in place, I then analyse Shakespeare's Second Tetralogy. It is essential to perceive what these plays imply about the antinomical nature of historical narratives, I suggest, if we are to fathom the radical scepticism apparent in the comedies and tragedies, with which the chapters that follow are concerned. In these histories, I argue, Shakespeare casts himself as a Cretan Liar. He is a historian who, through the discourse of folly, boldly declares: "All historians are liars!" Paradoxically, Shakespeare employs an intrinsically mendacious form, aesthetic semblance, to reflect upon the fictions that constitute historical fact.

Moving from the folly of barefaced lying to that of self-delusion, Chapter 5 argues that in *As You Like It*, *Twelfth Night* and *The Winter's Tale* the characters, who declare themselves to be wise on the grounds that they are free of the sway of love, are actually indulging in a form of self-love, which is every bit as foolish as the tribulations of lovers embroiled in the comic action. All three plays imply that one should, paradoxically, hope for an utterly unexpected future. But these plays also make clear the extreme unlikelihood of such a future occurring – a future in which Viola's injunction, 'Prove true, imagination, O prove true' (*Twelfth Night*, III. 4. 340–41), is fulfilled. Such scepticism is tempered, however, by the ways in which Shakespeare dramatises the dangers of a melancholic mindset, for which there is nothing new under the sun.

Shakespeare's melancholics perceive contingent events as mere examples of predetermined facts and general categories; as Orlando puts it when he attacks Jaques, the melancholic has 'studied' his 'questions' from 'a painted cloth' (*As You Like It*, III. 2. 251–52). For this reason, Shakespeare's melancholics are often unable or unwilling to hope for unexpected, radically new experiences, preferring to stay captive to the past. And this has near-tragic consequences in *The Winter's Tale*, in which Leontes is all too ready to perceive his wife as another faithless woman, another Cressida. Crucially, he, like Jaques and Malvolio, remains, if not an obdurate fool, at least comparatively unenlightened by the comic action: at the close of the action, he still espouses an idealising aesthetic, of which Montaigne and Erasmus are devoutly critical, an aesthetic that makes the inhuman demand of formal perfection on humans – 'Hermione was not so much wrinkled, nothing | So aged as this seems' (V. 3. 27–28).

The final chapter argues that *Hamlet* and *King Lear* offer Shakespeare's most extensive thinking-through of the paradoxical wisdom of folly. By employing Socratic irony and critiquing predetermined values and ideas, these tragedies fashion a self-critical aesthetics. *Hamlet* and *King Lear* craft an aesthetics of deformity and derangement in order to illustrate the complicity of 'neat and cleanly' (*1 Henry IV*, II. 5. 415) artworks in muting the privations of the world from which they sprang. Far from imposing order upon chaos as one might imagine aesthetic form to do, these plays turn order into chaos; they stage the dangers inherent in instrumental ways of thinking – measuring and categorising an object, person or discourse, these plays imply, is in no way the same as understanding it. As Adorno writes, the 'irrationality in the principle of reason is unmasked by the avowedly rational irrationality of art' (*AT*, p. 54). In other words, these tragedies use the purposeful purposelessness of aesthetic semblance to expose the dangers inherent in purposeful ways of thinking and communicating. While, for Prince Hal, 'in everything, the purpose must weigh with the folly' (*2 Henry IV*, 153–54) – that is, 'folly' is only justifiable if it has a 'purpose' – Shakespeare's philosophy of folly is at pains to show that the folly must 'weigh' the purpose: Shakespeare's folly puts the serious world's ways of understanding on trial and finds them wanting.

1.2 Folly and Critical Theory

This is not the only study to hinge on the idea tacit in Posthumous's memorable epanalepsis: 'Or senseless speaking, or a speaking such | As sense cannot untie'. It is, of course, the very 'stuff' that 'madmen | Tongue and brain not' – or at least, the 'experience' (*HM*, p. xxx) thereof – that Foucault attempts to reconstruct in his 1961 study, *History of Madness* (*Histoire de la folie à l'âge classique*), which is premised on the idea that 'there can be no reason without madness' (*HM*, p. xxv) and no reasonable utterance without 'senseless speaking'. Foucault's paradigm-shifting insight in this book is a Shakespearean one: namely, that sanity defines itself against insanity and reason against unreason.

Whereas Erasmus, Montaigne and Shakespeare are at pains to point out that there is nothing more foolish than considering oneself wise, Foucault goes so far as to argue that asserting one's sanity actually always reveals a trace of insanity; with Pascal in mind, he concerns himself with 'that "other trick" that madness plays – that "other trick" through which men, in a gesture of sovereign reason [...] lock up their neighbour [and] communicate and recognise each other in the merciless language of non-madness' (*HM*., p. xxvii). Like any act of categorisation, identifying someone as insane is, in a sense, irrational. Not only does it place an absolute faith in the powers of 'sense' to gain mastery over that which, by definition, it cannot understand, but it also fails to recognise that, as Montaigne reflects in the opening pages of his *Essays*, 'man is a wonderful, vaine, divers, and wavering subject: it is very hard to ground any directly-constant and uniforme judgement upon him' (*E*, Book 1, Chapter 1, p. 2). Such absolute standards are ultimately at odds with the essential intermittency of being.

Shakespeare's interest in the paradoxical wisdom of folly, which is evident from the earliest plays to the last, is based on the idea that putting one's faith in the certainties, categories and fictions of unitary identity, which it is in authority's best interest to maintain, is itself an act of *folie* – a word with a semantic range that encompasses both madness and folly. It transpires that the political and philosophical clout of Shakespeare's 'witless wisdom'[23] lies in its capacity to estrange the everyday world and its customs by exposing the serious as ridiculous, the sincere as insincere and laughter as a very serious matter indeed. As Leszek Kołakowski reflects:

> The philosophy of Clowns is the philosophy that in every epoch shows up as doubtful: what has been regarded as most certain; it reveals the contradictions inherent in what seems to have been proved by visual experience; it holds up to ridicule what seems obvious common sense, and discovers truth in the absurd.[24]

Crucially, Shakespeare's representation of folly does not simply turn the rational world topsy-turvy, as is commonly assumed. But by breaking causal patterns and interrogating the formation of meaning, it furnishes the reader with perspectives that tear holes in the fabric of the received wisdom of the everyday world.

In order to fathom the philosophical vision of a writer, who reflects with his tongue in his cheek: 'Alas, 'tis true I have gone here and there, | And made myself a motley to the view' ('Sonnet 110', 1–2), this study brings Renaissance folly into dialogue with a tradition of western thought that has, hitherto, neither been the subject of philosophical analysis, nor been brought into dialogue with Shakespeare's philosophy. This way of thinking runs from the philosopher-fool, Socrates, through to Montaigne and on to Nietzsche, but it ultimately finds its most sustained expression in the anti-theoretical philosophies of Foucault and Adorno. Far from fashioning watertight theoretical systems, these thinkers share a playful and paradoxical awareness that 'the truth of ideas is bound up with the possibility of their being wrong, the possibility of their failure' (*M*, p. 144). In other words, this diverse group of thinkers shares a striking capacity for a sort of 'Negative Capability'.[25] It suggests that the condition of being in uncertainty is philosophically valid, whereas dogmatically insisting upon the universality of one's systems, categories and identities is intellectually indefensible and dangerously irrational.

In *Minima Moralia: Reflections on Damaged Life*, Adorno suggests that it is the dialectician's role to enable the expression of the disquieting ideas latent in the fool's loquacious utterance, an utterance that picks up on the nonsensical elements in the serious world's assumptions, cherished discourses, concepts and institutions:

> The dialectic cannot stop short before the concepts of health and sickness, nor indeed before their siblings, reason and unreason. Once it has

> recognised the universal ruling order and its proportions as sick [...] then it can see as healing cells only what appears, by the measures of that order, as itself sick, eccentric, paranoid – indeed, 'mad' [*verrückt*]; it is true today, as in the Middle Ages, that only fools tell their masters the truth. The dialectician's duty is thus to help this fool's truth to attain its own reason, without which it will freely succumb to the abyss of sickness implacably dictated by the healthy common sense of the rest.
>
> (MM, pp. 81–82; [*MM*, p. 73])

Folly refuses to operate according to norms, for as Adorno writes in his later work, *Negative Dialectics*: 'Folly is truth in the form by which people are struck when, in the midst of untruth, they will not abandon truth' (ND, p. 396 [*ND*, p. 404]). The paradoxical wisdom of folly, in other words, has a negative or critical potential because it exposes the untruths that constitute the wholesome certainties upon which the workaday world depends.

The significance of Adorno's claim should not be underestimated, not least because the 'fool's truth' recalls the critical, rather than systematising, impulse of 'modern philosophy', a 'practice which', for Foucault, 'finds its function of truth in the criticism of illusion, deception, trickery and flattery' (*GSO*, pp. 353–54). The dialectics to which Adorno alludes are, of course, the negative dialectics with which his name is associated. In contrast to traditional dialectics, negative dialectics does not attempt to subsume two discrete identities into a larger one. Instead, it discovers the inner contradictions of supposedly stable identities and immutable categories. Negative dialectics, therefore, provides a way of understanding the peculiar philosophical movement of the paradoxical wisdom of folly, which lies primarily in its capacity to lay bare the contradictions inherent in the ostensibly immutable customs, values and discourses of the prevailing order.

Yet characterising the fool as a critical theorist *avant la letter* is not unproblematic, for as Jan Kott reflects:

> The position of a jester is ambiguous and abounds in internal contradictions arising out of the discrepancy between his profession and his philosophy. The profession of a jester, like that of an intellectual, consists in providing entertainment. His philosophy demands of him that he tell the truth and abolish myths.[26]

Standing outside of the pseudo-truths of everyday life, which, to this day, blinker the wise and the foolish alike, fools and poets neither fashion enduring epistemological systems, nor expound their ideas in humourless treatises. Rather, as Foucault memorably writes in *The Order of Things*, the 'words of the poet' are akin to those of the 'madman' or 'fool' because they 'unceasingly renew the power of their strangeness and the strength of their contestation'; they inhabit an area 'on the outer edge of our culture and at the point nearest its essential divisions'.[27] As Nietzsche intuited, the poet and the fool reside on the extreme edge of reason's domain as outsiders looking in. 'The lunatic, the lover, and the poet' reflects Shakespeare's Duke Theseus 'Are of imagination all compact' (*A Midsummer Night's Dream*, V. 1. 7–8).

1.3 Shakespearean Fools

'Foolery, sir, does walk about the orb like the sun, it shines everywhere' (*Twelfth Night*, III. 1. 33–34). As Feste's characteristically shrewd adaptation of Cicero's famous aphorism suggests, folly is ubiquitous. And Shakespeare's drama includes a host of covert fools, most of whom have yet to receive extensive analysis.[28] These include Hal and his fellow drinkers, who engage in scurrilously digressive badinage while playing 'the fools with the time' (*2 Henry IV*, II. 2. 120); the aristocrats and their servants in *Love's Labour's Lost*, whose love of role-playing, logic-chopping and the double entendres of their repartee clearly recall the language of the fool; and Hamlet, who appropriates the grotesque bodily imagery and nonsensical speech of the jester in order to craft his 'antic disposition' (I. 5. 170).

If, moreover, one extends the notion of the Shakespearean fool to include the traditional negative connotations of the word,[29] as someone duped, suffering under misapprehension or an unbeliever – as in Psalm 53, 'The fool hath said in his heart, | *There* is no God' (*KJV*, 1–2 [emphasis original]) – then it becomes clear that in Shakespeare's drama, '*Stultorum infinitus est numerus*' (*Vulgate*, Ecclesiastes, 1. 15): the number of fools is infinite. From the early knockabout farce, *The Comedy of Errors*, the very title of which attests to the dramatic and humorous potential of mistaken identity, to *King Lear*, which wrings pathos from both the king's initial mistake – to divide his kingdom – and his subsequent insanity, which mutates into 'matter and impertinency mixed, | Reason in madness' (*Lear*, IV. 6. 170–71), Shakespeare unflinchingly dramatises human error. His tragedies commonly hinge on misapprehension: be it Macbeth's failure to interpret the witches' equivocations correctly or Othello's 'jealous confirmations strong' due to 'Trifles' – or inconsequential follies – 'as light as air' (*Othello*, III. 3. 326, 325), the protagonists of a Shakespearean tragedy suffer acutely as a result of their own folly and are, as Montaigne puts it, commonly 'tormented by the opinions they have of things, and not by things themselves' (*E*, Book 1, Chapter 40, p. 127). Comedy relies on misunderstanding followed by a timely clarification and recognition, whereas in tragedy this recognition happens too late.

What G. K. Chesterton aptly describes as Shakespeare's 'thoughtless wisdom'[30] is a philosophy of folly that manifests itself most explicitly in the wise fools: Touchstone in *As You Like It*; the enigmatic Feste in *Twelfth Night*; Lavatch in *All's Well That Ends Well*; and the Fool in *King Lear*. These jesters claim the privilege of the licensed fool to speak profound, subversive or intolerable truths in the guise of gratuitous nonsense. Wise fools combine 'mangled forms' (*As You Like It*, II. 7. 41–42) of utterance with a riddling linguistic exuberance. They use 'tricksy word[s]' to consistently 'defy the matter' (*The Merchant of Venice*, III. 5. 59–60), putting the serious world on hold by rehearsing a dizzying array of counterfactual possibilities. Because they inhabit little fictions with which they lay bare the absurdities of the workaday world, fools are proudly perched, as Nietzsche puts it in his 'Dionysos-Dithyramben', '*auf Lügen-Regenbogen*': 'on rainbows of lies'. But to limit the analysis of wise folly in Shakespeare to jesters and clowns as previous studies have done is to fail to perceive the vital structural and thematic significance of folly, with which this study primarily is concerned. To be sure, folly is not a facet of the plays. Rather, it is what constitutes their ironic detachment from the values of the early modern age and, more importantly, what accounts for their continued capacity to estrange their audiences and readers from the *doxa*, false opinions, which mediate their respective presents.

Despite Bell's contention that until the advent of Shakespeare's professional jesters, clowning in the plays 'is comparatively circumscribed, relatively unthreatening and unenlightening',[31] a glance at some of Shakespeare's early comedies shows that his professional jesters have a genealogy that stretches back to the earliest plays – clowns of one sort or another can be identified in almost all the plays.[32] In *The Two Gentlemen of Verona*, possibly Shakespeare's first play, Lance, his early experiment with the intriguing figure of the stage clown, is given the play's most memorable moment, a set-piece tirade against his incontinent and coldly stoical dog (II. 3. 1–29). Lance's loyalty to 'the sourest-natured dog that lives' (5) burlesques the acts of devotion, often to equally unresponsive recipients, committed by the eponymous gentlemen. And although this clown overflows with a travesty of Christian compassion – 'I have sat in the stocks for puddings he [Crab] hath stolen' (IV. 4. 26), the hapless manservant complains, and this certainly does makes him appear foolish – he is wise enough to know the true nature of his master, the self-serving would-be rapist, Proteus: 'I am but a fool, look you, and yet I have the wit to think my master is a kind of knave' (III. 1. 263). As Shakespeare's fools never tire of reminding their audiences, onstage and off, the 'wise man knows himself to be a fool' (*As You Like It*, V. 1. 29–30). Indeed, for Indira Ghose, the key question posed by fools is "Who is the real fool"?[33] Certainly, this sort of reflexivity distinguishes Lance from non-Shakespearean clowns, such as Wagner in Christopher Marlowe's *Dr Faustus*, who like Lance parodies his master's actions, but unlike Lance lacks the Shakespearean clown's combination of wry irony, humility and insight.

This topsy-turvy logic is also found in the poignant conclusion of the knock-about farce *The Comedy of Errors*. In order to multiply the possibilities for misunderstanding, Shakespeare added to his source, Plautus's *Menaechmi*, a pair of identical twin servants, the Dromios; these twins may have been beaten black and blue through the course of the play, but it is they who offer at the close a utopian glimpse of a world organised according to common humanity rather than the false strictures of primogeniture; as they enter the abbey, the site of comic *anagnorisis*, Dromio of Ephesus refuses to calculate who should take precedence and step through the door first. He states: 'We came into the world like brother and brother, | And now let's go hand in hand, not one before another' (V. 1. 425–26). The Dromios transcend their situation, achieving a level of philosophical suggestion beyond their ken.

Yet the desire called utopia in Shakespeare's drama not only dovetails with the historical situation in which it was conceived, but is also undermined by structural and dramatic ironies, which ultimately thwart the construction of any castles in the sky. Consider Jack Cade's nonsensical manifesto to the rebelling artisans in *2 Henry VI*:

> CADE: There shall be seven half-penny loaves, sold for a penny. I will make it a felony to drink small beer. All the realm shall be held in common [...] there shall be no money. All shall eat and drink on my score, and I will apparel them in one livery that they shall agree like brothers.
>
> (IV. 2. 60–61, 64–66)

Cade's Land of Cokaygne is clearly stuck in Southwark, where the grip of commodity capitalism is evident from the fact that the notion of cheaper bread can be posited only within the framework of finance, despite Cade's decree to abolish money. The subversive political potential of his manifesto is curbed both because he remains a pawn in York's game and because the characterisation of this medieval rebel, with his 'anti-intellectualism and promotion of irrationality', [34] evokes the early modern satirical type of the clownishly ignorant Puritan.

Cade's egalitarian aims, which are mingled with clownish physical desires for cheap beer and food, are also present, albeit in a different form, in the old fool Gonzalo's utopian vision in *The Tempest*:

> GONZALO: I'th'commonwealth I would by contraries
> Execute all things. For no kind of traffic
> Would I admit, no name of magistrate;
> Letters should not be known [...]
> No occupation, all men idle, all;
> And women too [...].
>
> (II. 1. 147–50, 154–55)

This enchanted vision of how things could be in a 'brave new world' (V. 1. 186) if they were set topsy-turvy and executed by 'contraries' is as much at odds with how things are on the island as Cade's vision is disengaged from the realities of medieval (or early modern) London. Prospero demonises Caliban as a 'thing of darkness' (V. 1. 279) and administers regular physical abuse to his slave; Gonzalo is laughed to scorn by his companions, who see the island as a potential site of domination, something to be owned and used. Indeed, the deformed Caliban has theatrical credit: Trinculo observes that in England 'this monster [would] make a man' (II. 2. 28–29). But the similarities between Cade's rabble-rousing and Gonzalo's ideal 'commonwealth' are manifest: they both argue for common ownership, no commerce, no law, no wage-labour and no writing.

In his transformation of the sources of these two statements – one is drawn from the age-old popular dream of the Isles of Plenty and one from Montaigne's 'Of the Cannibals' – Shakespeare offers not only a kind of 'utopian realism',[35] a sort of speculation that is orientated towards the future while nonetheless tempered by present realities, but he also provides a realistic appraisal of the utopian impulse. Shakespeare neither affirms the radical reforms, endorsed by both popular culture and Montaigne's sceptical humanism, nor wholly censures them. What these ironies do suggest, however, is that Shakespeare baulks at concrete blueprints of utopia. This is because they are bound to reflect the world as it is – in the manner of Cade's longings for a cornucopia – and because they remain as hopelessly out of sync with the current situation as Gonzalo's fantasy.

Although, like the Dromios, the Porter in *Macbeth* is a servant, is implicated in folly, mediates between characters and only appears in one scene, he is nonetheless a 'great clown'.[36] In fact, his speech offers a hermeneutic key with which to unlock significant events, themes and images in the rest of the play; his very identity as a 'devil porter' (II. 3. 16) clearly resonates with the infernal imagery that runs through the play. After welcoming to 'th'everlasting bonfire' (19–20) a host of over-reachers, including an 'equivocator [...] who committed treason enough, for God's sake, yet could not equivocate to heaven' (7–10) and a 'farmer who hanged himself on th'expectation of plenty' (4–5), the Porter quibbles about the anaphrodisiac effects that the excessive consumption of alcohol can have:

PORTER: [...] drink, sir, is a great provoker of three things.
MACDUFF: What three things does drink especially provoke?
PORTER: Marry, sir, nose-painting, sleep, and urine. Lechery, sir, it provokes and unprovokes: it provokes the desire but it takes away the performance. Therefore, much drink may be said to be an equivocator with lechery: it makes him and it mars him; it sets him on, and it takes him off; it persuades him, and it disheartens him, makes him stand to, and not stand to; in conclusion, equivocates him in a sleep, and, giving him the lie, leaves him.

(II. 3. 25–33)

Equivocation, bending the truth through deliberately ambiguous statements, is also of manifest importance to the tragedy as a whole; what Macbeth calls the 'double sense' (V. 8. 20) of the Witches, the crafty ambiguities that lace their nonsense rhymes, is what undoes him. Although their comment that he should 'laugh to scorn | The power of man, for none of woman born | Shall harm Macbeth' (79–81) appears unambiguous; it transpires, of course, that Macduff, who sends the usurper to meet his maker, was delivered by Caesarean section, 'from his mother's womb | Untimely ripp'd' (15–16).

Indeed, the disjunction between 'desire' and 'performance', upon which the Porter's lewd gag is based, is the very disjunction pondered by Macbeth in the opening scenes of the play: does he dare to enact his desires and commit regicide? He reflects on the painful gap between 'desire' and 'performance' through something of a self-equivocation:

> If it were done when 'tis done, then 'twere well
> It were done quickly: if th'assassination
> Could trammel up the consequence, and catch
> With his surcease success [...].
>
> (I. 7. 1–4)

As Frank Kermode astutely observes, Macbeth's language here enacts the 'dizzying gap between thought and deed',[37] or that between desire and performance – the repetition of the past tense, 'done', implies that he has already made up his mind.

It could be argued that this is a case of the hungover clown's patter undermining the seriousness of the main action by travestying its concerns – perhaps the play is, after all, merely letting off steam through the safety valve of comedy. But this is not the case because the play's main concerns are themselves recurrently expressed, implicitly and explicitly, through the phallic imagery and metaphors that also find expression in the Porter's extemporisation. Consider Macbeth's reflection:

> I have no spur
> To prick the sides of my intent, but only
> Vaulting ambition, which o'erleaps itself
> And falls on th'other.
>
> (I. 7. 25–28)

When Lady Macbeth goads her husband to murder Duncan – 'When you durst do it, then you were a man; | And, to be more than what you were, you would | Be so much more the man' (I. 7. 49–51) – she connects virility with Macbeth's, admittedly impressive, capacity for atrocious violence. Elsewhere in the play, she needles him by suggestively eliding social 'ambition' (I. 5. 19) with his physical strength and virility. In fact, it is Lady Macbeth who sets up the disjunction between 'desire' and 'performance' that the Porter will later play on. 'Art thou afeard | To be the same in thine own act and valour | As thou art in desire?' (I. 7. 39–41), she asks her husband. When, moments before the 'Porter of Hell Gate' scene, she accuses Macbeth of being flaccid, 'infirm of purpose' (II. 7. 51) for feeling remorse at killing Duncan, the dramatic relevance of the Porter's digressive improvisation is immediately apparent.

Since the term did not come into being until 1825, it is hardly surprising that this play fails to conform to the theory of "comic relief".[38] Far from offering *relief* from its central concerns and obsessive imagery, the Porter's demotic patter reiterates them in such a way as to imply that the concerns of the serious world are themselves risible; Shakespeare uses the Porter's brand of black comedy to provide a commentary on the dangerous desires and fatal misconceptions that govern the behaviour of the play's protagonists. The serious point of this humour is that it exposes the absurdity of such desires and conceptions – to borrow a phrase from the Porter's speech: comic interludes in Shakespeare tend to give 'the lie' to the serious world.

Shakespeare's professional jesters, however, commonly offer a critique of their world that has resonances far beyond it. Consider Touchstone's digressive aria in response to Corin's simple question: 'And how like you this shepherd's life, Master Touchstone?' (*As You Like It*, III. 2. 11–12), which confounds reason even as it peddles a motley 'philosophy':

> TOUCHSTONE: Truly, shepherd, in respect of itself, it is a good life; but in respect that it is a shepherd's life, it is naught. In respect that it is solitary, I like it very well; but in respect that it is private, it is a very vile life. Now in respect it is in the fields, it pleaseth me well; but in respect it is not in court, it is tedious. As a spare life, look you, it fits my humour well; but as there is no more plenty in it, it goes much against my stomach. Hast any philosophy in thee, shepherd?
>
> (12–20)

This exuberant nonsense perhaps recalls the mock-philosophical dialogues between Strepsiades and a travesty of Socrates in Aristophanes's *The Clouds*, a comedy in which a farcical philosopher attempts to educate a rustic in the subtleties of natural philosophy, poetry and law. While Touchstone may fail to answer Corin clearly, he wastes time brilliantly, liberating the audience on stage and off from the 'briers' by which, as Rosalind accurately remarks, life in the 'working-day world' (*As You Like It*, I. 3. 9–10) is beset.

Touchstone's inspired gibberish parodies the relativism that is inherent in attempts at precise definition. It is a deft sideswipe at dogmatic philosophers of all times. Sebastian Brandt, Erasmus and Sidney – in his seriocomic masterpiece of literary theory, *An Apology for Poetry*[39] – all ridicule philosophy's tendency towards otiose formalism, and I shall return to Shakespeare's critique of it in my reading of *Hamlet*. Because Touchstone's opinion, what he is 'truly' stating, is obfuscated by his attempt to achieve clarity through definition, and because this 'parody appears to make distinctions where none really exist and exaggerates their number',[40] this spate of quibbling makes a mockery of definition; its humour lies in the incongruity between the response's spurious pseudo-scholastic form and the simplicity of the question posed.

This wise fool's ironic relativism, moreover, hints at his role within the play. A touchstone, as Kiernan Ryan reminds us, is 'a substance used to test the quality of gold and silver alloys rubbed upon it, and the fool in *As You Like It* serves figuratively as a touchstone for the credibility and values of the diverse viewpoints the play presents us with'.[41] Touchstone's tireless shifting of perspectives epitomises the polyphonic interplay of antithetical intentions and opinions voiced by the protagonists and antagonists in Shakespeare's drama. The myth that Touchstone's critical quibbling humorously disenchants is the myth of the significance and necessity of philosophical method. The punch-line of his mockery of man's drive for absolute conceptual clarity though rigorous definition is: 'Hast any philosophy in thee, shepherd?'

Indeed, the discourse of folly recurrently employs the foolish citation of an authoritative author (or discourses) to make a mockery of them; *Gargantua and Pantagruel* furnishes the reader with an illuminating example of this. At a stroke, Rabelais scatologically debases Scholastic seriousness and, with it, the profundity of Scholastic philosophy as a discourse; concluding his cod-academic discussion about the youthful Gargantua's precise experimentation with the best thing to wipe one's arse on, which, it transpires, is 'the neck of a goose' (*GP*, Book 1, Chapter XIII, p. 57), the narrator bolsters the Prince's scientific findings by commenting: 'such is the opinion of *Master John* of *Scotland*, aliàs *Scotus*' (*GP*, Book 1, Chapter XIII, p. 57).

Notes

1. *Sämtliche Werke*, ed. by Giorgio Colli and Mazzino Montinari, Kritische Studienausgabe, 6 vols (Munich and Berlin: Deutscher Taschenbuch Verlag/ de Gruyter, 1988), VI, p. 378: 'Only fool! Only poet! | Only colourful speech. | speaking through fool's masks. | climbing around on bridges of lying words, | on rainbows of lies | between false heavens | wandering about, prowling about – | *only* fool, *only* poet'! The emphases and irregular punctuation are original [my translation].
2. Philip Sidney, *An Apology for Poetry: or the Defence of Poesy*, ed. by R. W. Maslen (Manchester: Manchester University Press, 2002), p. 103.
3. *Praisers of Folly: Erasmus, Rabelais and Shakespeare* (London: Gollancz, 1964), p. 10.
4. Jonathan Bate reads folly in *King Lear* in the light of Montaigne's 'Apologie of Raymond Sebond' and the *Praise*. Bate argues that all three texts share a comparable anti-stoical standpoint; see 'Shakespeare's Foolosophy', in *Shakespeare Performed: Essays in Honor of R. A. Foakes*, ed. by Grace Ioppolo (Newark: University of Delaware Press, 2000), pp. 17–33. Donald Wehrs draws intriguing parallels between the suspicions about 'cool reason' (*A Midsummer Night's Dream*, V. 1. 6) apparent in Erasmus's theology, Shakespearean comedy, 'contemporary cognitive science, Levinasian ethics and Kristevan psychoanalysis, which conceives of subject formation in terms of a mutually modifying dialogue between the body and discourse, nature and culture'; see 'Touching

Words: Embodying Ethics in Erasmus, Shakespearean Comedy, and Contemporary Theory', *Modern Philology*, 104 (2006), 1–33 (p. 2).

5. See *Shakespeare's Great Stage of Fools* (Basingstoke: Palgrave, 2011) and Diminter Daphinoff, 'Shakespeares Narren' in *Der Narr: Beiträge zu einem Interdisziplinären Gespräch* (Freiburg: Universitätsverlag, 1991), pp. 57–71.
6. Shakespeare's Great Stage of Fools, p. 6.
7. See *The Fool and His Sceptre: A Study in Clowns and Jesters and Their Audience* (London: Edward Arnold, 1969).
8. See *The Fools of Shakespeare: An Interpretation of their Wit, Wisdom and Personalities* (New York: McBride and Nast, 1913).
9. See *Wise Fools in Shakespeare* (Liverpool: Liverpool University Press, 1955; repr. 1977).
10. The most significant of these are those of Karl Friedrich Flögel and Enid Welsford. Flögel's expansive study, which M. M. Bakhtin cites repeatedly in *Rabelais and His World*, examines the role that the grotesque comic had in the formation of various societies from Ancient Greece to Imperial China; see *Geschichte des Grotesk-Komischen: ein Beitrag zur Geschichte der Menschheit*, ed. by Max Bauer, 2 vols (Munich: Georg Müller, 1914 [1788]). But in terms of the sheer breadth of her research, Welsford's work remains unsurpassed: she provides a typology that traces the development of the fool in culture and literature from Greece, via Persia, through Shakespeare, Erasmus, Lodge and Jonson to Charlie Chaplin and the Marx brothers. Her study places fools firmly in a history of ludic customs, and it emphasises the fool's ability to mediate between 'the world of fact and the world of imagination'; (*The Fool: His Social and Literary History* (London: Faber and Faber, 1935; repr. 1968), p. 29.
11. See C. L. Barber, Shakespeare's Festive Comedy: A Study of Dramatic Form and its Relation to Social Custom (Princeton, NJ: Princeton University Press, 1959; repr. 1990).
12. See Phoebe Jensen, *Shakespeare and the Popular Tradition in the Theater*, trans. by Robert Schwartz (Baltimore, MD: Johns Hopkins University Press, 1979).
13. See *Shakespeare's Festive World*, trans. by Janet Lloyd (Cambridge: Cambridge University Press, 1993).
14. See Mock Kings in Medieval Society and Renaissance Drama (Oxford: Oxford University Press, 1991).
15. See *Religion and Revelry in Shakespeare's Festive World* (Cambridge: Cambridge University Press, 2008; repr, 2010).
16. Bristol uses Bakhtin's theories to emphasise the social and political resonances of Shakespeare's unique engagement with fools, folly and the ludic; see 'In Search of the Bear: Spatiotemporal Form and the Heterogeneity of Economies in *The Winter's Tale*', *SQ*, 42 (1991), 145–67; 'Charivari and the Comedy of Abjection in *Othello*', in *True Rites and Maimed Rites: Ritual and Anti-Ritual in Shakespeare and his Age*, ed. by Linda Woodbridge and Edward Berry (Urbana: University of Illinois Press, 1992), pp. 207–224. Manfred Pfister provides an alternative reading of Bakhtin, which pays particular attention to the subversive function of the fool in literature; see 'Comic Subversion: A Bakhtinian View of the Comic in Shakespeare', *Deutsche Shakespeare Gesellschaft Jahrbuch,* (1987), 27–43.
17. For instance, Much of the humour generated by Shakespeare's hapless sleuth, Dogberry, Hornback shows, depends upon the original audiences' familiarity with the 'notable clown type' of the 1590s: 'the stupid or ignorant puritan, a

religious zealot typed by his rusticity, misspeaking and inane logic'. Hornback contends that Dogberry is used as a 'super subtle satiric rebuttal of the Ramist method' – a method that reduced complex philosophical problems to numbered lists and confused understanding with memorisation (*The English Clown Tradition from the Middle Ages to Shakespeare*, Studies in Renaissance Literature, 26 (Cambridge: Brewer, 2009), pp. 102, 138.

18. See 'Emblems of Folly in the First *Othello*: Renaissance Blackface, Moor's Coat and 'Extravagant and Wheeling Strangers: Early Blackface Dancing Fools, Racial Representation, and the Limits of Identification', *Exemplaria*, 20 (2008), 197–223.
19. Barber, p. 245. Laroque argues that festive customs increased social cohesion; see *Shakespeare's Festive World*, pp. 1–16. Following Welsford's contention that 'there is nothing essentially subversive, immoral, blasphemous or rebellious about clownage' (*The Fool*, p. 8), Willeford (*The Fool and his Sceptre*, p. 135; *Wise Fools in Shakespeare*, p. 99) and Bente Videbæk (*The Stage Clown in Shakespeare's Theatre*, Contributions to Drama and Theatre Studies, 69 (Westport, CT: Greenwood, 1996)) argue that foolery ultimately consolidates the dominant order.
20. Mousley seeks to create a 'new literary humanism' that is derived partly from the ideas of Renaissance humanism rather than from the more conservative agenda of liberal humanism, and partly from the ideas of first and Second Generation Frankfurt School thinkers. Mousley argues that philosophical wisdom is encrypted in the speech of characters on the margins of society: 'Literary humanist wisdom often comes from below rather than above, in the shape of women or wise fools or designated individuals, such as Shylock [...], who speak back to the dominant culture about its inhumanity, its dehumanising instrumentalism or its deficient versions of humanism' (*Re-Humanising Shakespeare: Literary Humanism, Wisdom and Modernity* (Edinburgh: Edinburgh University Press, 2007), p. 141); see also, 'The New Literary Humanism: Towards a Critical Vocabulary', *TPr*, 24 (2010), 819–839.
21. Grady attempts to reconstruct an 'alternative Montaignean theory of early modern subjectivity' that uses 'Adorno, Horkheimer [and] Lacan [...] rather than the Machiavellian French post-structuralism that has set the agenda for cultural materialism' (*Shakespeare, Machiavelli and Montaigne: Power and Subjectivity from Richard III to Hamlet* (Oxford: Oxford University Press, 2002), p. 24); this argument develops those initially made in *Shakespeare's Universal Wolf: Studies in Early Modern Reification* (Oxford: Clarendon, 1996), p. 9.
22. Schweppenhäuser argues that a prototypical form of what might be called Critical Theory is identifiable, for the first time in Western literature, in Erasmus's *Praise of Folly*: see 'Narrenschelte und Pathos der Vernunft. Zum Narrenmotiv bei Sebastian Brandt und Erasmus von Rotterdam', *Neophilologus*, 71 (1987), 559–574 (p. 570).
23. Ryan, *Shakespeare's Comedies* (Basingstoke: Palgrave, 2009), p. 94.
24. Leszek Kołakowski, quoted in Jan Kott, *Shakespeare Our Contemporary* (New York: Norton, 1974), p. 131.
25. 'To George and Tom Keats, 21 Dec. 1817', in *The Selected Letters of John Keats*, ed. by Grant F. Scott (Cambridge: Harvard University Press, 1959; repr. 1983), pp. 59–61 (p. 60).
26. Kott, p. 119.

27. *The Order of Things: An Archaeology of the Human Sciences*, trans. by anon. (Basingstoke: Routledge, 2002; repr. 2012), p. 55.
28. Bente Videbæk mentions Shakespeare's covert fools, but only analyses Hamlet and Phillip Falconbridge; see *The Stage Clown in Shakespeare's Theatre*, esp. pp. 1–16.
29. See *OED*, definition no. 1; M. A. Screech points out that 'In the Old Testament, "fool" often implies sinner; folly and "foolishness", sinfulness'. He adds, 'the principal Hebrew words translated as "fool" in the Authorised Version are *halal* (boaster), *evil* (fool), *nabal* (an empty or vile person), *sakal* (a thick-head)' (*Laughter at the Foot of the Cross* (London: Penguin, 1997), p. 81).
30. G. K. Chesterton, '*A Midsummer Night's Dream*', in *On Lying in Bed and Other Essays*, ed. by Alberto Manguel (Calgary: Bayeux Arts, 2000), pp. 193–204 (p. 200).
31. *Shakespeare's Great Stage of Fools*, p. 12.
32. There is a greater number of '*Clowne*' roles in the Folio and the Quarto editions of Shakespeare's plays than any other type of character. The precise significance of them, however, varies significantly from play to play. Despite their different roles in their respective plays, both Feste and the prolix Gravedigger in *Hamlet* are given the speech prefix, 'Clowne'. In the Folio, 20 separate characters are given this speech prefix, whereas 7 are in the Quarto; see Helge Kokeritz, ed., *Mr William Shakespeares Comedies, Histories and Tragedies* (London: Oxford University Press, 1955) and Michael B. Allen and Kenneth Muir, eds., *Shakespeare's Plays in Quarto: A Facsimile Edition from the Henry E. Huntington Library* (Berkeley, CA: University of California Press, 1981).
33. 'Jesting with Death: Hamlet in the Graveyard', *TPr*, 24 (2010), 1003–1018 (p. 1008).
34. Hornback, *The English Clown Tradition*, p. 112.
35. Kiernan Ryan, *Shakespeare's Universality: Here's Fine Revolution* (London: Bloomsbury, 2015), p. 126.
36. Bell, p. 236.
37. *Shakespeare's Language* (Harmondsworth: Penguin, 2000), p. 206.
38. *OED*, quoted in Hornback, *The English Clown Tradition*, pp. 12–13.
39. See *The Shyppe of Fooles*, trans. by Alexander Barclay (London: Wynky[n] de Worde, 1509), pp. 4–5 (*et passim*); *PF*, p. 10; *An Apology for Poetry*, pp. 89–90.
40. Peter Mack, *Reading and Rhetoric in Montaigne and Shakespeare* (London: Bloomsbury, 2010), p. 86.
41. *Shakespeare's Comedies*, p. 213.

2 Humanism and Shakespearean Folly

2.1 Introduction

> There is in human nature generally more of the fool than of the wise; and therefore those faculties by which the foolish part of men's minds is taken are most potent.[1]
>
> —Francis Bacon

> The riddles of God are more satisfying than the solutions of man.[2]
>
> —G. K. Chesterton

Despite its centrality to the philosophical vision of other Renaissance writers, Shakespeare's fascination with folly has seldom been regarded in philosophical terms. Yet, in Shakespeare, folly is not simply an attitude that occasionally comes to the fore to question just how reasonable reason is; rather, what he and his fellow philosophers of folly – Erasmus, More, Rabelais, Montaigne, Jonson and Cervantes – found intriguing about the discourse of folly was how it made certain modes of thinking and forms of writing possible. The paradoxical wisdom of folly is, after all, the possibility of the impossible.

Unlike Erasmus's considerable influence on Shakespeare's friend and collaborator Ben Jonson,[3] the Dutchman's effect on Shakespeare has received comparatively little attention. Although this book brings to light some tantalising analogues between Erasmus's works – particularly the *Praise of Folly* – and Shakespeare's plays, its primary intention is to uncover their intellectual kinship. Thus, this chapter opens by tracing the metamorphosis of Stultitia. It contends that her three personae correspond, albeit fairly broadly, with the three main types of philosophical insight with which Shakespeare's dramatization of folly furnishes us. Next, I consider Thomas More's prescient critique of reason's self-destructive tendencies. Specifically, I consider the consequences of More's use of authorial self-interpolation and a speaker, whose name, Hythloday (Nonsense-Speaker) – like Stultitia (Folly) from *Utopia*'s partner text – disavows any unequivocal claim to authority, which his tall tale about a place called nowhere might otherwise make. I then examine More's juxtaposition of a friar and a fool, before considering a tension at the heart of the discourse of folly: namely, that between a worldly pragmatism that punctures pretensions and a kind of intellectual superiority, which refuses to sully itself by involvement in the inanities of the everyday world.

This chapter concludes with a twofold analysis of Montaigne's *Essays*, which, it is commonly agreed, exerted a considerable influence on Shakespeare's later drama. On the one hand, I illustrate the ways in which Montaigne's *Essays* – in particular, his 'Apologie of *Raymond Sebond*', 'Of Custom', 'Of Canniballs' and 'Of Experience' – transmit Erasmian themes and theories of writing. On the other, I show the remarkable way in which a central tenet of Adorno's aesthetic and political theory, identity critique, is presaged in Montaigne's discussion of the limitations of reason. Throughout what follows, I attend closely to the aesthetic and ideological consequences of the diverse (and innovative) forms – mock encomium, fictionalised travel narrative, essay and, of course, drama – through which folly finds expression in this period. I conclude by suggesting that what these forms share is precisely what appealed to Adorno about the essay: they offer a mode of expression that does not seek to universalise or establish a system. All four types of writing, after all, share a remarkable capacity to vividly evoke and criticise the particular, while retaining an ironic, almost Socratic, self-awareness. Not least through their use of foolish or self-effacing narrators, these texts sidestep any claims to authority, claims that they are certain of the truth. Perhaps the most obvious example of what I mean is furnished by the *Praise of Folly*: one would hardly expect any sort of philosophical insight to arise from an action as manifestly foolish as praising folly. But one would, naturally, be quite wrong.

2.2 Stultitia's Metamorphosis

Erasmus's Stultitia has three distinct incarnations. In the first section of the *Praise of Folly*, she undertakes an almost carnivalesque levelling of the differences that divide humanity, pointing out the physical nature its members share before arguing to the end that: 'No profit grows where is no pleasure ta'en' (*The Taming of the Shrew*, I. 1. 38). In the second, she caustically attacks the hypocrisy and venality of the powers that be. And in the third, she morphs into a Christian fool, extolling the folly of the cross. Her first persona turns 'diseases to commodity' (*2 Henry IV*, I. 2. 243), suggesting that were it not for humanity's universal folly, life would not be worth living.[4]

She celebrates mankind's shared corporeality and flaws and begins by asking her audience to give her the licence to speak freely – 'bestowe on me your eares [...] not those eares that ye carie to sermons, but those ye geue to plaiers, to jesters, and to fools' (*PF*, p. 8). After suggesting that she is 'the distraibtrix and dealer of all felicitee' (*PF*, p. 8), Stultitia launches into a mock genealogy, in which she contends that her father is Plutus, the 'golden god of riches [...] at whose onely becke as aforetymes, so now also, bothe holy and vnholy thynges be tourned topset turuie' (*PF*, p. 11). Not only do the events of Jonson's satire *Volpone*, which paraphrases the *Praise of Folly* and was performed by the King's Men in 1605, revolve around mankind's insatiable desire for gold, 'the world's soul' (I. 1. 3), but Shakespeare, in an invective which impressed Marx because of its economic accuracy, was also to extemporise about gold's transformative possibilities thus: 'Thus much of this will make | Black white, foul fair, wrong right, | Base noble, old young, coward valiant' (*Timon of Athens*, IV. 3. 27–30). Yet the tantalizing dance of capital is not the only thing that beguiles – or bedevils – humankind. So too do Stultitia's 'handmaides', who include 'Selfeloue',[5] 'Voluptuousnes' and 'Dronkenes' (*PF*, p. 11). By her own estimation at least, she is 'the geuer of all thynges to all men' (*PF*, p. 14), a comment that recalls Paul's observation that God 'giveth to all life, and breath, and all things' (*KJV*, Acts 17. 25). In discussing the universal illusion by which mankind is duped, Stultitia evokes what, for Erasmus and Christians to this day, is the necessary condition for existence: God's Grace. In copious style, she delineates the ways in which all actions, institutions and ideologies are beholden to her: they are all premised on the illusion that man possesses control of things, that he has the power to act independently and that what he does is cosmically significant.

The truth, according to Stultitia in the first part of her *sermon joyeux*, is quite the contrary: life consists of nothing other than the flourishing of certain follies – childhood is foolish, as is adolescence, and so too is manhood. The wiser a man becomes, 'the lesse and lesse he liveth' (*PF*, p. 15). Too much reading, she suggests, is liable to make one repress the bodily drives that make everyone tick. Old age, during which man becomes 'vrksome to others [...] and hateful also to hym selfe' (*PF*, p. 15), follows this decline. And no one could bear this, were it not for folly; it is only by 'becom[ing] childisshe again' that the elderly can face 'Obliuion' with a 'dronken longe forgetfulnesse of thynges passed', without fear of what is to come (*PF*, p. 17).[6] The illusion of love enables men and women to 'take into [their] mouthe the snaffle of wedlocke' (*PF*, p. 15) – what right-thinking woman would venture to undergo the 'perillous throwes of childbearing, or trauaile of their bringing vp' (*PF*, p. 16)? Stultitia uses the levelling potential of the human body when she points out that the organ that 'engendre[s] gods and men' is but a 'silie membre [...] so foolishe as maie not without laughter be spoken of' (*PF*, p. 15), but although Bakhtin is quite right to consider the *Praise* to be 'one of the greatest expressions of carnival laughter in world literature',[7] critics interested in the corporeal elements of the *Praise* have over-emphasised the importance of Stultitia's first persona,[8] which cannot, of course, be viewed in isolation from the structural ironies generated by her other two personae.

The insights of Stultitia's first incarnation correspond with those of Shakespeare's discourse of folly in two ways. First, they remind the reader that, from cradle to grave, the aspirations, achievements and sorrows of the serious world are simply scenes in a 'great plaie of follie' (*PF*, p. 36), or as *Lear* has it – quite possibly quoting Chaloner's 1549 translation of the *Moriae Encomium* – scenes on a 'great stage of fools' (*Lear*, IV. 6. 87). The second main type of philosophical insight that Shakespeare's discourse of folly furnishes us with is a sense of man's shared corporeal nature, in all its absurdity, with all its unpleasant abjections. Needless to say, the adepts of the discourse of folly, such as Pantagruel or Falstaff, are attuned to the body. Bodily processes are shared by the philosophically and non-philosophically minded and by rich and poor alike. For this reason, Terence Cave views them as key to the 'non-transcendent humanity' of the works of Erasmus, Ronsard, Rabelais and Montaigne.[9] In fact, when the latter writes in 'Of Experience' that 'on the loftiest throne in the world we are sitting only on our rump' (*F*, Book III, Chapter XIII, p. 1044), he almost appropriates the court fool's role of deflating his master's grandeur by reminding him of his physicality.

In Erasmus's case, however, his interest in the body as a stubbornly pre-philosophical addendum springs from his concern that the subtlety of arguments of contemporary theologians, along with their asceticism, negates the key role that the body plays in Christianity, a role that is obvious from the doctrines of the Incarnation and the Resurrection and the sacraments of communion and marriage. In Shakespeare, however, such comments serve to scupper the pretentions of speculation that regards itself as having transcended the body; the most remarkable instance of this is found in Shylock's famous plea for equality: 'Hath not a Jew eyes? Hath not a Jew hands, organs, dimensions, senses, affections, passions; [...] if you prick us do we not bleed? If you tickle us do we not laugh?' (*The Merchant of Venice*, III. 1. 50–54). Everyone shares similar bodily features, physical vulnerability and the same ability to transcend this vulnerability through that involuntary physical response of laughter, which Rabelais justly considers to be the unique and 'proper' feature of humankind (*GP*, Book 1, 'Prologue', p. 23).

About one third of the way through, Stultitia's oration changes tone. It slides away from pointing out the ways in which man lives a life unknowingly dedicated to folly to a caustic critique of the hypocrisies of the powers that be. The satirical railing of Thersites or Timon plainly resonates with this critique of authority. Erasmus can get away with it only because he has donned the persona of Stultitia: 'what worde comying out of a wyseman's mouthe were a hangying mattier, the same yet spoken by a foole shall muche delight euin hym that is touched therewith' (*PF*, p. 50).

Despite his deliberate disengagement from direct critique by using a persona, Erasmus's enemies still managed to wrest Stultitia's critique out of its seriocomic context and accuse him of heresy,[10] an accusation that was levelled at most of the great thinkers of the early modern age. Stultitia's erudite attack on human vanity encompasses all estates of man, from judges to priests, and from mercenaries to philosophers, with the exception of the poor and despised. Her *bêtes noires*, however, are Doctors of Divinity and theologians, for they are 'a neste of men [...] crabbed and waspelyke' (*PF*, p. 78):

> [...] propped vp with theyr owne Arrogance and Selflikyng, as if they dwelled amonges the sterres, or loked downe from aloft, and in a manner toke compassion vppon other seely men lyke wormes crepyng by the grounde. Namely whiles thei are hedged in on all sides, with such a gard of Magistral deffinicions, conclusions, corollaries, explicite and implicite propositions [...].
>
> (*PF*, p. 78)

This brand of theology misconceives the egalitarian simplicity of the teachings of the New Testament. The apostles, Stultitia comments, 'had need to be enstructed by a new spirite, in case vpon these matters they were compelled to argue with this new kynde of doctors' (*PF*, p. 80). What is more, such abstruse and self-satisfied speculation fails to grasp the fact that Christian faith is manifested through deeds, not through words.[11] The theologians, mendicants and priests whom Erasmus attacks are, in the words of Lear's fool: 'more in word than matter' (*Lear*, III. 2. 81). In part, at least, Stultitia is attacking Scholasticism, the theoretical core of the Catholic Church in the early sixteenth century, which employed Aristotelian dialectics to resolve Scriptural ambiguities. Critics interested in the role of Erasmus's works in the Reformation have tended to emphasise this section of the *Praise of Folly*, since it attacks the superstition and corruption of the Church just as much as the fruitless subtleties of Scholasticism.[12]

More important for our purposes, however, is how Stultitia debunks self-satisfied modes of speculation, which, peering down from dizzying heights of abstraction on the vast majority of humankind, view laymen as though they were 'wormes crepyng by the grounde'. Such anti-intellectualism is apparent in the canon of folly before Erasmus's genius for irony transformed it; after the author himself, the first fools aboard Sebastian Brandt's *Narrenschiff* are the learned, 'douctures' and 'clerkes', who are exhorted to:

> Consyder our olde faders: note wel theyr diligence:
> Ensue ye theyr steppes: obtayne ye such fame,
> As they dyd lyuynge: and that by true Prudence.
> Within theyr hartys they planted theyr scyence
> And nat in plesaunt bokes.[13]

In both books, 'Laughter purifies from dogmatism, from the intolerant and petrified; it liberates from fear and intimidation':[14] the power of the church, which underwrote intellectual endeavour until the Reformation, is rendered risible by evoking the disjunction between lived faith apparent in the teachings of the Patriarchs and Apostles and the book-learning of modern doctors of divinity. In this connection, something of the anti-systematic impulse that Catherine Bates detects in Nietzsche can be discerned both in Stultitia's seriocomic invective and Brandt's didactic satire:

> Any presumption of mastery or control over nature on the part of human beings was utterly vain – an absurd grandiosity based on nothing more substantial than the intellect's own flattering and entirely self-generated estimate of itself. The human mind didn't deliver truth so much as illusions that were structured to look like truths. It surveyed the surface of things and gave the name reality to what was no more than its own particular way of seeing.[15]

The crucial difference between the two works, however, is the claim to authority that each makes: 'What Brandt, with the whole authority of the author of the *Narrenschiff*, proclaims as a vain outrage to be fought against, Erasmus lets Stultitia say'.[16] In other words, Erasmus was Democritus to Brandt's Heraclitus.

That pretentious ratiocination and jargon-addled specialism obscure what they purport to explain is an anti-philosophical insight common in Shakespeare's dramatization of folly. When he speciously cites a pseudo-religious fictional authority's pedantic insight, which is anything but insightful, and appropriates it as a syllogistic justification of his sacrilegious impersonation, Feste makes a mockery of such sophistry:

> FESTE: [...] as the old hermit of Prague, that never saw pen and ink, very wittily said to a niece of King Gorboduc, 'that that is, is.' So I being Master Parson, am Master Parson; for what is 'that' but 'that' [...]?
>
> (*Twelfth Night*, IV. 2. 11–14)

This inspired perversion of philosophical doctrine is not that far removed from the discourse of the self-serving theologians, against whom Stultitia inveighs for bending the Scripture to have heretics burnt at the stake or to justify war (see *PF*, p. 89–90) – an outrageous perversion of Christian doctrine, which was as common then as it is now. As Gerhard Schweppenhäuser contends, beneath Erasmus's satire, there 'implicitly appears humanistic pathos [about] the suffering and violence stupidity causes',[17] a pathos that is clearly discernible in Shakespeare's plays.

Early in his career, in *Love's Labour's Lost*, Shakespeare experiments with the idea that philosophy is utterly removed from the drives and desires of everyday existence: the arrival of the Princess and her ladies causes the self-denying intentions of students at the King's 'little academe' (I. 1. 13) to fall at the first hurdle. The antithesis of the nonsense spoken by the old hermit of Prague and the schoolmen derided by Stultitia's second persona is a philosophy of the sort espoused by her first persona, a philosophy that is sensitive to man's embodied nature, a kind of thinking that Montaigne memorably describes as 'intellectually sensible and sensibly-intellectuall' (*E*, Book 3, Chapter 13, p. 625).

Stultitia's self-reflexive critique of Grammarians like Erasmus, philosophers, theologians and scholars is founded on the idea that 'in all humaine thynges there is so great darkness and diuersnesse as nothing maie be clearly knowne out nor discouered' (*PF*, p. 63). Anybody who claims to know the true nature of things with any degree of certainty is at best deluded and at worst a hypocrite – like the venal lawyers, pardoners and kings whom she vehemently attacks. The three incarnations of Stultitia are not separate entities. After all, her critical attack on the vanity of the sciences paves the way for the third part of her oration, where she morphs into a Christian fool, extolling the paradoxical wisdom of holy folly. The argument of the *Praise* is bound up with its movement, which Roland Bainton summarises with admirable clarity:

> The irrational is shown to be the rational. Yes, but the irrational is shown to be the rational only because the rational is shown to be irrational and all those disciplines so neatly reduced by men to order are but striving after the wind.[18]

The final section is based on the idea that folly is the only attribute that the finite and the infinite, human and divine, share:

> Now all these texts that I have alleaged, doe thei not plainly testifie, that mortall men beyng fooles, are godly also? And that Christ hym selfe mindying the relefe and redempcion of mankyndes folie, although he was the ineffable wisdome of the father, became yet a manner foole?
>
> (*PF*, p. 118)

God's primary folly is the incarnation, in which He 'clothed Himself in vile man's flesh | So that he might be weak enough to suffer woe'.[19] By the standards of worldly logic, this action, through which the immortal became mortal, is foolish or even mad. It is in this connection that Paul comments: 'the foolishness of God is wiser than man; and the weakness of God is stronger than man' (I Corinthians, 1. 25).

As Nicholas Cusanus, whom Erasmus and Montaigne both read, explains in *De docta ignorantia* (1440), what reason can positively know can consist only of 'measurement' and this is 'limited to the reality it has in a finite mind'.[20] Reason cannot fathom the 'infinite' or 'maximum', since 'in every inquiry men judge of the uncertain by comparing it with an object presupposed certain, and their judgement is always approximate; every inquiry is, therefore, comparative and uses the method of analogy'.[21] The relative nature of all human sciences comes to the fore in Cusanus's contribution to the canon of folly, *De idiota* (1450), which contains perhaps the earliest example of a fool wisely giving the lie to the values of the marketplace. Citing holy writ, the Idiot deflates man's pretensions to knowledge:

IDIOT: Because I told thee that wisedome cries out in the streets, and her cry is, that she dwells in the most high places, this now will I endeavour to shew thee. And first tell me what doest thou see here done in the Marketplace?

ORATOR: I see in one place moneyes telling, in another wares a weighing, and over against us, oyle a measuring. [...]

IDIOT: These are the workes of that reason, by which men excell beasts; for bruit beasts can neither number, weigh, nor measure.[22]

When the archetypal fool for love, Antony, reflects that 'there's beggary in the love that can be reckoned' (*Antony and Cleopatra*, I. 1. 15), he too suggests that what really matters cannot be calculated or measured. Likewise, in 'The Phoenix and the Turtle', Shakespeare's neo-platonic evocation of romantic ecstasy, 'Reason' is 'in itself confounded' (41) by the fact that:

Property was thus appalled
That the self was not the same.
Single nature's double name
Neither two nor one was called.

(37–40)

At a stroke, an individual's identity, the most basic predicate of calibrating reason not to mention a good deal of philosophy, is destroyed. Reason's capacity to measure is voided: 'Number there in love was slain' (28), and thus 'Love hath reason, reason none' (47).

For Erasmus, the true Christian imitates in their worship and their acts God's self-bankrupting love as best they can:[23]

> [...] no maner fooles are in apparence more ideotelike, than suche as are totally rauisshed, and enflamed with the ardent zeale of Christian charitee. So laueshly thei deale their goodes abrode, forgette all iniuries doen vnto theim, suffer theim selues to be decieued, put no difference between friends and foes, abhorre all pleasures and delites of the bodie [...]. Briefely, [they] seme to be so astonned and past all commen senses, which men liue by, as if their soules dwelled not in those bodies thei beare about with theim, but rather in some other mansion place [...] to the common iudgement of men [they] appeere to be [in] a verie madnesse, or rauying of the wittes [...] the apostles were iudged by the wicked Ethnikes to be drunkards [...] and Paul likewise was holden for madde, of Festus.
>
> (*PF*, p. 121)

By pointing out that the apostles also appeared ridiculous, Stultitia praises the foolish appearance and selfless behaviour of 'fools for Christ's sake' (I Corinthians, 4. 10). Shakespeare and his collaborators have Erasmus's best friend Thomas More confess that he is 'a very unthrift' because he has 'purchased [...] strange commodities' of 'Crutches [...] and bare cloaks, | For halting soldiers and poor needy scholars', making himself 'the poorest chancellor | That ever was in England' (*Sir Thomas More*, V. 3. 64, 52, 57–58, 47–48).[24] Conversely, the motivations of worldly fools, dedicated merely to getting by in the sublunary world, are rendered incomprehensible, even irrational.

Rabelais's *Gargantua and Pantagruel*, on which the influence of Erasmus is well chronicled,[25] expounds the same paradox with such brilliance as to warrant extensive quotation. Pantagruel, the foolosopher Prince, persuades Panurge to take the advice of a fool, Triboulet, by making the following argument:

> [H]e who narrowly takes heed to what concerns the dexterous Management of his private Affairs, domestick Businesses and those Adoes which are confined within the streight-lac'd compass of one Family: who is attentive, vigilant, and active in the oeconomik Rule of his own house [...] and who knows warily how to prevent the Inconveinces of Poverty, is a called a worldly Wise Man, though perhaps in the second Judgment of the Intelligences which are above, he is esteemed a *Fool*. So on the contary, is he most like [...] to be not only *sage*, but to *presage* Events to come by Divine Inspiration, who laying aside those cares which are conduciable to his body or his fortunes, and as it were rids all his senses of Terrene Affections [...]. All which neglects of Sublunary Things are vulgarly imputed *Folly*.
>
> (*GP*, Book 3, Chapter 37, p. 446)

Without wealth, the capacity to dissimulate, or scholastic arguments, these fools *live* their faith, embodying the radical egalitarian kernel of the New Testament, particularly apparent in the 'Sermon on the Mount' and Paul's writings. As Schweppenhäuser shows, the *Praise* uses irony to critique the emergent conceptions of bourgeois reason, whereas Brandt's *Narrenschiff* (1494) exonerates forward planning from charges of folly, and – in absolute contrast to Erasmus – associates thriftiness with godliness.[26]

Those interested in Erasmus's 'theology of ecstasy' have tended to emphasise the role of this final section of the *Praise* at the expense of the others;[27] but this description of holy fools lies in juxtaposition to Stultitia's attack on the learned, which, in turn, is connected to the bodily follies of the first section: 'Only through insight into the ambivalence between self-praise and self-denunciation can the paradoxical form of folly, and with it the organizing principle of the work, be unlocked'.[28] Rabelais employs his grotesque characters in a seriocomic exploration of the self-abnegating generosity of 'fools for Christ's sake' and of God himself. When the prodigal trickster Panurge is made 'Laird of Sulmygourdin in Dyposidie' by Pantagruel, he 'wastes' his substantial income:

> Now his Worship, the new *Laird*, husbanded this his Estate so providently well and prudently, that in less than fourteen days he wasted and dilapidated all the certain and uncertain Revenue of his Lairdship for three whole years: Yet he did not properly dilapidate it [...] in founding monastrays, building of churches [...] but spent it in a thousend little Banquets and jolly collations, keeping an open house for all Comers and Goers [...] borrowing money before-hand, buying dear, selling cheap, and eating corn (as it were) whilst it was but grass.
> (*GP*, Book 3, Chapter 2, p. 305)

Because he borrows with high interest and sells for cash, what Rabelais fallaciously terms the 'Mysteries of *Practical Arithmetick*' are evidently lost on this imprudent trickster. He lives for the moment, entertaining 'good fellows' and 'pretty wenches' (*GP*, Book 3, Chapter 2, p. 305) regardless of the cost. Enacting something of the boundless generosity at the core of the New Testament for himself, the Prince is 'in no way offended at the matter, angry, nor sorry' by his friend's 'Lavishness' (*GP*, Book 3, Chapter 2, p. 305).

Erasmus emphasises that although holy fools appear foolish in the eyes of the world, they are, like the lovers in 'The Phoenix and the Turtle', experiencing a tantalizing

> [F]oretaste of future blessedness, by which we are totally absorbed into God and shall live in future more in him than in ourselves. [...] what Plato calls madness, being rapt out of himself; he exists in the object of his love [...] he is brought in to a new kind of teaching, very different from all the current convictions of the wise and foolish alike.
> (*CWE*, 3, p. 127)

This passage, from his 'Letter to Maarten van Dorp' (May 1515), which is often appended to editions of the *Praise*, succinctly reiterates his argument from the final pages of the *Praise* (see *PF*, pp. 126–29). Referring to Plato's conception of poetic rapture, a state in which poets 'are seized by a divine spirit, which inspires them to rise above human limitations',[29] Erasmus suggests that fools offer a radical third way of knowing, one that goes beyond sublunary categories. He conceives of Greek philosophy as something that foreshadows Christian theology; texts from a pagan prehistory prefigure the teaching of the Gospel. While it would demand a full-length study in its own right, the anachronistic significance of Greek thought in Christianity had a considerable impact on the early modern mindset. A hundred years after the Dutchman's death, John Donne, for instance, argues along strikingly similar lines: 'it is evident, that in *Trismegistus*, and in *Zoroaster*, and in Plato and some other Authors of that Ayre, there seem to be clearer, and more literall expressings of the Trinity, than are in all the prophets of the old Testament'.[30]

Shakespeare, however, goes a step further than Erasmus in his use of the ironies it is possible to generate from the supra-rational wisdom of God's folly. In the *Praise*, a fool, who makes only spurious claims to authority, extols the paradoxical wisdom of folly, whereas in *A Midsummer Night's Dream*, Bottom brilliantly bungles St Paul's description of the ineffable joys of Salvation – 'But as it is written, The things which eye hath not seen, neither ear hath heard, neither came into man's heart, are, which God hath prepared for them that love him' (*Geneva*, I Corinthians 2. 9) – when he expresses his ostensibly inexpressible dream:

> BOTTOM: [...] I have had a most rare vision. I have had a dream past the wit of man to say what dream it was. Man is but an ass, if he go about t'expound this dream. Methought I was – there is no man can tell what. Methought I was, and methought I had – but man is but a patched fool if he will offer to say what methought I had. *The eye of man hath not heard, the ear of man hath not seen, man's hand is not able to taste, his tongue to conceive, nor his heart to report, what my dream was.* I will get Peter Quince to write a ballad of this dream. It shall be called Bottom's Dream, because it hath no bottom, and I will sing it in the latter end of a play, before the duke. Peradventure, to make it the more gracious, I shall sing it at her death.
>
> (IV. 1. 196–211[my emphasis])

For several reasons, Bottom's nonsense is astonishing. Awakening from his dream, in which he has fulfilled that age-old human fantasy of inhabiting an alternative body but nonetheless remained steadfastly himself, Bottom travesties Paul's memorable evocation of how man cannot grasp the joys of heaven – accidentally performing the limitations of human knowledge even as he describes them. As in Erasmus, a manifest fool, albeit not one who openly admits to being such, points out the absurdities of attempting to know the unknowable.[31]

In this respect, Bottom's inspired gibberish implies something similar to what Theseus, with characteristic self-assurance, formulates towards the end of the play: there are states of being, including dreaming, the lover's infatuation and poetic inspiration, that 'apprehend | More than cool reason ever comprehends' (V. 1. 5–6). Because of Bottom's malapropisms, however, even the doctrine of learned ignorance is submitted to the play's jubilant irony. Bottom's fears of idiotically endeavouring to explain away the unexplainable – 'man is but an ass, if he go about to expound this dream' – are undermined by the simple structural irony that Bottom has, quite literally, just been an 'ass'. Nonetheless, this sentiment foreshadows Shakespeare's closing act of authorial disavowal:

PUCK: If we shadows have offended,
Think but this, and all is mended:
That you have but slumbered here,
While these visions did appear;
And this weak and idle theme,
No more yielding but a dream,
Gentles do not reprehend.

('Epilogue', 1–6)

Man is an ass, Shakespeare implies, if he takes umbrage at *A Midsummer Night's Dream*, since drama seldom unequivocally affirms any one position. In fact, the way that the play idles away the time helps to constitute its philosophical vantage point, its otherness to the ideals of the waking world. Although Bottom considers it impossible to 'expound' the significance of his dream, he nonetheless sees its literary potential. However, the song he envisages, which is the ballad of 'Bottom's Dream' to being sung after the death of Thisbe, flagrantly violates theatrical decorum. While the performance of it remains an unrealised possibility in *A Midsummer's Night's Dream*, the mere mention of this ballad makes a mockery of both the high seriousness of Ovid's original and that of *Romeo and Juliet*, Shakespeare's tragedy of the same year based on the same tale.

2.3 Dialectics and Utopian Enlightenment

More's *Utopia*, one of the canonical texts of Renaissance folly and a possible influence on *The Tempest*,[32] Shakespeare's own deeply ambivalent comment on utopia, confronts the order of things considered rational today, almost as much as it tested the mores of Tudor England. Yet at first glance the satire of Book One has lost its topical resonance, its power to alarm and offend; for instance, when Hythloday reflects that 'Normally sheep are placid and eat very little, but now I hear that they have become so voracious and fierce that they have started eating men' (*U*, Book I, p. 66), the significance of this topical attack on the enclosures dictated by the burgeoning wool trade could easily be overlooked.

For two reasons, however, this is not the case. First, by employing the memorable image of ravenously carnivorous sheep, Hythloday uses the kind of seriocomic sugar-coating that Erasmus defends in his famous letter to Dorp. The object of the *Praise of Folly* is 'to teach and delight',[33] since 'truth by itself is a trifle astringent, and thus when made palatable finds an easier entrance into the minds of men' (*CWE*, 3, p. 113). Second, this image epitomises the self-destructive impulse at the heart of early modern (and present-day) capitalism. 'England', Hythloday comments, 'used to seem exceptionally prosperous; now the unchecked greed of a few is destroying that prosperity' (*U*, Book I, p. 67). This self-destruction is caught up with the kind of rationality that is premised on self-preservation at all costs; as Horkheimer and Adorno note, 'the not merely theoretical [*ideelle*] but practical tendency towards self-annihilation has been inherent in rationality from the start' (DA, p. 7; [*DE*, p. xix]).

But as Alain Badiou's and Slavoj Žižek's recent studies show,[34] such rationality finds its antithesis in the communism and pacifism of Jesus's and St. Paul's teachings, which are central to Erasmus's understanding of Christian folly. The image of voracious 'sheep' is clearly ironic, since sheep are commonly used as a metaphor for the Christian faithful. It encapsulates what R. W. Chambers long ago considered to be the formula at work in *Utopia* as a whole: 'With nothing save Reason to guide them, the Utopians do this; and yet we Christian Englishmen, we Christian Europeans, do this'.[35] That reason has the paradoxical ability to create the 'instruments' (*CWE*, 36, p. 402) of its own annihilation is, in fact, pointed out by Erasmus in his long pacifist essay, 'Dulce Bellum Inexpertis' (*CWE*, 36, p. 399–440), which is one of *Utopia*'s sources.[36]

Insofar as it presages much of what has still to be openly acknowledged, More's text looks back on the present day from its position somewhere in the future. This becomes clear when *Utopia* is considered in relation to the thesis of Horkheimer's and Adorno's *Dialectic of Enlightenment*: 'Myth is already enlightenment, and enlightenment reverts to mythology [*schon der Mythos ist Aufklärung, und: Aufklärung schlägt in Mythologie zurück*]' (DE, p. xviii; *DA*, p. 6) This is not to say, however, that St Thomas More was a harbinger of modernity. Rather, within his model of social progress lies a diagnosis of the tendencies latent in enlightened societies, which cause them to revert to barbarism; humankind's confidence in their intellectual convictions and instrumentality not only enables their enlightenment, but also causes repression and fear to a hitherto unimaginable extent.

Furthermore, the first aspect of the *Dialectic of Enlightenment*'s thesis is also apparent in *Utopia*. Despite being written by a Christian martyr, before the emergence of the vocabulary of scientific enquiry,[37] *Utopia* nonetheless examines the workings of the market using 'schemes and models'.[38] The second aspect of Adorno and Horkheimer's thesis is discernible if we trace the history of the literary genre that More's neologism, *utopia*, came to signify. *Utopia*, like Bacon's *New Atlantis*, displays a remarkable faith in the capacities of technology and social organisation to ensure human happiness. Yet, in the latter-day dystopias of Zamyatin, Huxley and Orwell, it is precisely technology and social organisation – the two things that have enabled man to dominate nature to an unprecedented extent – that thwart the possibility of his happiness. What had promised to liberate, now oppresses.

At the start of their book, Horkheimer and Adorno quote Francis Bacon's 'In Praise of Knowledge', which contends that the chief aim of knowledge is for man to be able to "control [nature] by action" (DE, p. 1; *DA*, p. 10).

This early philosophical formulation of enlightened man's instrumental relationship with nature is prefigured in *Utopia*. Not only do the Utopians battery-farm their chickens, but they also ensure the maximum possible agricultural yield through a precise categorisation and division of land; Utopian town planning, with its large boulevards and identical houses, displays a striking anticipation of the Haussmannization of Paris and, therefore, knowledge of the relationship between spatial design and social control. And the notoriously pragmatic attitude of the Utopians towards war – it should be avoided at all costs and preferably won by stealth (see *U*, Book I, pp. 135–44) – chimes with what Adorno and Horkheimer write about Odysseus, whom they consider to be a proto-bourgeois individual (DE, pp. 24–62; *DA*, pp. 41–88) because he eschewed the brute strength and endurance of the chivalric hero and used stealth, organisation and craftiness to complete his aims.

Of course, More's new genre partly has its roots in Edenic myths like the land of Cockaygne (see *CWM*, 4, p. clxvii), but his Utopia is no Big Rock Candy Mountain. In place of the cornucopian abundance, sexual licence and freedom of movement and expression, which is apparent, for instance, in Rabelais's Thélème with its daring injunction, '*Do what thou wilt*' (*GP*, Book 1, Chapter 57, p. 157), there is austerity, surveillance and strict control of travel, expression and sexual relations. In Utopia, 'liberation' from fear, the fundamental aim of 'Enlightenment understood in the widest sense as advance of thought' (*DE*, p. 1; DA, p. 9),[39] proves to be chimerical. As ostensible Enlightenment 'reverts' to superstition, the people remain passive and fearful. Although the Utopians need not fear a spectacular execution like the Tudor thieves of the First Book, they must, as Stephen Greenblatt shows, fear shame and slavery. More shames his readers by forcing them to compare the chaotic misery of their society with the order and formal freedom of the pagan utopians.[40]

Indeed, the expectation that the Utopians 'make good use of their free time' (*U*, Book II, p. 98), the micro-organisation of their every waking hour and an insistence on sociability presages the *Dialectic of Enlightenment*'s arguments about the illusory nature of freedom in modern society:

> Formal freedom is guaranteed for everyone. No one has to answer officially for what he or she thinks. However, all find themselves enclosed from early on within a system of churches, clubs, professional associations, and other relationships, which amount to the most sensitive instrument of social control.
>
> (*DE*, p. 120; DA, p. 158)

It is not just in Book Two, More's concrete model for social improvement, that we can discern anticipations of the *Dialectic*: in the first section, Hythloday illustrates how, after the enclosures of the landlords, the persecution of those left homeless as vagabonds is, as he later puts it, 'a conspiracy of the rich against the poor' (*U*, Book II, p. 157). Morton suggests that the English could test out the practices of the Polyerites ('People of Much Nonsense' [*U*, Book I, p. 71]) on 'vagabonds', upon whom 'so far none of our measures have been successful' (*U*, Book I, p. 73), by turning them into slaves and distinguishing them, terrifyingly, by 'badges' (*U*, p. 72).

More thematises the misinterpretation of Hythloday's comments: the whole point of his attack on the judicial system, of course, is that such people are victims of wider social forces. They become vagabonds, who are, like Poor Tom, 'whipped from tithing to tithing, and stock-punished, and imprisoned' (*King Lear*, III. 4. 124–25), as a direct result of the aristocracy's profiteering (*U*, Book I, 64–73). And this irony throws into relief a pattern of thought that is comparable to the sort Horkheimer and Adorno observe at work in anti-Semitism, in which people are attacked on the grounds of the very powerlessness or weakness – political or physical – that social conditions foist upon them (see *DE*, p. 137–39; DA, 177–78). 'Like Marx's early *Economic and Philosophical Manuscripts*', Greenblatt argues, 'More's work propounds communism less as a coherent economic program than as a weapon against certain tendencies in human nature'.[41] In fact, what *Praise of Folly* and *Utopia* are grasping for is a form of expression in which they can express something comparable to Critical Theory and what Schweppenhäuser writes about the *Praise* could equally well apply to *Utopia*; he contends:

> [T]he *Praise of Folly* is an introduction to reason's unsystematic self-reflection on its problematic realization. The criticism of reason, which is the motive of this work, refers already to the advanced forms of self-critical reason of the present.[42]

By using strategies of ironic disassociation, these humanists can attack the injustices of their world and model alternatives: in More, Utopian communism; in Erasmus, a life led according to the principles of holy folly. But this detachment means that what they offer does not have to be an impervious system. Both *Utopia* and *Praise of Folly* are, like Critical Theory 'incompatible with the idealist belief that any theory is independent of men and even has a growth of its own',[43] not least because Hythloday's ostensibly idealistic thought actually advocates adherence to the teaching of the Gospel, the expression of which is found in deeds rather than words. Both texts critique early modern society, debunking certain customs that shape the behaviour of individuals, who profess to be Christians, but act, frequently in bad faith, in a manner antithetical to that expounded in the Gospel.

2.4 Playing the Fool in Utopia

Utopia employs narrative techniques comparable to those of Stultitia's oration. Despite – or perhaps because of – the connotations their names hold, both speakers furnish the reader with a critique of the world as it is and offer suggestions about how the world could one day be. And like the *Praise* and many of Erasmus's *Colloquies*, *Utopia* is open-ended, without a clear-cut conclusion. Indeed, the ultimate significance of this thoroughly slippery and ambiguous text remains radically indeterminate. 'Explaining why *Utopia* is the sort of text it is', its most recent editor and translator, David Wootton, writes, 'is not the same as fixing its meaning, for the whole point of *Utopia* is that whenever we feel we have a grip on it, it slips from our grasp'.[44]

This is not least because both texts appear so critical of the dominant order of things: Stultitia seems to see pretensions to certainty as mere vanity, whereas Hythloday recurrently emphasises the fact that 'whenever you have private property, and money is the measure of all things, you will find society can scarcely ever be just or prosperous' (*U*, Book I, p. 86), a comment that 'At a stroke dismisses the elaborate ideology of status and custom that provided the time-honored justification for the uneven distributions of wealth in society'.[45] To have absolute faith in the veracity of Hythloday's narration, however, would be to take a fool's word as gospel. As David Wootton observes, *Utopia* is a Silenic text. This notion is central to Renaissance folly and finds fuller exposition in my next chapter, but essentially Wootton means that *Utopia* is characterised by a sense of duplicity: it is like the Silenus head, insofar as it 'holds out the possibility that our ways of thinking about the world are fundamentally unstable; that the "right" viewpoint may be parasitic on the "wrong"'.[46] This is most visibly evoked when the Anemolian ambassadors come to Utopia:

> They had gold rings on their fingers, and sparkling strings of gems and pearls hung from their caps. In short, they were dressed in exactly the way the Utopians dress slaves to punish them, and children to amuse them. [...] So [the Utopians] bowed low to the lowliest servants [...] as if they were great lords, while they mistook the ambassadors themselves, since they were wearing gold chains, for slaves, and showed them no respect at all.
>
> (*U*, Book II, p. 112)

Discussing the topsy-turvy, Silenic nature of 'all humaine thynges' (*PF*, p. 37), Stultitia reflects that, when one opens the Silenus head, what was once infamous becomes glorious: '*quod infame, gloriosum*'.[47] The misapprehension of the Utopians opens up the Silenus head: the beggarly 'slaves' are venerated, while the distinguished ambassadors are thought to be mere 'slaves'. Evidently, a 'transvaluation of values' has taken place. More significantly, however, this transvaluation also offers a satirical *devaluation* of the standards of this world, begging the question: 'What's aught, but as 'tis valued?' (*Troilus and Cressida*, II. 2, 52). As Cusanus shows, far from being natural and intrinsic, value is relative, extrinsic and ratified by custom alone.

This line of argument is supported by the exchange between a Friar and a Fool at Morton's table. Even Hythloday, the 'Nonsense-speaker' himself, is unsure as to whether to relate this 'ridiculous' (*U*, Book I, p. 74) anecdote.

The fool quips that Friars are the same as vagabonds and have thus been dealt with by the Cardinal's idea that they should be 'arrested and forced to work' (*U*, Book I, p. 75). Despite his profession, the monk fails to take the joke in good humour and becomes excessively angry: 'He called his opponent a rascal, a slanderer, a tittle-tattle, and a "Son of perdition". He quoted terrible threats at him out of the Bible' (*U*, Book I, p. 75). Refusing to calm down, he evokes Papal authority: 'we have a bull that decrees that anyone who mocks us is immediately excommunicated' (*U*, Book 1, p. 76). Wootton is quite right to point out that:

> The friar and the fool are a silenus statue, offering two contrasting readings of the Bible. The one claims to be a follower of Christ, but is in fact irascible, ill-educated, and quick to appeal to papal authority. The other presents himself as a mere jester, but quoting scripture 'was just the sort of thing he was good at'.[48]

Yet the ironies of this exchange, with its erudite fool and an ignorant friar,[49] reach beyond their local context. The Friar's actions, when tested against the wisdom of the fool, confirm the wisdom latent in the fool's joke; for all their faults, the Utopians delight in fools and have nothing but 'contempt' (*U*, Book II, p. 131) for those who mock or attack them.[50]

In fact, the wisdom of this vignette operates in much the same way as the overall philosophical and social vision of *Utopia*, which, on one hand, is a series of learned jokes, but, on the other, deals with the serious topic of secular power. Certainly, by forcing readers to shuttle between the manifest inequalities of Tudor England, which are attacked in Book I, and the life of the Utopians, which is unreliably narrated in Book II, the relative merits and failings of both societies are diagnosed. Moreover, as Fátima Vieira observes, the whole genre of literary works that have stemmed from More's neologism are essentially playful, since 'utopia is, in fact, a game, and implies the celebration of a kind of pact between the utopist and the reader: the utopist addresses the reader to tell him about a society that does not exist, and the reader acts as if he believes the author'.[51]

2.5 Playing and Mocking

> Is that the king? I think you are fooling me. He seems to be a man in an embroidered garment.
>
> —Thomas More[52]

The enduring charisma of fools, creatures who reside outside the domain of reason, lies in their ability to expose the fault lines of reason: Stultitia shows how man is blinded to his better nature by *philautia*, while Hythloday argues persuasively that once money is abolished, then 'Conflict and crimes are eliminated from society, just as a cancer is cut from the body'

(*U*, Book II, p. 158). For him, 'The mother of all mischief' is the deadly sin of pride, '*superbia*' (*CWM*, 4, p. 242), because of which man is happy with his 'good fortune' only when it 'is compared with the miseries of others' (*U*, Book II, p. 158, 159).

Yet because the fool is estranged from the explicit values of the society in which he finds himself, this perennial outsider habitually displays a lack of commitment to any one ideology – the court fool is ultimately politically powerless, despite the ways in which his mockery exposes the hypocrisy of those with political clout; and his ephemeral nature is further emphasised by disorientating strategies of rhetorical disassociation of Erasmus and More. The former dons the mask of Stultitia 'to embrace the whole world of things under the name of foolishness and to show that the whole sum of human felicity depends on Folly' (*CWE*, 3, p. 126); the latter uses the complex play between the real More and the narrative's Morus, who relates what a man called 'nonsense-speaker' had to say, to critique a model of reason based on self-preservation by comparing it to a place that does not exist.

Shakespeare's mercurial fool Feste best embodies this disengagement from the rules that govern the serious world:

Enter MARIA and [FESTE, *the*] *clown*

MARIA: Nay, either tell me where thou hast been or I will not open my lips so wide as a bristle may enter in way of thy excuse. My lady will hang thee for thy absence.

FESTE: Let her hang me. He that is well hanged in this world needs to fear no colours.

(*Twelfth Night*, I. 5. 1–5)

Feste refuses to remain obedient to the whims of his mistress's; although Maria upbraids him for his absence, Feste immediately renders her concerns absurd though his scurrilous punning; his quibble debases the authority that the powers that be possess to punish disobedience.

Like Feste, Hythloday values his autonomy. Despite Morus's and Peter Gilles's arguments that he should put his good humanist education and practical experience of the (new) world to good use by becoming an advisor to a prince, he stubbornly refuses to be committed to any particular king or country. In the Latin, this is evoked by wordplay; Gilles qualifies his suggestion to Hythloday that he should serve a king thus: 'I meant not that you should be in servitude [*seruias*] but in service [*inseruias*] to kings', but Hythloday replies that 'there is only one syllable less than the other' (*CWM*, 4, p. 54, 55) – tellingly, Ralph Robinson's 1556 translation omits this potentially subversive wordplay. Hythloday's 'do[ing] as he please[s]' (*U*, Book II, p. 61) recalls – perhaps deliberately – both Erasmus's assiduous avoidance of commitment to one particular cause or state and his desire for intellectual autonomy, a desire that is encapsulated in his remarkable motto: '*Concedo nulli*, [I yield to none]' (*CWE*, 12, p. 548), coined at around the time of the second edition of *Utopia* (1517–18); evidently, the most eminent theologian of his age, Erasmus, preferred not to join factions.

Hythloday follows Plato both in arguing that 'Unless government shared the moral values and the rational approach of the philosopher it would not, because it could not, apply his advice' and in believing that such commitment 'would do the philosopher harm. It would divert him to no purpose from intellectual pursuits, and it would be bound to compromise his moral integrity'.[53] What Morus calls Hythloday's 'eccentric wisdom' (*U*, Book I, p. 83) would be out of place at court, since kings – apart from those in Rabelais – are primarily interested in expanding their realms. Yet Hythloday's idealism comes across as egotistical, perhaps even a sublimated form of self-love. He uses an analogy of a philosopher who 'sees people out in the streets, being soaked by a thunder storm', but cannot 'persuade them to get out of the rain and take shelter' (*U*, Book I, p. 85), to express his critical relation to the universal unreason in which he finds himself. This one sane spectator, he continues, on a scene of universal madness: 'will achieve nothing if they go out and join them [the madmen]' (*U*, Book I, p. 85). In this, he adopts an attitude that corresponds very closely to Lucretius's and Stultitia's Menippean perspective on 'the innumerable tumults, and businesses of mortall men' (*PF*, p. 70). Not without a degree of self-satisfaction, Lucretius reflects that

> Nothing is more delightful than to possess lofty sanctuaries serene, well fortified by the teachings of the wise, whence you may look down on the others and behold them all astray and seeking the path of life: – the strife of wits, the fight for precedence, all labouring night and day with surpassing toil to mount upon the pinnacle of riches and lay hold on power. O pitiable minds of men, O blind intelligences.[54]

The Utopians' idea that human happiness consists mainly of avoiding pain, which Greenblatt argues is lifted from Lucretius,[55] is evidently not the only thing that More borrows from *De rerum natura*. Taking such conspicuous pleasure in one's intellectual superiority, however, sounds suspiciously like the conduct of proud people, who measure their success by the misery of others.

In contrast to Hythloday's elitism, Morus suggests that kings may in fact be guided by philosophy:

> [B]ut not by this ivory-tower theorizing, which makes no allowances for time and place. There's another philosophy, better suited to politics, which recognizes the play that's being staged, adapts itself to playing a part in it, revises what it has to say as the drama unfolds, and speaks appropriately for the time and place. [...] Play your part in it as best you can.
>
> (*U*, Book I, pp. 83–84)

This debate is significant, because it is a dialectic that runs throughout the discourse of folly in both Shakespeare and Erasmus. It seems one must choose between being a player in the drama like Morus or an outsider mocking the very conceits that the drama is based on, but whose mockery falls on deaf ears. For Stultitia, a philosopher in isolated superiority risks becoming one of 'The vnkyndest kynde of men liuyng, [a] foolelosopher' (*PF*, p. 10). She is talking about people like Jaques, who are so busy censuring the folly of others that they forget to recognise their own. Such people deny themselves a hand in any achievable social change, unlike hard-nosed pragmatists like Morus, who believe that 'if you cannot transform things for the better, you can at least make sure that they are no worse than necessary' (*U*, Book II, p. 84). The discourse of folly in Erasmus and Shakespeare debunks 'ivory-tower theorizing' as useless.

It would, therefore, be credible to view Hythloday as akin to the philosophers satirized by Stultitia, were it not for his response to Morus:

> Christ forbade dissimulation, and he commanded those truths that he had whispered into the ears of his disciples should be preached openly on street corners. Most of what he taught is much more at odds with the common customs of humankind than the policies I recommended in my speech.
>
> (*U*, Book I, p. 85)

There is no escaping the fact that the type of pragmatism, with its protean personae, that the worldly wise Morus advocates is as much at odds with the kernel of Christ's teaching as the 'customs' of Christian society are. Unable to change their 'behaviour to conform with Christ's commands', preachers have 'adapted his commands to their behaviour as if his standards were flexible' (*U*, Book I, p. 85). In this *volte-face*, Hythloday's desire for social reform modelled on Utopian society becomes a concrete set of practical measures, which, although more idealistic than Morus's Machiavellian role-playing, nonetheless still fail to live up to Christ's ideal example.

2.6 Essaying Folly

> Only the fools are certain and assured.
>
> —'Of the Education of Children'[56]

In his 'Apologie of *Raymond Sebond*', Montaigne has a revelation. He becomes aware that he is 'A new figure: an unpremeditated and accidental philosopher' (*F*, Book 2, Chapter 7, p. 487). Anne Hartle shows that, far from being incoherent, 'accidental' philosophy, 'in contrast with deliberate philosophy', is 'non-authoritative and purely human'.[57] It is 'human' because it mocks thinkers soaring up to dizzying heights of abstraction – often by reminding them that they are flesh and blood; and it is 'non-authoritative' because it makes no claim to general validity. 'Others fashion man', writes Montaigne, 'I repeat him; and represent a particular one' (*E*, Book 3, Chapter 2, p. 451). 'Montaigne', writes Hartle, 'invented the essay because he needed a new form to express not a "teaching" or a "system of thought", but a way of being'.[58] The peculiarities of an individual's existence are essentially incommensurate with the totalising impulse of the systematic reason with which people attempt to make sense of the world.

Montaigne is every bit as scathing in his attacks on the serious philosophy of his day as More and Erasmus are:

> It is a thing worthy consideration, to see what state things are brought unto in this our age; and how Philosophie, even to the wisest, and men of best understanding, is but an idle, vaine and fantasticall name, of small use and lesse worth, both in opinion and effect.
>
> (*E*, Book 1, Chapter 25, p. 76)

In contrast to much philosophy, the *Essays* do not offer a general theory, which is to be imposed on the contingent particulars of experience; instead, they offer a response to the contingent particulars of experience, taking as their basis and incorporating into their method what Adorno calls the 'non-identical': that which is left by the wayside whenever one unequivocally identifies someone or something.

Perhaps it is for this reason that the *Essays* defy summarisation. Since no brief consideration could do them justice, I will limit myself to illustrating the ways in which some of the *Essays* provide a conduit through which Erasmian ideas passed into Shakespeare's drama.[59] Aside from their striking formal affinity with Erasmus's *Adages*,[60] the preoccupation of the *Essays* with the particular features of their object adheres to Erasmus's dictum, which he employs in defence of the adage as a philosophical form: 'in the domain of literature, it is sometimes the smallest things which have the greatest intellectual value' (*CWE*, 31, p. 14). And it is just this attention to peculiarities of particulars that interests Adorno about the essay – a form that owes its very name to Montaigne's trials or *essais* of experience. As Ruth Calder argues, in offering a 'moral self-portrait' of an individual, Montaigne follows Erasmus by rejecting 'a universalizing mimesis [...] in favour of the particular, the personal, the idiosyncratic'.[61] Yet Montaigne's 'ill-formed' or grotesque representation of his thoughts and movements remains strikingly philosophical.

Erasmus's sustained polemic against the abuses of the clergy is premised on pointing out that the holy orders, especially the mendicant ones, view their dogma as divine, but fail to follow the explicit teachings of the Gospel. In his adage, 'Dulce Bellum Inexpertis', Erasmus suggests that 'nothing is too villainous or too cruel to win approval, if custom recommends it' (*CWE*, 35, p. 408). He then furnishes the reader with copious exempla, the most notable of which is the contention that in some civilisations 'it was thought pious to feast on the flesh of one's intimate friends' (*CWE*, 35, p. 408). What passes for piety is not innate; it is a consequence of custom.

Furthermore, 'Of the Caniballes' furnishes us with one of Montaigne's most illuminating discussions of hypostatisation, which focuses on the same taboo as Erasmus. Taboos are taboo, of course, precisely because they cannot be incorporated into existing models of knowledge, and in this respect, they are non-identical. Both thinkers ask how is it possible that something that seems manifestly abhorrent, such as cannibalism, can be perfectly acceptable in some cultures. Montaigne's conclusion is justly famous:

> I finde (as farre as I have beene informed) that there is nothing in that nation [America] that is either barbarous or savage, unless men call that barbarisme which is not common to them. As indeed, we have no other ayme of truth and reason, than the example and Idea of the opinions and customes of the countrie we live in.
>
> (*E*, Book 1, Chapter 30, p. 101)

He comes to the dispassionate conclusion that what is thought to be right and wrong is simply a consequence of custom – and thus of where and in what time one happens to be born. '[T]ruth' and 'reason' are historically formed rather than innate. Thus, what is considered to be barbarous is merely what is radically different from one's own opinions. For Erasmus, this is a consequence of *philautia*, that universal folly of the human race: 'What race is so savage, or tongue so uncouth, as not to consider all others beneath it? What bodily form is so brutish as not to appear most beautiful to itself?' (*CWE*, 31, p. 158). Erasmus and Montaigne expose what is taken to be innate moral superiority as blinkered stupidity, whereas More's Hythloday goes even further, contending that the happiness of the Utopians can primarily be attributed to their 'willingness to learn from others' (*U*, Book I, p. 89). The chief resource of More's brave new world is not the gold out of which the Utopians make their 'chamber pots' (*U*, Book II, p. 110). Rather, it is the possibility of alternative ways of interacting with each other and understanding the world.

In his essay, Montaigne, like Erasmus, comes to the conclusion that it is not culturally sanctioned cannibalism that is irrational. Rather, it is the violent assertion of the innate superiority of one's customs: 'Whatsoever is beyond the compasse of custome, wee deeme likewise to bee beyond the compasse of reason, God knowes how, for the most part, unreasonably' (*E*, Book 1, Chapter 30, p. 51). The manner in which 'a long habit of not thinking a thing wrong gives it the superficial appearance of being right'[62] and causes humans to become enthralled by ideas of their own making is given explicit consideration in 'Of Custom'. Montaigne sees custom, despite being mutable and relative to one's society, as a force of gargantuan strength. It is indeed 'That monster Custom, who all sense doth eat' (*Hamlet*, III. 4. 159).

What is important here is not so much the question of direct influence, but how Montaigne and Shakespeare have responded to a common intellectual heritage, steeped in Erasmian ideas, and come to a similar conclusion. They both see custom as mediating almost every aspect of social relations and experience: 'there is nothing in mine opinion, that either she [custom] doth not, or cannot: and with reason doth Pindarus, as I have heard say, call her the Queen and Empresse of all-the world' (*E*, Book 1, Chapter 22, p. 50). A paradox apparent throughout his critique of cultural conventions is discernible here. While he is critical of treating transient cultural conventions as if they were natural, he not only bolsters his arguments against custom by continually invoking the authorities of the past, but he also recurrently inveighs against novelty and innovation in its various guises.

More's Hythloday, however, attacks conservatives who evoke custom as if it were 'an unanswerable argument' (*U*, Book I, p. 62) on the grounds that: "Our present policies seemed good enough to our ancestors, and we can only wish we were as wise as they" (*U*, Book I, p. 62), but who 'don't feel a moment's hesitation in abandoning those of their policies that worked really well' (*U*, Book I, p. 62). This implies, quite correctly, that what we understand to be customary is changeable. In fact, what is really important about Montaigne's conception of custom is that he sees it as something ubiquitous. Even the laws of nature are a consequence of custom:

> The laws of conscience, which we say to proceed from nature, rise and proceed of custome [...] the chiefest effect of her power is to seize upon us, and so to entangle us, that it shall hardly lie in us to free ourselves from her hold-fast, and come into our wits againe.
>
> (*E*, Book 1, Chapter 22, p. 50)

Custom is deception because it inculcates a false sense of authenticity. What are merely opinions 'seeme to be the generall and naturall' (*E*, Book 1, Chapter 22, p. 51); even the 'laws of conscience' are a result of the ossification of mutable words into immutable 'nature'. Don Quixote is mad precisely because of his rigid adherence to chivalry, to custom, albeit the custom of a bygone age:[63] 'there is', comments the (less than) ingenious Hidalgo, 'no disputing, or drawing of conclusions against the customes of the time' (*DQ*, Book IV, Chapter XII, p. 255).

Shakespeare, of course, dramatises the perils of custom with characteristic ambivalence, but in various ways associates it with irrationality. In *King Lear*, Edmund rails:

> Thou, nature, art my goddess; to thy law
> My services are bound. Wherefore should I
> Stand in the plague of custom, and permit
> The curiosity of nations to deprive me,
> For that I am some twelve or fourteen moonshines
> Lag of a brother? Why bastard? Wherefore base?
>
> (I. 2. 1–6)

This is a reasonable request. But it comes from a character whose unnatural, illegitimate birth is mirrored by his unnatural, parricidal behaviour. Unlike Montaigne, Edmund construes 'nature' in a proto-Darwinian sense as something diametrically opposed to, rather than formed by, custom. Yet this construction of nature is undermined by the reversion to 'nature' that Edmund professes. Because it is custom that prevents illegitimate or younger children from inheriting, he rejects the ensnaring 'curiosity of nations', their fastidious adherence to custom.

Othello claims that 'The tyrant custom, most grave senators, | Hath made the flinty and steel couch of war | My thrice-driven bed of down' (I. 3. 227–29). This metaphorical fusing of custom with tyranny may have been derived from Erasmus's *Colloquies*, in one of which 'Custom' is described as 'more powerful than any tyrant' (*CWE*, 40, p. 835) – Shakespeare's school almost certainly used the *Colloquies* (as well as *De Copia* and the *Adages*) to teach intermediate-level Latin.[64] But Othello's sinister personification of custom as a tyrant develops the metaphor to suggest more strongly several things that the play as a whole shows: it implies that custom is a 'tyrant' because it is all-controlling, and dangerously irrational, given to pursuing whims as if they were absolutes. Like a tyrant, it is undemocratic, since it is supported and perpetuated by the ruling elite; the uncustomary love between Desdemona and Othello is destroyed partly because it is considered unnatural. Brabantio repeatedly invokes the concept of nature to show that his daughter's love is 'Against all the rules of nature' (I. 3. 102; see also 63, 97). Nature is exposed as nothing other than the cultural construct it was and still is. The ostensible "facts" about the nature of things and people, facts that make up the knowledge of the worldly-wise, are shown to be deceptive, whereas a discourse that consciously interrogates the dubious wisdom of custom, the discourse of folly, gains credibility. Indeed, perhaps the cardinal virtue of the discourse of folly lies precisely in the ways it penetrates the façade of custom.

2.7 Identity Critique

In his *Essays*, Montaigne aims to capture one particular man's continually fluctuating experience of the world. In the opening pages, he dispels the assumption that it is possible to determine 'the rules of nature', which Brabantio invokes for instrumental ends: 'Surely, man is a wonderful, vaine, divers, and wavering subject: it is very hard to ground any directly-constant and uniforme judgement upon him' (*E*, Book 1, Chapter 1, p. 2). And later, in 'An Apologie of *Raymond Sebond*', Montaigne argues along similar lines to Cusanus. In this essay, he uncharacteristically refers to the key ideas and texts of biblical folly, which were discussed earlier in this chapter; he even informs the reader that he writes with Ecclesiasticus's terse rhetorical question to mankind, which is rendered by the Authorized Version as 'Why is earth and ashes proud?' (*KJV*, 10. 9), engraved in the beam above his head.

He defends Sebond's thesis that the natural world is a general revelation, whereas the Bible offers specific revelations, on the grounds that knowledge does not make a man good: 'The simple and the ignorant (saith St. *Paul*) raise themselves up to heaven, and take possession of it; whereas we, with all the knowledge we have plunge ourselves downe to the pit of hell' (*E*, Book 2, Chapter 7, p. 278).

This corresponds to the praise of the simple-minded that Folly's third persona offers – the only clear rule, it seems, is that there are no clear rules. As Cusanus also argued, man should attempt to fashion a negative awareness of the limits of his knowledge:

> In few, *there is no constant existence, neither of our being, nor of the objects*. And we and our judgement and all mortall things else do uncessantly rowle, turn and passe away. Thus can nothing be certainely established, nor of the one nor of the other; both the judgeing and the judged being in continuall alteration and motion. We have no communication with being; for every humane nature is ever in the middle betweene being borne and dying.
>
> (*E*, Book 2, Chapter 7, p. 340)

Yet as Cave shows, this idiosyncratic defence of natural theology is more interested in sounding the depths of Pyrrhonist thought, 'a philosophy constantly in suspense, affirming no single opinion or position other than that of perpetual enquiry', [65] than defending Sebond. Montaigne engages with the age-old Christian *topos* of the mutability of the world. But the difference is that he views nature, both in the sense of the natural world and human nature, in a Heraclitian manner. The consequence of this is that 'if everything is in a state of flux, so too is language; in which case, nothing is knowable in the sense that nothing can be expressed immutably and clearly'.[66]

Alongside his criticism of the solidification of historically contingent actions into immutable customs, Montaigne presages Adorno's threefold critique of identity thinking. For Albrecht Wellmer, the central preoccupation of Adorno's philosophy lies in working out how the 'non-identical' can be employed as a tool for the 'critique of identity',[67] a critique formulated with precision in Adorno's *Lectures on Negative Dialectics*:

> The concept is always less than what is subsumed under it. When a B is defined as an A, it is always *different from* and *more than* the A, the concept under which it is subsumed by way of a predicative judgment. [...] However, in a sense every concept is at the same time more than the characteristics that are subsumed under it. If [...] I speak of 'freedom', this concept is not simply the unity of the characteristics of all the individuals who can be regarded as free on the basis of a formal freedom within a given constitution [...] the concept of freedom contains a pointer to something that goes well beyond those specific

> freedoms, without our necessarily realising what this additional element amounts to.
>
> (*LND*, p. 7 [Adorno's italics])

Every identity – that is, a positive "fact" or the identity of a "thing" – upon which cognition depends, is shadowed by that which it is not, its 'non-identity', in a threefold way.

First, the simple fact that two things are never quite the same is overlooked by the identifying gesture or 'predicative judgment', which seeks to classify the particular as an example of a given category, rather than enquire into the particularities of the object. Second, the concept of a thing is extraneous to the thing itself – to put it simply, the periodic table is not the chemical elements themselves. Third, in grand, abstract concepts – such as freedom, salvation or love – the concept far exceeds any possible positive objective experience of it. Freedom evidently does not simply mean comparative legislative freedom for most people in the West, any more than the overall concept of love signifies a specific romantic assignation between two (or more) people. For these reasons, it is possible to maintain that concepts are always 'less than' and 'more than' what is 'subsumed under them'; the argument attests to the innately paradoxical procedure of identifying something, of saying what something is by referring it to what it is not.

While Adorno's 'critique of identity' may sound pretty abstract, it is necessary to bear in mind that he considered the horrors of the twentieth century and the catastrophes of history to be a direct result of 'identity thinking', a type of thought that denies difference and the provisional nature of categories. It is, however, necessary to think and speak using identity, although this does not mean that identity is 'natural'. Simon Jarvis argues that, for Adorno, 'the thought of reconciled non-identity',[68] which is a mode of speculation that remains aware that the foundations of identity are built on the quicksand of non-identity, resists the totalitarian tendencies of what Adorno calls 'idealist-identitarian' (*ND*, p. 47) thought. Because 'Dialectical thinking wants to say what something is, whilst identity thinking says what something falls under, of what it is an example or representative – what it is therefore is not itself' (*ND*, p. 149), the reconciliation of non-identity with the subject is only possible through dialectics.

Strikingly, in the 'Apologie', Montaigne likewise suggests that the very nature of cognition hinders itself:

> [T]he privilege whereof our soule vaunts, to bring to her condition whatsoever it conceiveth, and to despoile what of mortall and corporall qualities belongs unto it, to marshall those things which she deemed worthie her acquaintance, to disrobe and deprive their corruptible conditions, and to make them leave as superfluous and base garments, thicknesses, length, depth, weight, colour, smell, roughnesse,

> smoothnesse, hardnesse, softnesse, and all sensible accidents else, to fit and appropriate them to her immortall and spirituall condition [...].
> (*E*, Book 2, Chapter 7, p. 268)

It is in the nature of subjectivity, Montaigne suggests, to assimilate or to 'bring to her condition' whatever it apprehends. Thus the mind renders the object an exemplum of a preconceived category, which belies the mutability that so perplexes Montaigne. The object's specific features are displaced by presupposed attributes, which, unlike 'mortall and corporall qualities', are not historically contingent. Bodies rot, but 'qualities' do not. To enable objects to be conceptualised – not to mention exchanged with other objects, likewise 'disrob[ed]' of their real features – they must be measured in some way. Montaigne thus scorns realism, which views these external, quantifiable features of 'thicknesses, length, depth, weight, colour, smell, roughnesse, smoothnesse, hardnesse, softnesse' as metaphysical forms, seeing them instead as fictions imposed on the object that hinder an immanent understanding of the thing itself.

Montaigne elsewhere anticipates the third part of Adorno's identity critique – the argument that the possibilities inherent in grand, abstract concepts reach beyond any possible specific experience of them: 'We easily pronounce puissance, truth, and justice; they be words importing some great matter, but that thing we neither see nor conceive' (*E*, Book 3, Chapter 8, p. 279). In order to suggest that the full import of humanly fashioned concepts is inconceivable, Montaigne echoes the passage from Paul's First Epistle to the Corinthians, which emphasises the inexpressible joys of salvation thus: 'the Eye hath not seen, nor ear heard, neither have entered into the heart of man, the things which God hath prepared for them that love him' (*KJV*, 2. 9) – the passage Shakespeare's Bottom so brilliantly bungles.

In the same essay, Montaigne paraphrases an argument made by the Grammarian Priscian:

> Our contestation is verball. I demaund what Nature, voluptuousnesse, circle, and substitution is? The question is of words, and with words it is answered. A stone is a body: but he that should insist and urge: And what is a body? – A substance. And what is a substance? and so goe-on, should at last bring the respondent to his Calepine or wits end. One word is changed for another word, and often more unknowne. I know better what *Homo* is then I know what *Animal* is, either mortall or reasonable.
> (*E*, Book 3, Chapter 8, p. 602)

Juliet, when she comments 'What's in a name? That which we call a rose | By any other word would smell as sweet' (*Romeo and Juliet*, II. 1. 85–86), is not the only early modern character to be aware of the diremption of *res* and *verbum*. Even the concept of 'nature', Montaigne suggests, is a linguistic construct.

In the 'Apologie' he extols Erasmian simplicity by suggesting that reason's discourses hinder rather than help man's understanding of the object, or own nature:

> It is credible that there are natural laws, as may be seen in other creatures; but in us they are lost; that fine human reason butts in everywhere, domineering and commanding, muddling and confusing the face of things in accordance with its vanity.
>
> (*F*, Book 2, Chapter VII, p. 532)

It is through the open-ended essay, which does not seek to appropriate the object of its discourse, that speculation can be unshackled from identity-thinking; the essay makes no claims to 'totality' (*TEF*, p. 165); it establishes no 'system' (*TEF*, p. 160). 'These universall judgements', which characterise 'deliberate philosophy', reflects Montaigne, 'say nothing at all' (*E*, Book 3, Chapter VIII), whereas the essay offers the 'provisional ordering of an encounter', in which 'the self and the object define each other, but only in a temporary way'.[69]

For this reason, in his discussion of the 'Essay as Form', Adorno quotes the Hungarian philosopher György Lukács's *Soul and Form*; the integrity of the essay as a form of speculation inheres in its anti-systematic nature:

> 'The essayist dismisses his own proud hopes which sometimes lead him to believe that he has come close to the ultimate: he has, after all, no more to offer than explanations of the poems of others, or at best of his own ideas. But he ironically adapts himself to this smallness – the eternal smallness of the most profound work of the intellect in face of life'.
>
> (*TEF*, p. 158)

No universal judgement is possible in this form, for it is bound to its ever-changing object. For Erich Auerbach, this realisation enables Montaigne to get to the heart of the human condition: 'Of all his contemporaries he had the clearest conception of the problem of man's self-orientation; that is, making one's self at home in existence, without fixed points of support'.[70] Montaigne himself reflects on the comparative poverty of the essay form with a scatological metaphor. He takes no pride in his disordered discourse. It is abject shit: 'the excrements of an ould spirit, sometimes hard, sometimes laxative; but ever indigested' (*E*, Book 3, Chapter 9, p. 531).

The essay offers its readers no 'hierarchy of concepts' (*TEF*, p. 166); as Auerbach contends, Montaigne sees that the problem with 'systems of moral philosophy' lies in 'the tendency of their methodology to disguise the reality of life'.[71] Adorno openly attacks the 'tendency' for method to obscure the multifarious nature of existence and the dynamic nature of thought. Not only does he inveigh against philosophy's 'metamorphosis [*Verwandlung*] into method' (MM, p. 13; [*MM*, p. 15]), but he also views the essay as the primary historical form that attacked dry formalism: 'Doubt about the unconditional priority of method was raised, in the actual process of thought, almost exclusively by the essay' (*TEF*, p. 157). Montaigne's fellow essayist, William Cornwallis, cuts to the chase when he comments that Montaigne 'speaks nobly, honestly, and wisely, with little method, but much judgment'.[72]

In a characteristically paradoxical vein, Adorno reflects that 'The law of the innermost form of the essay is heresy. By transgressing the orthodoxy of thought, something becomes visible in the object, which it is orthodoxy's secret purpose to keep invisible' (*TEF*, p. 171). By making no claims to universality and by fashioning an anti-systematic and anti-philosophical mode of speculation, Montaigne's essays estrange the very building blocks of thought – in the sense of both the everyday cognition of objects and people and of orthodox philosophical thought. In the preceding analysis, it is a sense of negativity that Erasmus's, Montaigne's and Shakespeare's discussions of the human condition share: they imply that at the heart of being human is an inability to get to the essence of things, but that a partial and necessarily imperfect understanding of the human condition lies in the realisation that one is flawed – that one is, in a sense, a fool.

True folly, Erasmus, Montaigne and Shakespeare suggest, consists in attempting to establish unequivocal positivistic knowledge of the nature of things, one's essential self, or God: 'Only fools are certain and assured'. To follow the famous humanist mantra, *gnōthi seauton*, and to know one's self is to have an awareness of the limitations of concepts, language and cognition itself. What is remarkable about negativity of these authors, however, is that it is tempered by comic self-awareness; their ambivalent laughter makes a mockery of both the serious world's philosophical systems and their own scepticism, which they behold from a healthily ironic position of the sort David Hume famously recommends in his *Treatise of Human Nature*: 'A true sceptic will be diffident of his philosophical doubts, as well as of his philosophical conviction'.[73] 'If I have a desire to laugh at a foole', reflects Montaigne with his tongue in his cheek (and in an inadvertent paraphrase of Seneca): 'I neede not seeke one farre; I laugh at my selfe' (*E*, Book 2, Chapter 25, p. 387).

Notes

1. 'Of Boldness', in *The Major Works*, ed. by Brian Vickers (Oxford: Oxford University Press, 2008), pp. 361–363 (p. 362).
2. 'The Book of Job', in *On Lying in Bed and Other Essays*, ed. by Alberto Manguel (Calgary: Bayeux Arts, 2000), pp. 172–180 (p. 176).
3. Jonson's most obvious engagement with the *Praise of Folly* occurs in *Volpone*. The trickster Mosca summarises it in his song, which starts: 'Fools, they are

the only nation | Worth men's envy or admiration' (*Volpone*, I. 2. 66–67). See Ben Jonson, *The Alchemist and Other Plays*, ed. by Gordon Campbell (Oxford: Oxford University Press, 1995; repr. 2008); subsequent quotations are given in the text. See also Peter G. Bietenholz, *Encounters with a Radical Erasmus: Erasmus' Work as a Source of Radical Thought in Early Modern Europe* (Buffalo: University of Toronto Press, 2009), pp. 116–122.

4. *Ibid.*, pp. 51–84.
5. 'Selfloue' is the foremost of Stultitia's 'handmaides'. In his adage, 'Philautoi', Erasmus observes: 'it [self-love] is a deeply rooted fault which makes people approve of everything belonging to themselves' (*CWE*, 31, p. 311). The irony at work in the *Praise* is that by praising herself Stultitia is committing an act of self-love, which, in her second guise, she later bitterly attacks as a vice.
6. Echoes and correspondences between Shakespeare and Erasmus have received some critical attention, most notably from John Evans ('Erasmus' Folly and Shakespeare's *King Lear*: A Study in Humanist Intertextuality', *Moreana*, 27 (1990), 3–23) and Claudia Corti ('Erasmus' Folly and Shakespeare's Fools', *Silenos: Erasmus in Elizabethan Literature*, ed. by Claudia Corti, Studi di Letterature Moderne e Comparate, 1 (Pisa: Pancini, 1998), pp. 13–36). Although the spirit of Erasmus's *Praise* haunts the tone and key ideas of these plays, the only scene in which a direct influence can be discerned with some degree of certainty is when Falstaff attempts to divert the Lord Justice's attention from his misdemeanours. Echoing Ecclesiastes (1. 18), Falstaff claims that Hal has a 'perturbation of the brain' (*2 Henry IV*, I. 2. 106), caused by 'much grief from study' (105). The prince has 'a kind of sleeping in the blood' (102). This recalls the stultified philosophers and theologians – ironic self-representations in Erasmus's satire; they waste their youthful years on abstractions and grow old before their time: the 'sharp 'truailing of the braine' is responsible for the 'little by little sokying vp the liuely iuice of the spirits' (p. 19). Furthermore, the Lord Chief Justice's characterisation of Falstaff as the epitome of old age – 'Have you not a moist eye, a dry hand, a yellow cheek, a white beard, a decreasing leg, an increasing belly? Is not your wind short, your voice broken and your wit single, and every part of you blasted with antiquity?' (165–169) – echoes Folly's memorable anatomy of aging discussed in Chapter 4; see also Roy Battenhouse, 'Falstaff as Parodist and Perhaps Holy Fool', *PMLA*, 90 (1975), 32–52 (p. 35); this article also appears in *Christian Irony in Shakespeare's Histories*, ed. by Peter Milward, 2 vols., Renaissance Monographs, 37–38 (Tokyo: Renaissance Institute Sophia University, 2009), I, pp. 107–145.
7. *Rabelais and His World*, trans. by Helene Iswolsky (Bloomington, IA: Indiana University Press, 1984), p. 14.
8. Donald Gwynn Watson concludes his reading of the role of the carnivalesque in the *Praise* by conflating Folly's first and third incarnation: 'Erasmus has incorporated the spirit of Carnival into the meaning and philosophical celebration of Christ' ('Erasmus' *Praise of Folly* and the Spirit of Carnival', *Renaissance Quarterly*, 32 (1979), 333–353 (p. 353)); Claudia Corti argues that Erasmus displays a 'fondness for the overthrow of accepted values that characterises carnival' ('Introduction', in *Silenos: Erasmus in Elizabethan Literature*, pp. 5–13). However, this line of argument is untenable for three reasons. First, these interpretations estimate the significance of *Praise* as a whole purely in the terms of folly's first persona. Second, in several places, Erasmus appears to oppose

carnivals; in his colloquy, 'A Fish Diet', the Butcher describes with horror the grotesque hedonism of 'revels' in a nearby town, which would not be out of place in Rabelais: 'an old fellow [...] carried head down to prevent his choking on vomit [...] he was vomiting wretchedly on the legs and feet of the hindmost carriers. Most were laughing, but in such a way as you would say without hesitation they were crazy' (*CWE*, 40, p. 707); likewise, in his adage, 'For sluggards it is always a holiday', he sees holidays as having become irreligious: 'For a true Christian every day is a holy day; while to the bad Christians who form the great majority, holy days are not so much holy as profane' (*CWE*, 33, p. 296). Third, as he repeatedly emphasises in his later letters, Erasmus is against the wholesale 'overthrow of traditional values', since he desires reform, not reformation (see J. A. Fronde, *Life and Letters of Erasmus: Lectures Delivered at Oxford 1893–1894* (New York: Scribner's, 1912), pp. 359–417; Roland H. Bainton, *Erasmus of Christendom* (London: Collins, 1969), pp. 298–337; Cornelis Augustijn, *Erasmus: His Life, Work and Influence*, trans. by J. C. Grayson (Toronto: University of Toronto Press, 1991), pp. 147–161).

9. Cave, p. 327.
10. See Fronde, p. 309–338; Bainton, pp. 209–241.
11. This belief is by no means unique to Erasmus. The Brethren of the Common Life, by whom Erasmus was brought up, practiced the *Devotio Moderna*, which combined monastic devotion with practical works, such as treating the sick and educating the young (see Bainton, pp. 8–25). Attacking theological jargon in a different context, towards the end of his life Erasmus writes to John Carondelet in 1523: 'You will not be damned if you do not know whether the Spirit proceeding from the Father and the Son has a single or a double principle, but you will not escape perdition unless you see to it in the mean time that you have the fruits of the Spirit, which are charity, joy, peace, patience, kindness, goodness, forbearance, gentleness, faith, moderation, self-control, and chastity' (*CWE*, 9, p. 252).
12. Marc Lienhard provides a cogent examination of all the critical work on Erasmus' ambivalent relationship with the radical sects, especially the Anabaptists, in Germany during the reformation. He argues that Erasmus's 'Philosophy of Christ' is the part of his thought that has the greatest affinity with radical ideas, but Erasmus's conception of Christian simplicity is far more tolerant; see 'Die Radikalen des 16 Jahrhunderts und Erasmus's in M. Mout, H. Smolinsky and J. Trapman, eds., *Erasmianism: Idea and Reality* (Royal Netherlands Academy of Arts and Sciences: Amsterdam, 1997), pp. 91–105.
13. *The Shyppe of Fooles*, trans. by Alexander Barclay (London: Wynky[n] de worde, 1509), p. 11.
14. Bakhtin, *Rabelais and His World*, p. 123.
15. *Play in a Godless World: The Theory and Practice of Play in Shakespeare, Nietzsche and Freud* (London: Open Gate Press, 1999), p. 47.
16. Gerhard Schweppenhäuser, 'Narrenschelte und Pathos der Vernunft. Zum Narrenmotiv bei Sebastian Brandt und Erasmus von Rotterdam', *Neophilologus*, 71 (1987), 559–574 (p. 570).
17. *Ibid.*, p. 569.
18. Bainton, p. 123.
19. John Donne, 'Holy Sonnet XI', in *John Donne's Poetry*, ed. by Arthur L. Clements, 2nd edn (New York: Norton, 1992).

20. *Of Learned Ignorance*, trans. by Germain Heron (Eugene, OR: Wipf and Stock, 2007), pp. 2, 7.
21. *Ibid.*, p. 8.
22. *The idiot in four books. The first and second of wisdome. The third of the minde. The fourth of statick experiments, or experiments of the ballance*. By the famous and learned C. Cusanus, trans. by John Everard (London: William Leak, 1650), p. 5; *idiotia*, incidentally, is how the Vulgate translates Paul's self-deprecating description of himself as moros or fool. In early modern English 'idiot' signified both a 'a simple or ordinary person' and a natural fool or 'A person so profoundly disabled in mental function or intellect as to be incapable of ordinary acts of reasoning or rational conduct' (OED, definition nos. 1a and 2a).
23. For a detailed analysis of this paradox, see M. A. Screech, *Laughter at the Foot of the Cross* (London: Duckworth, 1999), pp. 1–28; *Ecstasy and the Praise of Folly* (London: Duckworth, 1980), esp. pp. 36–42 and pp. 63–91; Walter M. Gordon, *Humanist Play and Belief: The Seriocomic Art of Desiderius Erasmus* (Toronto and London: University of Toronto Press, 1990), p. 6; Augustijn, pp. 20–50.
24. *Sir Thomas More* in *Shakespeare and Others: Collaborative Plays*, ed. by Jonathan Bate and others (Basingstoke: Palgrave, 2013), pp. 349–421 (p. 414–415).
25. Rabelais wrote to Erasmus, referring to him as his spiritual 'father and mother'; for a recent overview of the critical work on this and the question of influence, see Paul J. Smith, ('Jean Thenaud and François Rabelais: Some Hypotheses on the Early Reception of Erasmus in French Vernacular Literature', in Karl A. E. Enkel, ed., *The Reception of Erasmus in the Early Modern Period* (Leiden: Brill, 2013), pp. 211–237).
26. 'Narrenschelte und Pathos der Vernunft', p. 567.
27. Screech, *Ecstasy and the Praise of Folly*, p. 3; Gordon, pp. 223–253.
28. Schweppenhäuser, p. 568.
29. M. A. Screech, *Montaigne and Melancholy* (London: Duckworth, 1983; repr. 2000), p. 60.
30. *The Sermons of John Donne*, ed. by George R. Porter and Evelyn M. Simpson, 10 vols (Berkeley, CA: University of California Press, 1953–1962), VII, p. 57.
31. The influence of the *Praise* on *A Midsummer Night's Dream* in general and Bottom's in particular is discussed by Thelma N. Greenfield in '*A Midsummer Night's Dream* and *Praise of Folly*', *Comparative Literature*, 20 (1968), 236–244, and Catharine Birkenshaw in "Past the wit of man': *A Midsummer Night's Dream's* Debt to *Praise of Folly*', *Shakespeare in Southern Africa*, 5 (1992), 43–58. For Emily Stockard, however, these studies underestimate the crucial role of holy folly in the play; she contends that 'Titania's foolish love for Bottom mirrors God's foolish love for mankind': see 'Christian Folly and the Subversion of Hierarchy in *A Midsummer Night's Dream*', *R&L*, 29 (1997), 1–20 (p. 2).
32. Recognising Shakespeare's debt to contemporary utopias, Thomas Bulger goes so far as to contend that '*The Tempest* directly and fully examines Utopian ideas current at the time of the play's composition' and that it does so both thematically and formally ('The Utopic Structure of the *Tempest*', *Utopian Studies*, 5 (1994), 38–47 (p. 38).
33. Sidney, p. 86.
34. See *Saint Paul: The Foundation of Universalism*, trans. by Ray Brassier (Stanford, CA: Stanford University Press, 2003 [1997]), and *The Fragile Absolute – or, Why Is the Christian Legacy Worth Fighting for?* (London: Verso, 2000).

35. 'The Meaning of *Utopia*', in Sir Thomas More, *Utopia: A Revised Translation, Backgrounds, Criticism*, ed. and trans. by Robert M. Adams (New York: Norton, 1992), pp. 137–147 (p. 139).
36. John C. Olin, 'Erasmus's *Adagia* and More's *Utopia*', *Moreana*, 100 (1989), 127–136. Wootton discerns the influence of Erasmus's adage 'Among friends all is in common' at work in Hythloday's communism. See his 'Introduction' to *Utopia: With Erasmus' The Sileni of Alcibiades*, ed. and trans. by David Wootton (Cambridge: Hackett, 1999), pp. 1–48 (p. 19).
37. Wootton, 'Introduction', p. 19.
38. *Ibid.*, p. 21.
39. Lucretius writes that 'I proceed to unloose the mind from the close knots of superstition […] because the subject matter is so dark and the lies I write so clear, as I touch all with the Muses grace'; the enlightenment urge to free man from naive 'superstition' or mythology is at the core of this Epicurean thinker's philosophical project—as is an awareness of being able to get to the heart of things through imaginative rather formal discourse. (*De rerum natura*, trans. by W. H. D. Rouse, rev. by Martin Ferguson Smith, LOEB Classical Library, 181 (Cambridge, MA: Harvard University Press, 1924; rev. edn 1975), I. 931–935.
40. See *Renaissance Self-Fashioning: From More to Shakespeare* (Chicago: University of Chicago Press, 1980; repr. 2005), pp. 57–72.
41. Greenblatt, *Renaissance Self-Fashioning*, p. 37.
42. 'Narrenschelte und Pathos der Vernunft', p. 573.
43. Max Horkheimer, *Critical Theory: Selected Essays*, trans. by M. J. O'Connell and others (New York: Herder and Herder, 1972), p. 240.
44. Wootton, 'Introduction', p. 2.
45. Greenblatt, *Renaissance Self-Fashioning*, p. 37.
46. Wootton, 'Introduction', p. 27.
47. *Opera Omnia Desiderii Erasmi*, ed. by various, 9 vols (Amsterdam: E. J. Brill/ London: Elsevier, 1964–2005), III, p. 376. Chaloner omits this comment in his translation; see Miller, *PF*, p. 151.
48. Wootton, 'Introduction', p. 30.
49. The Friar's ignorance and willingness to misuse scripture to justify his cause are exposed by his mistake when he quotes 'The zeal of Thy house has eaten me up' to justify his anger; as the marginal gloss explains: '*Evidently the Friar, because of His Ignorance of Latin, Misuses "Zelus" (Zeal) as if It Were Neuter like "Hoc Scelus" (This Crime)* (*CWM*, 4, p. 85) [eds. italics and capitalisation].
50. More uses the word 'Moriones' (*CWM*, 4, p. 192) for fools or simpletons; this unusual word would have recalled Erasmus's pun on the author's name in the title of his *Praise* (*Moriae Encomium*).
51. 'The Concept of *Utopia*', in *The Cambridge Companion to Utopian Literature*, ed. by Gregory Claeys (Cambridge: Cambridge University Press, 2010), pp. 3–28 (p. 8).
52. *The Latin Epigrams of Thomas More*, ed. and trans. by Leicester Bradner and Charles Arthur Lynch (Chicago: University of Chicago Press, 1953), p. 205.
53. Brendon Bradshaw, 'More on *Utopia*', *The Historical Journal*, 24 (1981), 1–27 (p. 26).
54. *De rerum natura*, II. 6–14.
55. *The Swerve: How the Renaissance Began* (London: Bodley Head, 2011), p. 228.
56. This comment is found only in the C-Text (*F*, Book 1, Chapter XXVI, p. 135).

57. *Michel de Montaigne: Accidental Philosopher* (Cambridge: Cambridge University Press, 2003), p. 3.
58. *Ibid.*, p. 13.
59. Screech considers the transmission of various Erasmian preoccupations, including a respect for the body, in the course of his *Montaigne and Melancholy*; in *The Cornucopian Text,* Cave deals with Montaigne's use of Erasmus's theories of writing and their self-reflexive nature; see also Edmund J. Campion, *Montaigne, Rabelais and Marot as Readers of Erasmus* (Lewiston, NY: Edwin Mellen, 1995).
60. 'Villey has shown [...] that the form of the *Essays* stems from the collections of exempla and quotations, and aphorisms' (Eric Auerbach, *Mimesis: The Representation of Reality in Western Literature*, trans. by Willard R. Task (Princeton, NJ: Princeton University Press, 1953; repr. 2003), p. 295).
61. Ruth Calder, *From Grotesque to Silenus: Register and Satirical Self-Depiction in the 'Essais' of Montaigne* (unpublished doctoral thesis, Royal Holloway, University of London, 1993), p. 70.
62. Thomas Paine, *Common Sense* (Harmondsworth: Penguin, 2004), p. 3.
63. See Kaiser, pp. 277–296.
64. See T. M. Baldwin, *William Shakespeare's Small Latine & Less Greke*, 2 Vols (Urbana: University of Illinois Press, 1944), I, pp. 187–264. Angela Locatelli argues for the pervasive influence of Erasmus on the way rhetoric was taught in grammar schools and disseminated through teaching manuals ('The Land of "Plenty": Erasmus' *De Copia* and English Renaissance Rhetoric', in *Silenos: Erasmus in Elizabethan Literature*, ed. by Corti pp. 41–57 (p. 53)). Roger Stritmatter and Lynne Kositsky argue for a considerably greater influence of Erasmus's colloquy 'Naufragium' on *The Tempest* than had previously been discerned. They establish not only that the play quotes this colloquy verbatim, but also that the ostensibly historical sources, from which Shakespeare was believed to have borrowed, use Erasmus's fictional narrative (see 'Pale as Death: The Fictionalizing Influence of Erasmus's *Naufragium* on the Renaissance Travel Narrative', in Daniel Wright ed., *Discovering Shakespeare: A Festschrift in Honour of Isobel Holden* (Portland, OR: The Shakespeare Authorship Research Centre, 2009), pp. 143–152).
65. *How to Read Montaigne* (London: Granta, 2007), p. 40.
66. Screech, Montaigne and Melancholy, p. 76.
67. 'Adorno and the Difficulties of a Critical Reconstruction of the Historical Present', trans. by Frederik van Gelder, <www.amsterdam-adorno.net/T_wellmer_twa.pdf>, p. 2.
68. *Adorno: A Critical Introduction* (Oxford: Polity, 1998), p. 230.
69. Graham Good, *The Observing Self: Rediscovering the Essay* (London: Routledge, 1988), p. 4.
70. *Mimesis*, p. 311.
71. *Ibid.*, p. 312.
72. *The Essays by Sir William Cornwallis the Younger*, ed. by D. C. Allen (Baltimore, MD: Johns Hopkins University Press, 1946), p. 44.
73. *A Treatise of Human Nature*, ed. by Ernest C. Mossner (Harmondsworth: Penguin, 1985), p. 273.

3 Opening the Silenus

The Fool's Truth

3.1 Introduction

> All humaine thynges are lyke the Silenes or double images of Alcibiades, have two faces much vnlyke and dissemble that outwardly seemed death, yet looking within ye shoulde fynde it lyfe and on the other side what seemed lyfe, to be death: what fayre to be foule what riche, beggarly: what cunnyng, rude: what strong, feeble [...] Breifly, the Silenus ones beying vndone and disclosed, ye shall fynde all things [are] tourned into a new semblance.
>
> —Praise of Folly, p. 37

In *The Symposium*, Alcibiades suggests that Socrates is akin to a 'Silenus statue':[1] there is an absolute disjunction between the philosopher's foolish appearance in the world – his notorious ugliness, his incessant infatuations with beautiful young men, and his poverty – and the 'moderation', 'strength' and 'beauty'[2] of his innermost thoughts, which 'despised all things for which other mortals run their races' (*CWE*, 34, p. 263). These statues, observes Erasmus in his famous adage 'Sileni Alcibiades' (1515), were commonly carved in the shape of Bacchus's tutor, Silenus: 'the court buffoon of the gods of poetry' (*CWE*, 34, p. 264); they were 'small figure[s] of carved wood, so made that they could be divided and opened. [...] When they were closed they looked like a caricature of a hideous flute-player, when opened they suddenly displayed a deity' (*CWE*, 34, p. 262).

It is easy to see how this reversible image came to encapsulate the paradoxical wisdom of folly (not to mention, the folly of wisdom). Indeed, Erasmus's word for the reversal of values that the Silenus statue makes possible is '*praeposterum*', a rhetorical figure of reversal; and the English translation of this adage aptly uses the word 'topsy-turvy'.[3] Walter Kaiser explains the seemingly infinite self-generative ironies of the *Praise* by evoking the idea of the Silenus,[4] while Michael Screech examines its surprising centrality to Erasmus's 'ecstasy'.[5] David Wootton argues that More's *Utopia* must be interpreted as a Silenus,[6] whereas Terence Cave analyses the significant role this duplicitous little statue plays in shaping the philosophical content and literary form of Rabelais and Montaigne's works.[7] Claudia Corti even goes so far as to describe Erasmus's 'enormous' influence on early modern English literature with a deliberately Silenic image: 'embedded within Shakespeare, Nashe, Ascham, Wilson and Puttenham [...] lay Erasmus, with that ironic smile of his, as immortalised by Holbein'.[8]

Not least because Alcibiades behaves foolishly, the image of the Silenus head has been equivocal from its inception. Since Alcibiades wanders into the *Symposium* late and drunk, we can infer that while he may find Socrates's 'moderation' laudable, he does not feel compelled to imitate it, and his encomium of Socrates's wisdom and 'moderation' is decidedly double-edged. Alcibiades is both impressed and appalled that, despite his multiple attempts to entrap him, the philosopher refused to be sexually 'gratified' by him.[9] Socrates refused to 'strike a bargain' with him, in which knowledge is traded for sex;[10] as he points out, not only does Alcibiades misconceive the nature of love, but also this transaction does not make sense even by commercial standards, as Socrates would be trading the 'gold' of his knowledge 'in exchange for [the] bronze' of the latter's body.[11] At the end of the *Symposium*, Socrates contends that Alcibiades's 'Silenus-play' itself has a deceptive double nature: it furnishes the spurned lover with a way of venting his inner frustrations in the guise of praise.[12]

3.2 Theology and the Silenus

Erasmus was the first thinker to connect the Christian *via negativa* with the self-revelation of Socrates, who was considered by the Oracle at Delphos to know something precisely because he admitted that he 'knows nothing'.[13] If we trace the key arguments of the 'Sileni Alcibiades', which were translated into every major European vernacular, including English in 1543,[14] then many of his chief linguistic, social and theological preoccupations can be discerned. Initially, Erasmus argues that there is a difference between the inner core and outer appearance of true philosophers and apostles: 'they wear what is most contemptible [...] concealing their treasure with a kind of worthless outward shell and not showing it to uninitiated eyes' (*CWE*, 34, p. 264); such prophetic souls have drunk from 'the true fountain head [of] heavenly wisdom, against which all human wisdom is mere folly' (*CWE*, 34, p. 263). Their revelation confounds earthly intelligence – it is not that we are too naïve to get to the truth, but rather that we are too sophisticated.

Next he contends that Scripture, especially the New Testament, has a doubly Silenic nature. First, the reader must not 'pause at the surface' because all the allegories, ambiguities and textual instabilities make it seem 'ridiculous' (*CWE*, 34, p. 267). Instead, they must attempt to 'pierce the heart of the allegory' and 'open up the Silenus', so that they can 'venerate the divine wisdom' (*CWE*, 34, p. 267). Second, as Erasmus puts very clearly in the mouth of an educated layman in his *Colloquies*: 'What the Old Law taught under a veil, the New Law placed before the eyes' (*CWE*, 40, p. 167).

For Erasmus, then, the importance of the Old Testament and pagan texts like *The Symposium* lies in what is hidden beneath the surface. When read correctly, such writings display a partial and imperfect prefiguration of Christ's and his apostles's explicit teachings (see *CWE*, 3, p. 127 et passim).

Erasmus then rephrases the argument that he makes most explicitly in his *Enchiridion Militis Christiani* (1503), contending that in human nature there is perpetual strife between embodied existence and the being-for-the-Spirit that characterises Paul's 'fools for Christ's sake' (I Corinthians, 4. 10):

> In this world there are, as it were, two worlds, which fight against each other in every way, one gross and corporeal, the other heavenly and already practicing with all its might to become what it one day will be.
>
> (*CWE*, 34, p. 276)

The *coup de théâtre* of his essay, however, is when he posits a deliberately provocative question: 'what of Christ? Was not he too a marvelous Silenus? His appearance was not only human, but also a poor, even wretched human?' (*CWE*, 34, p. 264). In the figure of Christ there is an absolute disjunction between appearance and essence. God's embodiment provides a 'cheap', mortal 'setting' for that which is immortal and perfect, a 'glorious pearl' (*CWE*, 34, p. 264). It is ultimately for this reason that the Christian 'picks out what is least visible to the eye and pass[es] over all the rest or using them with a measure of contempt [...] he draws his principles of judgment entirely from what is within' (*CWE*, 34, p. 268).

Erasmus plays on the idea that if the mean is splendid, the foolish is wise and the insubstantial substantial, then the inverse must also be true. He regrets that earthly experience, reality, is akin to a reversed Silenus head. The essence is absurd and ugly, but the external appearance is grand. The holy essence of things has been etiolated: the ceremonies and sacraments of the Church Militant are akin to 'seeing the Silenus from the outside' (*CWE*, 34, p. 167). This incredulity at visual signifiers of faith and his critique of the hypostatisation of ceremonies in the Church corresponds with Reformist arguments, such as Luther's and Von Hutten's, against ostentatious displays of faith, which they saw as idolatrous attempts to represent the divine,[15] and with the deep unease that the medieval mystics felt about the iconography of their world.

At the conclusion, Erasmus's gloss itself opens up, betraying its double nature and suggesting that exegesis is always an indeterminate procedure: he who promises to get to the essence of things may just have been captivated by appearances all along. What Erasmus has been writing is seriocomic, since the adage has grown from a drunken praise of a man's wisdom for knowing nothing to a discussion of the way that mankind is universally taken in by appearances. 'Of course', writes Erasmus, 'it was Alcibiades in his cups, and his Sileni, that drew me to this very sober disputation' (*CWE*, 34, p. 281).

Erasmus even paints himself as a Silenic grotesque: with a characteristic act of self-effacement, he casts himself as a rash man, almost a fool, asking: 'whither has the flood of my language carried me away, so that I, who profess myself a mere compiler of proverbs, begin to be a preacher?' (*CWE*, 34, p. 281).

Michel Foucault argues that in Sebastain Franck's and Erasmus's works the Silenus epitomises the fact that:

> The abyss of folly into which men are plunged is such that the appearance that men find there is in fact its complete opposite. But there was more: the contradiction between truth and appearances was present in appearance itself, for if the appearance was coherent with itself, at least it would be an allusion to the truth, or some form of hollow echo.
>
> (*HM*, p. 30)

To put it another way, appearances are not wholly convincing in themselves, which is why we have a niggling sense that they are appearances rather than reality proper; for this reason, they cannot recall the essence of things. If they did, then their suggestion of their own incoherence would be part of this essence. For the historian of madness and deviancy, reality is abysmal: man is immured in a phantasmagoria, from which he cannot quite awake. And something not dissimilar to this is implicit in August Wilhelm Schlegel's comment that the Shakespearean fool offers an 'antidote to the emptiness and boredom of everyday life, a welcome interruption to traditional formalities'.[16] Clearly, if the serious world really were wholly fulfilling, there would be no call for the paradoxical wisdom of folly.

That appearances are not even 'coherent' with themselves proves essential to understanding Erasmus's use of the Silenus for explicit critique of civil authority, the trappings of which, Erasmus suggests, are nothing other than an artful piece of dissimulation, a costume (not quite) concealing man's bestial inner nature:

> Those of whom you would say, were you to inspect their outward bodily form, that they are human beings and distinguished beings too; open the Silenus, and inside you will find maybe a pig or a lion, a bear or a donkey.
>
> (*CWE*, 34, p. 268)

Such men are the opposite of the Silenic Christian Erasmus described: what was once 'riche' is shown to be 'beggarly'. Erasmus's capacity for critical thought is an attribute that the real-life Dutchman shares with his fictional doppelganger. In *Sir Thomas More*, More plays a practical joke on Erasmus, getting his manservant to pretend to be him to ascertain 'if great Erasmus can distinguish | Merit and outward ceremony' (III. 2. 39–40).[17] As it transpires, he can.

This *topos* of the inverted Silenus, with its disjunction between inner poverty and external grandeur, recurs throughout Erasmus' 'Sileni Alcibiades' and *The Praise of Folly* and can be discerned in Lear's 'reason in madness' (IV. 6. 171):

LEAR: Thou hast seen a farmer's dog bark at a beggar?
GLOUCESTER: Aye, sir.
LEAR: And the creature run from the cur? There thou mightst
behold the great image of authority: a dog's obeyed in office.
Thou rascal beadle, hold thy bloody hand!
Why doest thou last that whore? Strip thine own back;
Thou hotly lusts to use her in that kind
For which thou whipp'st her. The usurer hangs the cozener.
Through tattered clothes small vices do appear;
Robes and furred gowns hide all. Plate sin with gold,
And the strong arm of justice hurtles breaks;
Arm it in rags, a pigmy's straw does pierce it.

(IV. 6. 150–61)

In this indictment of hypocrisies of the legal system, Lear draws similar conclusions about the bestial essence that the signifiers of civil authority commonly hide. The powers that be can hide their moral poverty with costumes ('Robes and furred gowns hide all'), but even the minor misdemeanours of the poor can be discerned through their rags; as Shakespeare emphasises with his demotic analogy, however, those in authority are placed there by mere chance – in a certain context, even 'a dog's obeyed in office'. It is there that the demented king formulates explicitly what the action of the play implies; kings are but men and 'man, proud man', as Isabella reminds Angelo in *Measure for Measure*, is 'Dressed in a little brief authority' (II. 2. 118).

3.3 Silenic Style

In 'Of Physiognomy', Montaigne explicitly mentions Socrates's Silenic nature, suggesting that people these days would not appreciate him, since 'they perceive no charms that are not sharpened, puffed out and inflated by artifice' (*F*, Book III, Chapter 12, p. 965). His primary interest in Alcibiades's image, however, is in how it relates to the register in which the philosopher chose to speak:

> Socrates makes his soul move with a natural and common motion. [...] His mouth is full of nothing but carters, joiners, cobblers and masons. His are inductions and similes drawn from the commonest and best-known actions of man. Under so mean a form we should never have picked out the nobility and splendour of his ideas.
>
> (*F*, Book III, Chapter 12, p. 965)

Beneath the surface of Socrates's homely metaphors and the commonplaces, there is profound philosophical wisdom. Erich Auerbach argues that by the Renaissance the Silenus head had become a metonym for the humanist ideal of absolute clarity of expression; Montaigne and Rabelais saw it as representing 'Socratic style [which] meant [...] something free and untrammeled, something close to ordinary life, indeed, for Rabelais, something close to buffoonery'.[18]

This ideal is derived from Erasmus. He writes admiringly of Socrates that 'his language was simple and homely and smacking of common folk; for his talk was all of carters and cobblers' (*CWE*, 34, p. 263), which Montaigne echoes. As Ruth Calder argues, because his language mixed rough and ready expression with philosophical content, 'Socrates was seen as the archetype of the *Spondaioloios*'[19] or mixed mode, characteristic of Erasmus, Montaigne and Shakespeare. This register enables the 'common characteristic of *dissimulatio*',[20] found in Montaigne's twin rhetorical personae of Socrates and Horace, which consists of 'an understated, self-deprecating form of self-expression, and a profound, smiling irony in their judgments'.[21] Irony penetrates appearances; it brings 'human wisdom back down to earth' (*F*, Book III, Chapter 12, p. 966). Such a style furnishes Montaigne with the perfect form with which to posit what is perhaps the central tenet of his philosophy: namely, that the 'essence' of human beings is 'radically imperfect'.[22]

Thus Montaigne pits the demotic speech of his Socratic persona against windy self-aggrandisement and vanity; his copious discourse is not wholly senseless, because it is through it he expresses his wry sense of irony, which enables him to become 'a living Silenus'.[23] Like Socrates, Montaigne is 'always one and the same' (*F*, Book III, Chapter 12, p. 966), content with man's absurdity and the radical contingency of things. For this reason, in 'Of Experience', 'he contemplates his old, troublesome body with its disgusting excretions, and gazes upon it with the detachment of a wise and serene mind'. This is not to say, however, that he is some kind of ascetic, who renounces the outer world and his body. Rather, this process enables Montaigne to re-experience a sense of philosophical wonder at the most inconsequential and material of things. Existence, Montaigne realises, is not a riddle to be solved by reason: 'the more I frequent myself and know myself, the more my deformity astonishes me, and the less I understand myself' (*F*, Book III, Chapter 11, p. 958).

As I argued in the previous chapter, Montaigne makes the inadequacy of reason an object of philosophical inquiry. The idea of the Silenus, therefore, affects both the style of his self-deprecating self-presentation and his conception of philosophy as something that is intrinsically playful. But this playful character has been obscured and made 'inaccessible for children' (*E*, Book I, Chapter, 25, p. 76) by modern 'Sophists' who, through their 'quibbling' and abstruse formalism, have given philosophy a grotesque outer appearance; they have set 'Lady Philosophy [...] foorth with a wrimpled, gastlie, and frowning visage' (*E*, Book I, Chapter, 25, p. 76). However, the shining deity beneath this formidable – yet risible – exterior need be neither fastidiously sincere, nor something that has been transformed into an intangible method. Philosophy actually has a decidedly bacchanalian aspect:

> There is nothing more beauteous, nothing more delightfull, nothing more gainesome; and as I may say, nothing more fondly wanton: for she [Philosophy] presenteth nothing to our eyes, and preacheth nothing to our eares, but sport and pastime.
>
> (*E*, Book I, Chapter, 25, pp. 76–77)

Montaigne amplifies the playful nature of philosophy. His conception of philosophy corresponds to what Adorno, acknowledging Socrates, Montaigne and Nietzsche as his forerunners, was later to formulate so clearly as to warrant quotation at length:

> We can perhaps express this scepticism, this element of fallibility that philosophy must remain conscious of, and also of this spiritual element, by saying that, in contrast to all the methods that have been taught in the philosophical tradition, there is an essential element of play in philosophy. This is the element that the growing trend to make philosophy scientific would like to expel, whether in accordance with the laws of the natural sciences, or [...] those of the philological disciplines. From this angle, I think one of Nietzsche's greatest achievements was the emphasis he placed on the element of play in his philosophy. In this respect, if we set aside the Greeks, and especially Socrates, he really does stand out from the entire philosophical tradition, with the exception of the so-called moralists and their predecessor Montaigne [...] I would ask you not to think of this playful element of philosophy as something merely psychological, but, as I just said, as something essential to the discipline itself. This is because philosophy goes beyond whatever secure knowledge that it possesses, and because it knows this, and because it is fallible, it also possesses this playful element without which it could not be philosophy in the first place. It does not just flirt with playfulness in its motives or its methods; rather playfulness is deeply embedded within it and candidly so. I would go so far to say that without playfulness there is no truth. And I would say further that the element of chance inherent in play makes an essential contribution to the truth – as the thing that under the general spell of identity thinking reminds us of the unthinkable. In this connection, let me remind you of a saying that I have myself applied to art in a spirit of playfulness, when I said that art is the most serious thing in the world, but then again, not that serious.
>
> (*LND*, p. 90)

There is a palpable connection between playfulness and a dissatisfaction with the given nature of things, which arises from a realisation that things could be other than how they appear. Playfulness animates philosophical speculation by virtue of the fact that it 'goes beyond whatever secure knowledge it possesses', but it retains an awareness of its own fallibility.

3.4 The Casket Test

Erasmus suggests that one of the original functions of Sileni was to provide a 'humorous surprise [that] made the carver's skill all the more admirable' (*CWE*, 34, p. 262): the 'ugly outer folded back to reveal a golden statue of a god' (*CWE*, 34, p. 262). Likewise, Shakespeare delights in exploiting his audience's wider capacity for delusion – they are consistently taken in by appearances – by drawing attention to his own virtuoso skill at generating artifice. In the opening scene of *The Merchant of Venice*, for instance, Antonio displays a melancholic awareness that the world of appearances is not even, as Foucault in his discussion of the Silenus puts it, 'coherent in itself': 'I hold the world but as the world, Graziano – | A stage where every man must play a part, | And mine a sad one' (I. 1. 77–79). Like Erasmus's duplicitous Stultitia, who, moments after her discussion of the Silenic nature of things, reflects that 'All this life of mortall men, what is it els, but a certaine kynde of stage plaie? wheras men come forthe one in one araie, an other in another, eche playing his parte' (*PF*, p. 38), Antonio invokes the *theatrum mundi* topos.

Yet this theatrical self-awareness is not the only way in which *The Merchant of Venice* is strangely duplicitous. The play has two generic aspects: it is tragicomic. The play's dual *loci* are like Erasmus's Silenus turned inside out: underneath the peaceful appearance of Belmont lies the rancour and ruthless exploitation of the Venetian marketplace, while embedded in the demotic discourse of the clown's speech lies a grasp of the play's central concerns. When, for instance, Gobbo voices regrets about Jessica's conversion to Christianity – 'This making of Christians will raise the price of hogs. If we grow all to be pork-eaters we shall not shortly have rasher on the coals for money' (III. 5. 19–21) – he furnishes the audience with a *reductio ad absurdum* of the logic of the marketplace. His doctrinal ignorance implicitly illustrates how commodity, competition and exchangeability blind people to their better selves. The conversion of the Jews had an even more important significance than an increase in the price of bacon: it presaged the Second Coming of Christ.

The most obvious way in which the deceptiveness of Erasmus's Silenus is evoked, however, is through a game within the play: the seriocomic casket test. Portia's suitors must choose one of three caskets in order to marry her and acquire her fortune. Inside the winning casket lies a 'picture' of Portia (II. 7. 11). Each casket is inscribed with a riddle, which Morocco, the first to play the game, reads:

> This first of gold, who this inscription bears:
> 'Who chooseth me shall gain what many men desire'.

> The second silver, which this promise carries:
> 'Who chooseth me shall get as much as he deserves'
> This third dull lead, with warning all as blunt:
> 'Who chooseth me must give and hazard all he hath'.
>
> (II. 7. 4–9)

The correct interpretation of appearances, it seems, can enable us to fathom the essence of things. The audience is not informed which casket contains the image of Portia. They too are set an interpretative puzzle, which is only solved by a process of elimination, once two incorrect choices have been dramatised. Shakespeare assumes that his audience tends, in Paul's words, to 'look on things after the outward appearance' (II Corinthians 10. 7). Morocco, who asks Portia not to be deceived by appearance or 'complexion, | The shadowed livery of the burnished sun' (II. 1. 1–2), is a naïve realist, since he thinks essence corresponds to appearance. No one, he comments, could bear to encase the beautiful picture in 'gross' (50) lead. Besides, he loves himself well enough to know that 'A golden mind stoops not to shows of dross' (20). But when he opens the golden casket, he is disabused of his illusions. He is greeted with a skull – in the age of *vanitas* iconography, shorthand for the poverty of all human wealth and ambition, a reminder that 'all is vanity' (*KJV*, Ecclesiastes, 1. 1). In its riddling couplets, the scroll, placed in the 'empty eye' of the skull, extols the wisdom of correctly interpreted commonplaces (or adages of the ancients): "All that glistens is not gold; | Often have you heard that told" (65–66).

When it is Aragon's turn to play the casket game, he discloses its rules to the audience; he must not tell anyone which casket he chooses, and he must leave if he chooses incorrectly. Most seriously, 'if [he] fail[s] | Of the right casket', he may never 'woo a maid in way of marriage' (II. 9. 11–14). The significance this final and binding vow would have in a society based on rigid structures of primogeniture need hardly be pointed out. He is a little more successful in his interpretation. He will not choose gold, 'what many men desire':

> ARAGON: [...] the fool multitude, that choose by show,
> Not learning more than the fond eye doth teach,
> Which pries not to th'interior, but, like the martlet,
> Builds in the weather on the outward wall
> Even in the force and road of casualty.
>
> (25–39)

Like Montaigne in 'Of Physiognomy', Aragon does not assume that there is a correspondence between appearance and essence; later in the speech he employs the example of people who 'cozen fortune' and corruptly acquire 'dignity' (35–45) to prove this point. He chooses the silver casket. As its inscription predicts, he 'get[s] as much as he deserves' (48). He is presented with 'a portrait of a blinking idiot' (53). Here the Silenus has been reversed.

Its appearance is precious silver, while its essence is a grotesque portrait of a fool. There is another verse with this portrait, which suggests that those who think themselves wise – that is, not 'fool[s] of the multitude' – are actually foolish. Such is the self-satisfied knowledge of what Portia calls 'deliberate fools' (79); the riddle informs Aragon that such false knowledge characterises old men – those who have grown grey or 'Silvered o'er' (68). Despite being among Stultitia's greatest devotees, they consider themselves wise (*PF*, p. 17). The riddle allows him to marry ('Take what wife you will to bed'), but informs him that 'I [i.e. the blinking idiot] will ever be your head' (69–70).

Bassanio is a good Machiavellian. This prodigal son of Venice advises Graziano that one must manipulate appearances to give the right impression: sometimes one must 'Use all the observance of civility'; at other times, 'put on | Your boldest suit of mirth' (II. 2. 172–95). Perhaps because of this, when he comes to play the game, he is not taken in by appearances:

BASSANIO [aside]: So may the outward shows be least themselves.
The world is still deceived with ornament.
In law, what plea so tainted and corrupt
But, being seasoned with a gracious voice,
Obscures the show of evil? In religion,
What damnèd error but some sober brow
Will bless it and approve it with a text,
Hiding the grossness with fair ornament?

(III. 2. 73–80)

Aragon's arguments against duplicity in public life are reiterated. The legal system is corrupt and so are the clergy, who, as Erasmus' Folly also intuits, justify their vices with deceptive readings and self-serving interpretations of scripture (see *PF*, pp. 88–91). But Bassanio's critique of these duplicities is itself expressed through a piece of linguistic ingenuity. The word 'ornament', signifying deceptive rhetorical embellishment, is itself expressed though the rhetorical ornament of epiphora.

Bassanio then rejects the 'gaudy' gold casket as 'hard food for Midas' (101) and the silver because it is a 'pale and common drudge' (106). He *foolishly* chooses the outwardly unpromising lead and is appropriately rewarded. Inside he finds the picture, and with it the right to marry Portia:

What find I here?
Fair Portia's counterfeit. What demi-god
Hath come so near creation? Move these eyes?
Or whether, riding on the balls of mine,
Seem they in motion? Here the severed lips
Parted with sugar breath. So sweet a bar
Should sunder such sweet friends. Here in her hairs

The painter plays the spider, and hath woven
A golden mesh t'untrap the hearts of men
Faster than gnats in cobwebs. But her eyes–
How could he see to do them? Having made one,
Methinks it should have power to steal both his
And leave itself unfurnished. Yet look how far
The substance of my praise doth wrong this shadow
In underprizing it, so far this shadow
Doth limp behind the substance.

(III. 2. 114–29)

On the surface, it seems as though Erasmus's comment that 'All humaine thynges are lyke the Silenes or double images of Alcibiades' holds true in a straightforward way. The casket text has shown us that what 'outwardly seemed death [...] looking within ye shoulde fynde it lyfe and on the other side what seemed lyfe to be death: what fayre to be foule'. Beneath 'what men most desire', the gold casket, lies a skull; inside the leaden casket compared by Morocco to a shroud – lies the lifelike picture of Portia.

However, when we look deeper this is not the case. When Bassanio opens his Silenus he gets a painting, a 'counterfeit' (115). This is not altogether surprising, so long as we recall that 'Breifly, the Silenus ones beying vndone and disclosed, ye shall fynde all things [are] tourned into a new semblance [*breviter, omnia repente versa reperies, si Silenum aperueris*]'.[24] In fact, Bassanio's eloquent praise of Portia's beauty furnishes the audience with an *ekphrasis* – a vivid description of the beauties of a painting, an image of a person. Portia's radiant natural beauty, which finds its realisation in art alone, is expressed primarily through two negations. First, the life-like quality of her eyes cannot be positively described in the way her hair – 'A golden mesh t'untrap the hearts of men' – can. Second, Bassanio's description of this painting is as unequal – 'The substance of my praise doth wrong this shadow | In underprizing it' – as this inexpressibly beautiful painting is to capture Portia's radiance: 'so far this shadow | Doth limp behind the substance'. But this 'substance', which this painting – or rather this lover's *ekphrasis* of this painting by a 'demi-god' – cannot fully represent, is no 'substance' at all, for she is an actor in a play.

3.5 Self-Serving Mercy

For the Jews require a sign, and the Greeks seek after wisdom: But we preach Christ crucified, unto the Jews a stumbling block, and unto the Greeks foolishness.

(I Corinthians, 1. 22–24)

Because it underlies what Paul calls the 'great love wherewith He loved us' (Ephesians, 2. 4), the peculiar 'quality of mercy' (IV. 1. 179) is of paramount importance for understanding the concept of holy folly. Owing to His excessive mercies – most significantly, the Incarnation and the general resurrection – God appears foolish by the standards of the world. For Erasmus, as for St Paul, God's mercy is a truth that confounds earthly knowledge and logic, whereas in *The Merchant of Venice*, Shakespeare examines how seeming knowledge, infected with the pernicious logic of measurement and of *quid pro quo*, can blind people to their better intentions.

The most obvious evocation of mercy in Shakespeare is furnished by Portia's frequently anthologised courtroom speech. 'Mercy', she argues

> [...] becomes
> The thronèd monarch better than his crown.
> His sceptre shows the force of temporal power,
> The attribute to awe and majesty,
> Wherein doth sit the dread and fear of kings;
> But mercy is above this sceptred sway.
> It is enthronèd in the hearts of kings;
> It is an attribute of God himself,
> And earthly power doth then show likest God's
> When mercy seasons justice.
>
> (IV. 1. 184–93)

The disguised Portia's duplicitous testimony demonstrates how the relative truths of the marketplace can corrode even the supra-rational truth of God's foolish mercy; her speech is an inside-out Silenus: its passionate, erudite appearance hides the fact that the Christians of the play are as bereft of mercy as the individual this speech effectively condemns.

Mercy, Portia argues, is a key quality of the earthly Christian weakness that is actually transcendent strength: 'earthly power doth then show likest God's | When mercy seasons justice'. She suggests that the real power of kings lies in the mercy 'enthroned in [their] hearts'. This inner disposition is greater than their 'force of temporal power' and its outward signifiers, a sentiment that recalls a similar claim made in Erasmus's late sermon, *De Immensa Dei Misericordia* (1524): 'A king's power and majesty are often admired even by those who hate or envy him [...] clemency and generosity are loved even by those who have no need of them' (*CWE*, 70, p. 231). Unlike 'majesty', mercy is a universally admirable quality. Portia recalls four other Erasmian ideas. First, Erasmus holds that visual signifiers of faith or power, such as 'sceptres', are at best a necessary evil and at worst a mere deceptive stage property, which conceals a depleted or deformed essence; her appeal to Shylock's conscience, in addition to her suggestion that regal power lies in the heart, displays a typically Erasmian emphasis on an internalised form of faith.

Second, Portia suggests that the ethical way to live is through the imitation of Christ: man should be merciful because mercy is an 'attribute of

God himself'. The Gospel should be lived, not merely paid lip-service to. Third, she suggests that man should actively seek his 'salvation' (195) through his deeds of mercy, which 'mitigate[s] the justice' of Shylock's 'plea' (198). Shylock will not be saved unless he seeks out his salvation through deeds. Erasmus contends that divine mercy is what enables us to exist and that 'good' and 'justice' spring from an understanding of mercy (*CWE*, 70, pp. 132–35). Finally, Portia echoes Erasmus's emphasis on the reciprocity of mercy: 'any gift to another human being for the love of Jesus is made in a worthy cause' (*CWE*, 66, p. 137). She describes mercy as something that 'blesseth him that gives, and him that takes' (182). The use of anadiplosis reiterates the reciprocity it denotes. And in a covertly self-interested, but nonetheless effective, argument she reflects that mercy should temper justice, because men are judged by their deeds of mercy in life. She asks Shylock: 'how canst thou expect mercy giving none?' Shylock, however, remains steadfast in his insistence on the immutability of letter of the law: 'an oath, an oath! I have an oath in heaven | Shall I lay perjury on my soul? | No, not for Venice' (222–25). His conscience drives him in the opposite direction from Portia's.

Similarly, when Portia implores him for the sake of 'charity' (256), which Erasmus considers to be an offshoot of mercy (*CWE*, 70, p. 136), to use 'some surgeon [...] | To stop his wounds, lest he do bleed to death' (252–53). Shylock answers prosaically: 'I cannot find it. 'Tis not in the bond' (257). This legalistic logic is responsible for his downfall and, ethically speaking, for Portia's too. The paradox of this scene is that the action of the play hinges on an absolute Judaic adherence to the letter of the law, which is confounded by Christian folly. But it characterises Portia's dexterous quibbling just as much as it does Shylock's insistent demands that he is allowed to demand that his 'bond' is paid in full. Not 'a jot of blood' is to be spilt, if his 'bond' is to be kept to the letter; 'just a pound of flesh' (321), no 'less nor more' (320), is stipulated in the bond; and he is not to receive the compensation that Portia promised earlier because 'He hath refused it in open court. | He shall have merely justice and his bond' (333–34).

This paradox speaks volumes about the play as a whole. Kiernan Ryan and Zdravko Planinc both argue that the reason these Venetians hate Shylock is not because of their difference from him, but because of their similarity to him.[25] And in *Dialectic of Enlightenment*, Horkheimer and Adorno suggest that this hatred of one's reflection, so cogently examined in *The Merchant of Venice*, is the key to understanding Nazi hatred of the Jews: 'in the image of the Jew, which the racial nationalists hold up before the world, they express their own being. Their craving is for ownership, appropriation, unlimited power [...] at any price' (DA, p. 177; [*DE*, p. 137]). In his famous threat, Shylock himself acknowledges that the rage of the Christians is that of Caliban's in the mirror: 'The villainy you teach me I will execute, and it shall go hard but I will better the instruction' (III. 1. 60–61).

Planinc is correct to point out the hypocrisy of the Christian traders: 'Neither Antonio nor Bassanio produce wealth; they merely redistribute it [...].

And yet that is the ostensible basis of their hatred of money-lending Jews'.[26] In fact, the *state* of Venice itself does not produce anything. It, too, merely redistributes wealth. This is hinted at when the Duke hesitates to release Antonio from his bond: 'the trade and profit of the city | Consisteth of all nations' (III. 3. 30–31). Erasmus's adage, 'To extract tribute from the dead', in which he laments how 'money breeding money' (*CWE*, 32, p. 184) has become ubiquitous, voices comparable views to those tacit in *The Merchant of Venice*. Erasmus writes: 'I would accept a usurer sooner than this sordid class of merchants, who use tricks and falsehoods, fraud and misrepresentation, in pursuit of profit from any source' (*CWE*, 32, p. 185).

Antonio's business must be seen for what it is: namely, reckless venture capitalism. And Portia's testimony must also be seen for what it is: perjury – the 'plea' is both 'tainted and corrupt'. As Planinc shows, she engages in entrapment; she appears in court in a disguise, 'gives a false name and legal credentials';[27] is ignorant of the difference between 'contract law and civil law';[28] and is the wife of one of the interested parties.[29] It is safe to assume that her instrumental evocations of 'mercy' and 'charity' fall on deaf ears. Despite the fact that his losses have been common knowledge for some time, the Venetian Christians have conspicuously failed to give or lend Antonio 'the money he needed in time, though he had often done so for them in similar circumstances'.[30]

This play shows the audience how even the radically egalitarian concept of God's mercy, which applies to all people of all times and of all creeds, can be used in earthly testimony as a means to an end. In Shakespeare's Venice, even the concepts that ostensibly transcend the ruthless exploitation of the marketplace are not safe from it. The ironies of this play suggest that mercy cannot be realised in a world in which even the minds of the ostensibly faithful are ensnared by a 'mad passion for property [that] has gone so far that there is nothing in the wide world, sacred or profane, from which something like usury cannot be extracted' (*CWE*, 32, p. 185).

3.6 Epilogue

What Erasmus, Rabelais, Montaigne and Shakespeare all find so fascinating about the Silenus is its self-generative, self-reflexive possibilities. In Montaigne, Silenic style enables self-reflection, through which he becomes aware of his own limitations. Through Socratic 'ignorance' he reaches a negative truth: 'Ignorance that knows itself, that judges itself and condemns itself, is not complete ignorance' (*F*, Book II, Chapter 12, p. 451). Truth is not a consequence of human knowledge. Rather, a truth of sorts is found negatively, through the unlearning of received wisdom. The Silenic texts of Erasmus, Montaigne and Shakespeare all delight in lifting the veil of appearances to point out the untruth of the way things are, of what passes for reality.

Of course, the paradox at the core of the Greek Sileni is that they did not contain a holy essence, but rather a gold statuette, a representation of a deity; similarly, the lead casket in *The Merchant of Venice* contains a *semblance* of an *actor*. It should not be forgotten that it is Erasmus's Stultitia, in her encomium to folly, who invokes the idea of the Silenus as a metaphor for the truth of '[a]ll humaine thynges' and that she points out that when you open the Silenus 'ye shall fynde all things [are] tourned into a new *semblance*'. '[S]emblance' carries multiple connotations of dissimulation, especially in early modern English:[31] this duplicitous icon undermines its revelation that the reality is mere shadow play. But by doing so, it also embodies the need to have a sceptical attitude towards determinate values, even of the determinate value of universal indeterminacy.

Isabella suggests something comparable in *Measure for Measure*, when she informs Angelo that man is 'Most ignorant of what he's most assured | His glassy essence' (II. 2. 22–23). Shakespeare shies away from positing negative truths about man's essential 'ignorance' – the ambiguity in 'glassy' allows for an essence that is at once brittle yet solid, translucent yet reflective.[32] If the human essence is translucent, then there is a nihilistic inference to be drawn: appearances are an envelope around a void and, as such, all we have. Thus man becomes a perpetual actor, which is an appropriate enough creed for a dramatist. If, however, the essence is reflective, the distinction between appearance and essence is collapsed; we are faced with the proposition that the essence of things actually reflects back the monstrous, quotidian world of appearances. This also suggests that it is through speculative reflection on semblance that it is possible to get to the essence of things.

The fragile truth of the Silenus head may lie less in the uncovering of an essence, which is an image, and more in the process by which this uncovering of a false idol is reached. However quixotic this process may be, its profound strength and its peculiar truth lie in its obdurate refusal to resign itself to the given, to certain knowledge and to explicit values. In this connection, Adorno writes that 'Art is magic delivered from the lie of being truth. Its semblance disenchants the disenchanted world' (*AT*, p. 75). As I will endeavour to establish in the following chapter, the philosophical potential of Shakespeare's drama inheres in its capacity to expose the expedient fictions by which the serious world functions, while refusing to forget that it is itself a form of semblance.

Notes

1. Plato, *The Symposium*, ed. by M. C. Howatson and Frisbee C. C. Sheffield, trans. by M. C. Howatson (Cambridge: Cambridge University Press, 2008), 216c–217a.
2. *Ibid.*, 216c–217a.
3. Shakespeare's Foolosophy', in *Shakespeare Performed: Essays in Honor of R. A. Foakes*, ed. by Grace Ioppolo (Newark: University of Delaware Press, 2000), pp. 17–33 (p. 21).
4. See *Praisers of Folly: Erasmus, Rabelais and Shakespeare* (London: Gollancz, 1964), esp. pp. 60–62.

5. See *Ecstasy and the Praise of Folly* (London: Duckworth, 1980), p. 3; *Laughter at the Foot of the Cross* (London: Penguin, 1997), p. 91.
6. See 'Introduction' in *Utopia: With Erasmus' Sileni of Alcibiades*, ed. and trans. by David Wootton (Cambridge: Hackett, 1999), pp. 1–30.
7. See *The Cornucopian Text: Problems of Writing in the French Renaissance* (Oxford: Oxford University Press, 1979; repr. 2002), pp. x–40.
8. 'Introduction', in *Silenos: Erasmus in Elizabethan Literature*, Studi di Letterature Moderne e Comparate, 1 (Pisa: Pancini, 1998), pp. 5–13 (pp. 5, 6).
9. *The Symposium*, 218d–219e.
10. *Ibid.*, 218e.
11. *Ibid.*, 219a.
12. *Ibid.*, 222d.
13. *Ibid.*, p. 216c.
14. For an English translation, see Here folowith a scorneful image or monstrus shape of a maruelous stra[n]ge fygure called, Sileni alcibiadis, trans. by anon (London: John Gough, 1543).
15. For a concise introduction to these concerns drawn from the primary sources, see Ulrich Von Hutten, 'Ein Klangschrift Herren Ulrichs von Hutten' and Martin Luther, 'Von der Freyheyt eyniß Christen menschen', in *Die deutsche Literatur in Text und Darstellung*, ed. by Otto F. Best and Hans-Jürgen Schmitt, 17 vols (Stuttgart: Reclam, 1998), III, pp. 67–73; pp. 73–80.
16. *Kritische Schriften und Briefe*, ed. by Edgar Lohner, 7 vols (Stuttgart: W. Kohlhammer, 1967–75), VI, p. 139.
17. *Sir Thomas More* in *Shakespeare and Others: Collaborative Plays*, ed. by Jonathan Bate and others (Basingstoke: Palgrave, 2013), pp. 349–421 (pp. 381–385).
18. Erich Auerbach, *Mimesis: The Representation of Reality in Western Literature*, trans. by Willard R. Task (Princeton, NJ: Princeton University Press, 1953; repr. 2003), p. 279.
19. *From Grotesque to Silenus* (unpublished doctoral dissertation: Royal Holloway, University of London, 1987), p. 256.
20. *Ibid.*, p. 256.
21. *Ibid.*, p. 256.
22. Anne Hartle, *Michel de Montaigne: Accidental Philosopher* (Cambridge: Cambridge University Press, 2003), p. 160.
23. Calder, p. 3.
24. *Opera Omnia Desiderii Erasmi*, ed. by various, 9 vols (Amsterdam: E. J. Brill/ London: Elsevier, 1964–2005), IV, p. 428 a–b.
25. *Shakespeare's Comedies* (Basingstoke: Palgrave, 2010), p. 121; 'Reading *The Merchant of Venice* through Adorno', *Journal of Cultural and Religious Theory*, 8 (2007), 20–41.
26. Planinc, p. 23.
27. *Ibid.*, p. 37.
28. *Ibid.*, p. 37.
29. *Ibid.*, p. 37.
30. *Ibid.*, p. 21.
31. 'Semblance' primarily signifies the outward appearance of a thing or a person, but holds multiple connotations of dissimulation, especially in early modern English (compare *OED*, definitions nos. 1a, 2a and b, 3a and b, 4a and c, 5, 6, 7, 8).
32. Compare *OED*, definitions no. 1a, b, e.

4 Jesting at History

4.1 Introduction

> If one at a solemne stage plaie, would take vpon hym to plucke of the plaiers garments whiles theyr were saying theyr partes, and so disciphre vnto lokers on, the true and natiue faces of eche of the plaiers, shoulde he not (trow ye) marre all the mattier? And well deserue for a madman to be pelted out of place with stones? Ye shoulde see yet straightwaies a new transmutacion in thynges: that who before plaied the woman, should than appeare to be a man: who seemed youth, should shew his hore heares: who counrefaited the kynge, should tourne to a rascall, and who plaied god almightie became a cobbler as he was before. Yet take awaie this errour, and as soone take awaie all togethers, in as muche as the feigning and counterfaitying is it that so delighteth the beholders. So likewise, all this life of mortall men, what is it els, but a certaine kynde of stage plaie?
>
> —*PF*, pp. 37–38

It is primarily through the discourse of folly that the Second Tetralogy critiques the representation of history even as it dramatises it. What is significant about Shakespeare's rendering of history, I suggest, is the way in which it is self-critical, uncomfortable in its own skin. Although Shakespeare uses historical drama to de-mystify any false memories of a finest hour, he remains acutely aware that artworks are not privileged objects free from the sway of the prevailing ideology: they are shaped by ideology and have a hand in shaping it. This is especially the case with historical writing because, as Jonathan Baldo shows, the selection of what is worthy for dramatisation in a history play is itself an ideological act: 'any play based on chronicle histories, necessarily highly selective and truncated in its treatment, may easily assume the qualities of a cover-up as much as a rescue of memorable, heroic acts'.[1] And lending aesthetic form to the multiplicity of the past clearly risks imbuing the past with an artificial coherence and inferring meaning from a retroactively imposed narrative about a time that never quite existed.

Unlike historians, however, poets (and fools) make only provisional claims to authority. Thus, it is entirely fitting, albeit rather disconcerting, that these plays insistently remind their audiences that they are telling a story rather than establishing hard and fast historical facts. Discussing the folly of expecting to find certainties in historical writing, Philip Sidney's *Apology* is attuned to the way that poetry sidesteps making such unequivocal truth-claims:

> What child is there that, coming to a play, and seeing *Thebes* written in great letters upon an old door, doth believe that it is *Thebes*? If a man can arrive, at that child's age, to know that the poet's persons and doings are but pictures of what should be, and not stories of what has been, they will never give the lie to things not affirmatively but allegorically and figuratively written. And therefore, as in History looking for truth, they shall go away full fraught with falsehood, so in Poesy looking but for fiction, they shall use the narration but as an imaginative ground-plot of a profitable invention.[2]

Even a child is aware that drama does not present historical facts *per se*, for the representation of reality in fiction is necessarily ideal and 'allegorical'. Far from simply replicating the way things are, representation organises reality and offers an ideal picture 'of what should be'.

Therein lies the rub: representation's tendency to skate over the hard facts of reality is one of the recurrent concerns of Shakespearean drama, not just his histories. Chapter 5 illustrates how representational thinking is complicit in thwarting the possibility of happiness, whereas Chapter 6 shows how the aesthetics of derangement and deformity at work in *Hamlet* and *King Lear* work to foreground tragedy's own 'unreal luxury status as play';[3] these tragedies, in particular, expose the felicitous removal of the realm of make believe from the harsher realities of life – at the end of a tragedy, the actors rise from the dead and take a bow, but such a luxury is not, of course, afforded to their audience.

Not least because of its focus on the abject, incomplete and imperfect, in the Second Tetralogy, the discourse of folly problematises, ironises and resists representation's tendency towards abstraction and idealisation. It is, for instance, clear in the opening scene of *2 Henry IV* that Northumberland, who has betrayed his son, evokes an abstraction, time, in order to downplay his part in the rebellion: 'The times are wild; contention, like a horse | Full of high feeding, madly hath broke loose, | And bears down all before him' (I. 1. 9–11). Indeed, by giving the lie to such politically expedient abstractions, folly is an ethically charged aspect of the plays, one that ultimately enables Shakespeare to write drama that possess what Hugh Grady describes as an 'impure aesthetics'.[4] And an understanding of these aesthetics can take us closer to perceiving an unresolved tension at the heart of Shakespeare's antithetical historical practice.

For Adorno, it is *Don Quixote*, the last great text of Renaissance folly, that most presciently embodies the dialectic between art's freedom, which inheres in its removal from the world of purpose by virtue of its purposelessness, and its constraint – the way in which is it is mediated by the conditions in which it was composed:

> The object of bourgeois art is the relation of itself as artefact to empirical society; *Don Quixote* stands at the beginning of this development. Art, however, is social not only because of its mode of production, in which the dialectic of the forces and relations of production is concentrated, nor simply because of the social derivation of its thematic material. Much more importantly, art becomes social by its opposition to society, and it occupies this position only as autonomous art. By crystallising itself as something unique to itself, rather than complying with existing social norms and qualifying as 'socially useful', it criticises society by merely existing, for which puritans of all stripes condemn it.
>
> (*AT*, p. 296)

Quixote's folly, his purposive purposelessness, is comparable to that of bourgeois art in general. Through his hero's socially useless quest, Cervantes assays values of his society and of his cultural history, of the romances with which the errant Knight is infatuated. It is through the numerous extra-historical digressions of the Henriad that Shakespeare *stages* the power of purposelessness to oppose – and critique – the purposeful world. In *1&2 Henry IV*, the serious world's condemnation of art's freedom is exemplified in its attempts to set Falstaff to work and his banishment.

Unsurprisingly, studies of folly in the Second Tetralogy have been attracted to its most magnetic and enigmatic character, Falstaff; they compare him with Shakespeare's other wise fools,[5] place him in a genealogy of European trickster figures[6] or analyse him in the light of Bakhtin's theories about carnival.[7] Yet the significance of folly in these plays is by no means circumscribed by Falstaff's ample girth. Indeed, to treat him in isolation is to neglect both his crucial role within the text and the other,[8] less immediately apparent, but much more important, manifestations of folly. It is through the protean mode of folly that these texts stage the dialectic at the heart of Shakespeare's philosophy of history, that between art's freedom from social coercion and its complicity in it.

By mapping the metaphorical, structural and thematic integrity of folly in these plays, this chapter illustrates how Shakespeare uses the discourse of folly, a discourse that, for the most part, is added to his chronicle sources, to assiduously *avoid* claiming that his plays represent the past accurately. In the Henriad, Shakespeare fashions something comparable to Montaigne's silenic style, a demotic register with a kernel of philosophical insight that lays bare both the sheer absurdity of the grand claims to authority often made by historians and dramatises the grotesque essence of political sovereignty. As Richard F. Hardin astutely observes, these histories offer us 'the opacity of true history: contradictions, deceptions, rumours, without certainty that any doubts can ever be cleared up. Parents betray children; religion is at best ineffective, more often a pretext for policy; dishonour, injustice and fear are the real ruling powers'.[9]

Of course, Shakespeare's fascination with the ways in which political power is legitimated though performance has long been acknowledged – as Grady writes, in Shakespeare, 'political power grows, not from any deputation of authority from God to king and his subjects, but from the social acceptance of artfully produced illusions of legitimacy'.[10] However, in the interpretations of *Richard II*, *1&2 Henry IV*, and *Henry V* that follow, I show how Shakespeare – like Erasmus and More before him – employs the discourse of folly to draw attention to the performative aspect of political power; this 'life of mortall men', it transpires, is indeed 'but a certaine kynde of stage plaie'.

Initially, I examine how folly infiltrates the language, themes, action and imagery of *Richard II,* before showing how the candid speech of the plebeian gardeners is not only interwoven with images and ideas from the main plot, but is also concerned with the ethical ramifications of giving aesthetic form to contingent historical reality, a concern that surfaces recurrently in these acutely self-critical plays. Next, in an analysis of *1&2 Henry IV*, I argue that the theme of mendacity in these plays furnishes Shakespeare with a way of reflecting on the process of writing history;[11] I pay close attention to how the purposeful purposelessness of Falstaff in the tavern scene embodies on stage what Adorno means about purposelessness and art's inbuilt opposition to society. And this analysis is developed further in the reading of *Henry V*, with which this chapter concludes. In *Henry V*, two conflicting accounts of history – an authorised account, which attempts to fashion myths, and a fool's account, which debunks such myths – grind away at each other in dramatic attrition, *staging* the dialectical attrition that Adorno considers an essential aspect of 'complex artworks' (*AT*, p. 242).

4.2 Degeneracy

> So too should the historian write, consorting with Truth and not with flattery, looking to the future hope, not to the gratification of the flattered[12]
>
> —Lucian

To present day, the concept of degeneracy is frequently employed as a byword for a disregard for the values of the established order. In this respect, it has an affinity with the word folly in the sense of a dangerous, even sinful, misapprehension – as in the Richard's 'follies' (IV. 1. 275).[13] According to Bolingbroke, Richard was 'unhappied and *dis*figured clean' by Bushy and Green because they 'Made a divorce betwixt his queen and him' and 'Broke the possession of the royal bed' (III. 1. 10, 12–13 [my emphasis]). Making the platonic association between physical beauty and virtue, the usurper suggests that Richard is physically marked by his immoral behaviour. Ironically, of course, it is Bolingbroke himself who is responsible for Richard being 'Doubly divorced', breaking 'A twofold marriage: 'twixt my crown and me, | And then betwixt me and my married wife' (V. 1. 71, 72–73). And as the word's etymological root implies – it stems from the Latin *genus*, signifying 'birth, decent, origin; offspring; kind; race; family; nation; gender'[14] – to be de*gen*erate is to be 'One who has lost, or has become deficient in, the qualities considered proper to the race or kind; a degenerate specimen; a person of debased physical or mental constitution'.[15] In Richard's case, his degeneracy is bound up with property in general and primo*gen*iture in particular. He is a 'Most degenerate king' (II. 1. 263) for over taxing the commons and robbing his cousin Hereford of his 'patrimony' (238).[16]

Because it threatens the legitimacy of the royal *genus* and because the king's behaviour is supposed to be exemplary, the aberrant sexual behaviour of Holinshed's Richard attracts the chronicler's scorn. He comments, in an observation not found in his main source,[17] that Richard committed the 'filthie sinne of leacherie and fornication, with abhominable adulterie, speciallie in the king' (*NDSS*, 3, p. 408). To be degenerate is to violate the past by failing to fulfil the deep-rooted expectations of how you should behave in the present or how you will behave in the future. It is to shatter the petrified historical constructs of form and precedence, as Hal does in his mockery of chivalric conceits, which Hotspur reports to the King:

> he would unto the stews,
> And from the common'st creature pluck a glove,
> And wear it as a favour, and with that
> He would unhorse the lustiest challenger.
>
> (V. 3. 20–23)

Paving the way for *1&2 Henry IV*, in which it is of central thematic importance, the concept of degeneracy is subjected to close scrutiny at the close of *Richard II*.

Moments after Hotspur and Henry IV have discussed Hal's delinquent behaviour, the theme is replayed in Aumerle's thwarted attempt to depose Henry (his uncle), a degenerate king according to the rules of primogeniture. Aumerle's father, York, in what his wife regards a degenerate action, betrays his son to the king and is praised as a paradigm of constancy:

> O loyal father of a treacherous son!
> Thou sheer, immaculate, and silver fountain,
> From whence this stream through muddy passages
> Hath held his current and defiled himself.
>
> (V. 3. 57–61)

What is really significant about the idea of degeneracy in *Richard II*, however, is the way in which ideas of legitimacy become a disguise for wholly instrumental relations. In the final count, it is hard to say who is more degenerate: Hal or Henry, York or Aumerle. After all, the play dramatises the fall of a degenerate king's realm into the hands of one whose claim is degenerate because it breaks with primogeniture. In terms of legitimacy, then, the play's action lies somewhere between Scylla and Charybdis. Despite Richard's hysterical protestations to the contrary, 'the breath of worldly men' can 'depose | The deputy elected by the Lord' (III. 2. 52–53). As Katharine Eisaman Maus puts it: 'If being a king and having a kingdom were completely inseparable – if the realm, were, so to speak, permanently soldered to the monarch – usurpation would be an impossibility'.[18]

The discord with which the play opens, in which the 'ceremonious form of the appeal of treason'[19] is used to cloak Hereford's knowledge of Richard's complicity in Woodstock's murder, is followed by the scene in which John of Gaunt is upbraided by his brother's widow. She accuses him of being degenerate because he, one of 'Edward's seven sons', one of 'seven vials of his sacred blood' (I. 2. 11–12), fails to take revenge upon his brother's murderer:

> Thou dost consent
> In some large measure to thy father's death
> In that thou seest thy wretched brother die,
> Who was the model of thy father's life.
> Call it not patience, Gaunt, it is despair.
> In suff'ring thus thy brother to be slaughtered
> Thou show'st the naked pathway to thy life,
> Teaching stern murder how to butcher thee.
> That which in mean men we entitle patience
> Is pale cold cowardice in noble breasts.
>
> (25–34)

She attempts to motivate Gaunt's action in the present by recalling memories of an idealised past. The ironies of this marginal character's speech expose the self-serving core of the concept of legitimacy: she appeals to Gaunt's sense of pride and then his desire for self-preservation, rather than his desire to defend his *genus*. 'Old John of Gaunt', may indeed be 'time-honoured' (I. 1. 1) – as in Richard's formal epithet with which this play opens – but the common critical assumption that he embodies the values of the good old days of chivalry is undermined by the Duchess's speech.

In *Thomas of Woodstock*, the tyrant Richard is impressed that Trissillian, a 'Janus lyke' fawning lawyer and parasite, has thought up the idea of 'Blanke charters, to fill up our treasury, | Opening the cheasts of hoording cormorants | That laugh to see ther kingly soveraigne lacke' (*NDSS*, 3, p. 470 [III. 1. 1135–38]). Shakespeare reverses the significance of the bestial image of the gluttonous cormorant to describe the voracious greed of Richard's inner circle;[20] in a desperate plea for the king to, in Northumberland's words, 'make high majesty look like itself' (II. 1. 297), Gaunt piles one commonplace about the perils of prodigality onto another, suggesting that the ruthless pursuit of self-interest is self-destructive:

> He tires betimes that spurs too fast betimes.
> With eager feeding food doth choke the feeder.
> Light vanity, insatiate cormorant,
> Consuming means, soon preys upon itself.
>
> (II. 1. 36–39)

Invoking the licence granted to fools and dying men, Gaunt inveighs against the madness into which society has degenerated. He concludes his famous praise of England, 'This royal throne of kings, this sceptured isle' (II. 1. 40), thus:

> Is now leased out – I die pronouncing it –
> Like a tenement or pelting farm
> England, bound in with the triumphant sea,
> Whose rocky shore beats back the envious siege
> Of wat'ry Neptune, is now bound in with shame,
> With inky blots and rotten parchment bonds.
> That England that was wont to conquer others
> Hath made a shameful conquest of itself.
>
> (59–66)

Although Richard's 'blank charters' turn out to be not so much writing that conquers as writing that deposes, his legal discourse, which seeks to order reality, illustrates the darker side of reason's desire to categorise the world. The 'shame', to which Gaunt alludes, is connected to the king's degeneracy in two related ways.

First, because he exults in the works of man, Richard is idolatrous. This is significant because, as David Hawkes explains in his excellent study of idolatry and capitalism:

> The pursuit of fleshly pleasures or worldly goods indicates a misconstrual of the *telos* of the human being. To be carnal is to forget that the body is a means to a spiritual end. Such a fleshy consciousness will systematically reduce the spiritual to the material, the subjective to the objective. It is, in other words, a *fetishistic* consciousness.[21]

Such a '*fetishistic* consciousness' is dangerously foolish, since it misapprehends the world, seeing it as possessing cornucopian plenitude, whereas, in and of itself, without the hope of salvation and resurrection, the world is barren, and human activity bereft of significance.

Second, Richard's conduct is manifestly at odds with how a Christian prince should behave; as Erasmus argues at length in his manual about statecraft, *Institutio Principis Christiani* (1518), the earthly pomp and decadence in which tyrants revel can be measured only by the privations of their subjects (see *CWE*, 27, p. 225). In the terms of Shakespeare's Alexander Iden, Richard 'wax[es] great' as a result of 'others' waning' (*2 Henry VI*, IV. 9, 18–19). By being captivated by the signifiers of kingship, he actually negates its spiritual power. Erasmus explains this in theatrical terms: 'If all that makes a king is a chain, a sceptre, robes of royal purple, and a train of attendants, what after all is to prevent actors in a drama who come on stage decked with all the pomp of state from being regarded as real kings?' (*CWE*, 27, p. 215). This *praeposterum* reverses the transformation of a king into an actor by suggesting that when a sovereign becomes obsessed with the signifiers of temporal authority, then his authority becomes a mere performance.

Gaunt jokes about the similarities between his cadaverous appearance and his name, itself an Anglicization of Ghent, in such a way as to negate its metonymic significance in favour of its literal one. His humour subtly enacts the systematic reduction of the 'spiritual to the material, the subjective to the objective', which Hawkes sees as characteristic of idolaters. The object of Gaunt's former pride becomes the object of his scorn. The very names of the nobility attest to the way their identity – or *property* in the early modern sense of a distinguishing feature – is determined by what they own.[22] This piece of moribund humour is absent from Shakespeare's sources:

KING RICHARD: Can sick men play so nicely with their names?
JOHN OF GAUNT: No, misery makes sport to mock itself.
  Since thou doest seek to kill my name in me,
  I mock my name, great King, to flatter thee.
KING RICHARD: Should dying men flatter with those that live?
JOHN OF GAUNT: No, no, men living flatter those that die.
KING RICHARD: Thou now a-dying sayst thou flatter'st me?
JOHN OF GAUNT: O no: thou diest, though I the sicker be.
KING RICHARD: I am in health; I breathe, and see thee ill.
JOHN OF GAUNT: Now He that made me knows I see thee ill:
  Ill in myself to see, and in thee seeing ill.
  Thy deathbed is no lesser than thy land,
  Wherein thou liest in reputation sick.

(II. 1. 84–96)

Gaunt's name has become as polysemous as a word in the mouth of a fool. Although Richard dismisses this critique as the words of a 'lunatic lean-witted fool' (113), Gaunt turns reality on its head by playing on the dual significance of the word 'ill': the ill man is morally healthy, the healthy man is terminally ill in moral terms. Gaunt ironically adopts the position of one of Richard's flatterers so as to warn him about the deceptive nature of their eloquent counsel, as opposed to his riddling wordplay, which is as erudite as Lear's fool's castigations of his master and is removed from the inarticulate language of lunacy. Because his son returns to England specifically to make good his name, Gaunt's self-deflation has a residual significance: it creates a structural irony, which tacitly makes a mockery of Henry's project to reclaim his birth right.

To destroy the documentation of someone's existence is to write them out of history. And this is precisely what Richard's flatterers attempt to do to Bolingbroke; his sense of vulnerability to historical erasure is palpable when, in a kangaroo court, he indicts them for *logocide*. They have

> From my own windows torn my household coat,
> Razed out my imprese, leaving me no sign,
> Save men's opinions and my living blood,
> To show the world I am a gentlemen.
>
> (III. 2. 24–27)

The proliferation of first-person pronouns in connection with his property certainly supports Maus's argument about the interrelation of personal identity and ownership. Moreover, Bolingbroke's return makes it clear that the duplicity of words in the face of the reality they purport to signify is not simply a problem of representation. It shapes history.

4.3 Deformities

To examine the theme of deformity, it is necessary to consider the exchange between the Gardeners, absent from the sources, which puts the narrative of the nobles and gentry on hold. Yet far from providing comic relief, their exchange is rife with tensions that are also apparent in the serious action. As with the Clowns in *Hamlet*, the Porter in *Macbeth* and Falstaff's language of exuberant corporeality in *1&2 Henry IV*, these plebeian characters not only reflect upon the main action, but also betray an uncanny grasp of the significant patterns of imagery that run through the serious action of the play. They 'brush history against the grain',[23] deforming the received account of history by their very presence. These men, who work up to their elbows in mud but speak in elegant blank verse, display an intuitive grasp of a conflict at the heart of Shakespeare's representation of history: namely, the contradictory nature of historical narration.

The main problem of the positivist conception of history is that its own form belies it. As Lucan's, from whom Erasmus got his *theatrum mundi* trope,[24] 'How to Write History', admits, writing history is, in a certain sense, an aesthetic practice, since it involves 'superinduc[ing] upon events the charm of order'.[25] To write history is to give the formal organisation intrinsic in representation to the formless multiplicity of what has been.

Perhaps this tension accounts for the striking contrast between form and chaos in the exchange between the Gardener and his mate and, indeed, in the play as a whole:

GARDENER: [*To First Man*] Go, bind thou up yon dangling apricots
    Which, like unruly children, make their sire
    Stoop with oppression of their prodigal weight.
    Give some substance to the bending twigs.
    [*To Second Man*] Go thou, and, like an executioner,
    Cut off the heads of too fast-growing sprays
    That look too lofty in our commonwealth.
    All must be even in our government.
    You thus employed, I will go root away
    The noisome weeds which without profit suck
    The soil's fertility from wholesome flowers.
FIRST MAN: Why should we, in the compass of a pale,
    Keep law and form and due proportion,
    Showing as in a model our firm estate,
    When our sea-wallèd garden, the whole land,
    Is full of weeds, her fairest flowers choked up,
    Her fruit trees all unpruned, her hedges ruined,
    Her knots disordered, and her wholesome herbs
    Swarming with caterpillars?
GARDENER: Hold thy peace.
    He that hath suffered this disordered spring
    Hath now himself met with the fall of leaf.
    The weeds, which his broad spreading leaves did shelter,
    That seemed in eating him to hold him up,
    Are plucked up, root and all, by Bolingbroke.

(III. 4. 30–53)

This exchange offers a précis of the play's themes and imagery. Prodigal offspring that threaten to destroy the achievements of their fathers must be 'Cut off' to prevent lasting damage to the abundance of England, a 'sea-wallèd garden', which is infested with parasitical creatures and 'weeds'. In addition to echoing Bolingbroke's description of himself as a gardener and the king's flatterers as 'caterpillars of the commonwealth | Which I have sworn to weed and pluck away' (II. 3. 165–66), as with the image of the 'cormorants', Shakespeare inverts the significance of the 'caterpillars' in the second half of the source.[26] In the latter part of *Woodstock*, Trissillian's trickster-servant, Nimble, insults a group of common people, from whom he is extorting money, by calling them 'caterpillars' (*NDSS*, 3, p. 477 [III. ii. 1636]), whereas in *Richard II* the word is used by a worker to describe the venality of 'the Earl of Wiltshire, Bushy, Green' (54).

But this pervasive imagery of parasites is also significant because it is associated with dramatic representation in the period. The *second and third blast to the players* (1580), which is sometimes attributed to Shakespeare's collaborator Anthony Munday, like many of the contemporary anti-theatrical polemics, views theatre as a degenerate activity, which tempts its audiences, who 'prodigalie consume'[27] this commodity, to replicate the atrocities they see on stage. Real-life desires and emotions are all too easily infiltrated by represented ones. The audience's 'insatiable desire [for the] filthie plesure' of the theatre not only allures 'schollers [...] from their studies', but, worse still, is intrinsically idolatrous: 'we despise the Lordes table, and honor Theaters; at a worde, we loue al *things*, reuerence al *things*, [that] God alone seemeth vile to vs'.[28] And one need only think of the modern notion of the matinee idol to observe the continuing association between actors and idols, theatre and idolatry.

The polemicist continues, observing that players debase their patrons:

> Since the reteining of these *Catetpillers*, the credite of Noble men hath decaied, & they are thought to be couetous by permitting their seruants, which cannot liue of theselues, and whome for neerenes they wil not maintaine, to liue at the deuotion or almes of other men, passing from countrie to countrie, from one Gentlemans house to another, offering their seruice, which is a kind of beggerie [my emphasis].[29]

Obviously, the actor's art and the plays themselves are commodities. Thus they are objects of the implacable desire that characterises an objectifying consciousness, which, never satisfied, restlessly and relentlessly shifts from desiring one thing to desiring another. Paradoxically, however, it is though theatre, which is itself a commodity, that Shakespeare stages the dangers of fetishistic consciousness, which, as we have seen, reduces kingship to stage playing. The signifiers of authority captivate Richard. As Richard F. Hardin writes, 'Richard's tragedy is that he allows himself to be deluded, hence ultimately usurped, by his confidence in a symbol. What gives life to the symbol of the crown, what gives it is sacredness, is the King's living up to his role'.[30] Richard is akin to the idolatrous tyrant of the *Trauerspiel*, of whom Walter Benjamin writes: 'His unfaithfulness to man is matched by his loyalty to those things [the symbols of kingship] to the point of being absorbed into contemplative devotion to them'.[31] Simply put, Richard confuses *having* with *being*.

In striking contrast to the other plebeian characters in the rest of the Second Tetralogy, the Gardeners speak for the most part in elegant iambic pentameter – with 'law and form and due proportion'. This registers the play's obsession with form and formality in the face of material disorder, with the inexorable growth of weeds even in the most carefully maintained of gardens. Unsurprisingly, analogies between the state of the nation and the state of a garden, badly maintained or otherwise, abound in both of the play's two main sources. In *Woodstock*, Lancaster reflects on the duties and achievements of himself and his brothers, making the comparison between statecraft and gardening or farming:

> Princly Edwards sonnes In tender care
> Of wanton Richard & ther Fathers realme,
> Have toyld to purge faire Englands plessant field
> Of all those ranckorous weeds that choakt the grounds
> & left hir plessent meads like barron hills
>
> (*NDSS*, 3, p. 491)

Meanwhile, in Holinshed, horticultural degeneration acquires a providential significance: in the year of Richard's deposition, 'old baie trees withered, and afterwards, contrarie to all mens thinking, grew greene againe, a strange sight, and supposed to import some unknowne event' (*NDSS*, 3, p. 396).

Shakespeare, however, puts this providential rendering of history into the mouth of the Welsh captain, so as to gesture towards the way in which giving form to multiplicity, a process intrinsic to representation, can lead to manifestly erroneous conclusions:

> 'Tis thought the king is dead. We will not stay.
> The bay trees in our country are all withered,
> And meteors fright the fixèd stars of heaven.
> [...]
> And lean-looked prophets whisper fearful change,
> Rich men look sad, and ruffians dance and leap;
> The one in fear to lose what they enjoy,
> The other to enjoy by rage and war.
> These signs forerun the death or fall of kings.
>
> (II. 4. 7–9, 11–15)

The irony is, of course, that, for all his dire imagery of the *mundus inversus*, it is the Welshman's decision to leave that is in no small part responsible for the earth-shattering event he foresees in the stars. When the Gardener, silencing the protests of the First Man, suggests that Richard's fall is a result of his tolerance of a 'disordered spring', the tension between historical allegorisation, in which Richard indulges, and personal agency, which Bolingbroke exploits to the full, comes to the fore. Although the Gardener evokes images of autumnal, natural decomposition, he makes it clear that this fall is not part of an organic cycle. It is the consequence of an intervention – Bolingbroke has 'plucked up' these 'weeds', Richard's parasitical flatterers, 'root and all'. Shakespeare uses the Gardeners to reflect upon the history in which the other characters are embroiled; England, they suggest, is 'full of weeds' not because the land or some higher power somehow foresees Richard's fall, but because the lethal combination of Richard's prodigal kingship and Bolingbrook's 'boist'rous' (I. 3. 127) ambition has created chaos.

The Gardener's reflection, 'All must be even in our government', makes clear the link between statecraft and representation. The former must be even-handed and calm, while the latter lends 'even' form to multiplicity. But it also echoes the under-garrisoned York's abrupt reflection shortly before, after a series of self-interruptions, that 'All is uneven' (II. 2. 121) – his discontinuous utterance lapses from mainly iambic pentameters into a fragmented line consisting of a dactyl followed by a trochee,[32] reflecting metrically what his panicked observation denotes. On the one hand, if one reads the Second Man's comment literally, it poses a potentially incendiary question, showing how 'clowning creates openings both in the literary text and in the social structure that it purports to reflect'.[33] Why *should* this workman obey and be productive, when those assumed to be his moral superiors are tyrants?

On the other hand, the Second Man's rhetorical question – 'Why should we, in the compass of a pale, | Keep law and form and due proportion?' – emphasises the fact that 'due proportion' is conceivable only in an aesthetic form. Yet, as Richard later reflects – very much in the manner of Montaigne – life is at odds with both 'law and form':

> How sour sweet music is
> When time is broke and no proportion kept.
> So is it in the music of men's lives.
> And here have I the daintiness of ear
> To check time broke in a disordered string;
> But for the concord of my state and time
> Had not the ear to hear my true time broke.
> I wasted time and now doth time waste me,
> For now hath time made me his numb'ring clock.
>
> (V. 5. 42–50)

Even Richard's moments of intense personal crisis appear strangely formal:[34] this aesthete may be able to sense musical discord but can neither govern his state nor admit to himself his culpability in its degeneration into civil war. Much like the melancholics considered at length in the next chapter, Richard is an 'allegory monger',[35] preferring, in the manner of the *de casibus*,[36] to make himself a hapless victim of an abstraction, 'time', rather than admitting that he has been 'deposed' (III. 2. 153) as a result of his own prodigality.

* * *

Through voices associated with unreason, *Richard II* critiques its diverse and, at times, contradictory sources, rather than simply replicating their assumptions. And it comes as little surprise in a text so vitally attuned to its own method that Shakespeare provides a cue for its interpretation. Attempting to cheer up the Queen, who is suffering from a portentous 'unborn sorrow', the Bushy comments:

> For Sorrow's eye, glazèd with blinding tears,
> Divides one thing entire to many objects—
> Like perspectives, which, rightly gazed upon,
> Show nothing but confusion; eyed awry,
> Distinguish form.
>
> (II. 2. 19–21)

Moments later, when Green announces the rebellion, the suggestion that the Queen is worrying about nothing is disproven. What is more, it is clear that in *Richard II* Shakespeare views history 'awry'. As Lukas Lammers astutely observes: when 'Richard asks the Queen to tell his "lamentable tale" he explicitly asks for a particular version of his suffering to be passed on. Significantly, however, this tale does not simply coincide with what the play has shown'.[37] The deformity of an anamorphic painting, a thoroughly silenic type of painting, skews the viewer's perspective; it forces them to adjust the position from which they view it and implies that the serious world is mere vanity.

Ultimately, in *Richard II*, ideas of degeneracy and deformity work together to imply through dramatic action what Foucault explicitly theorises when he writes about the 'problem of the infamy of sovereignty, of the discredited sovereign' (*A*, p. 13). This, it transpires, is

> precisely the problem posed by [Shakespeare's] royal tragedies, without it seems the sovereign's infamy ever being theorised. [...] from Nero [...] down to the little man with trembling hands crowned with forty million deaths, who, from deep in his bunker, asks for two things, that everything above him be destroyed and that he be given chocolate cakes until he bursts, you have the outrageous functioning of the despicable sovereign.
>
> (*A*, p. 13)

Richard II is a play concerned with the 'ridiculous authority' (*A*, p. 13) of a degenerate sovereign: Richard is a pathetic man, usurped by a violent hypocrite, with a son who acts the fool. Crucially, it is the play's voices associated with unreason that tell the truth about the 'grotesque' nature of the foolish tyrant and the way that merely 'by virtue of their status, a discourse, or individual, can have effects of power that their intrinsic qualities should disqualify them from having' (*A*, p. 11).

As Foucault suggests, it is not in *Richard II* alone that Shakespeare uses the grotesque register to point out the tyrannical nature of those in power. Explicitly referring to festive custom of the Lord of Misrule, Angus suggests that Macbeth, a sovereign who maintains his power though atrocity, feels 'his title | Hang loose about him, like a giant's robe | Upon a dwarfish thief' (V. 2. 20–22). And, in a comment that transforms political reality into a pageant, Hamlet refers to Claudius as 'a king of shreds and patches' (III. 4. 99). But it is in *1&2 Henry IV* and *Henry V* that a grotesque register most clearly serves the important ethical function of foregrounding the violence, venality and hypocrisy of those in power, of those for whom history is normally written.

4.4 Echoes of Folly

> Well, thus play we the fools with the time while the spirits of the wise sit in the clouds and mock us.
>
> —*2 Henry IV*, II. 2. 120–21

The two plays that most explicitly represent the paradoxical purpose of purposelessness are, of course, *1&2 Henry IV*; in the second scene of the first play, Hal's 'praise-abuse'[38] of Falstaff's lifestyle furnishes the audience with an embedded ironic mock-encomium, which wastes time even as it castigates Falstaff for using his time improvidently:

FALSTAFF: Now, Hal, what time of day is it lad?
PRINCE HARRY: Thou art so fat-witted with the drinking of old sack, and unbuttoning after supper, and sleeping on benches after noon, that thou hast forgotten to demand that truly which thou wouldst truly know. What the devil hast thou to do with the time of day? Unless hours were cups of sack, and minutes capons, and clocks the tongues of bawds and dials the signs of leaping houses, and the blessed sun himself a fair hot wench in flame-coloured taffeta, I see no reason why thou shouldst be so superfluous to demand the time of day.

(*I Henry IV*, 1.2. 1–9)

Falstaff cannot inquire honestly about the time of the day because his errant lifestyle renders such a question irrelevant, even insincere. Falstaff, the Prince suggests, does not conceive of time as something that is quantifiable – as, reformed, he later does when he 'weighs time | Even to the utmost grain' (*Henry V*, II. 4. 138–39). Rather, emancipated from the tyranny of clock-time, 'the time of day', for Falstaff, the passing time is labile, discernible only through what one consumes and passes.

When the young Prince takes on the guise of is his father and inveighs against Falstaff, he suggests that Falstaff's sole purpose is eating and drinking:

PRINCE HARRY: [...] Thou art violently carried away from grace. There is a devil haunts thee in the likeness of an old fat man; a tun of man is thy companion. Why doest thou converse with that trunk of humours, that

> bolting-hutch of beastliness, that swollen parcel of dropsies, that huge bombard of sack, that stuffed cloak bag of guts, that roasted Manningtree ox with the pudding in his belly, that reverend Vice, that grey Iniquity, that father ruffian, that Vanity in Years? Wherein is he good, but to taste sack and drink it? Where in is he neat and cleanly, but to carve a capon and eat it? Wherein cunning, but in craft? Wherein crafty, but in villainy? Wherein villainous, but in all things? Wherein worthy, but in nothing?
>
> (*1 Henry IV*, II. 5. 407–18)

Falstaff's gargantuan body is described as being constituted by what it consumes; and what he eats and drinks is intimately associated with his moral dissoluteness. The most remarkable thing about the grotesque register, however, is the way in which it exposes the fragility of everyday categories of experience. Just as Giuseppe Arcimboldo can compose a likeness of Rudolf II (b.1552– d.1612) out of fruit and vegetables, so too can Hal vividly evoke his friend as a carnival meal, a roasted ox stuffed with sausage.

Indeed, here, as Gargamelle's labour in *Gargantua and Pantagruel*, the 'limits between animal flesh and the consuming human flesh are dimmed, very nearly erased. The bodies are interwoven and begin to be fused in one grotesque image of a devoured and devouring world'.[39] Strikingly, however, this is not the first time in the play that an image of such a world has been employed, for *1 Henry IV* actually opens with a grotesque image of a 'devouring world':

KING HENRY: So shaken are we are, so wan with care,
Find we a time for frightened peace to pant
And breathe short-winded accents of new broils
To be commenced in strands afar remote.
No more the thirsty entrance of this soil
Shall daub her lips with her own children's blood.

(I. 1. 1–6)

Just as in *Richard II*, the language of the digressive, extra-historical, scenes contains uncanny echoes of the serious action, while the serious action appears to be infected with the language of folly. As with the duplicitous metaphor of the Silenus considered in Chapter 3, here what appears to be glorious – the language of Kings and nobles – has an absurd aspect, whereas the language of the body, of folly, gains a certain gravitas from the fact that it is duplicated in the speech of those who attempt to censor it. While Henry's image of the 'land' as a monstrous mother, one who feasts on the blood of her children, grimly evokes the self-destructive nature of civil war, it does so through an image of drinking. Although his use of the word 'broils' signifies 'A confused disturbance, tumult, or turmoil; a quarrel', as a verb, this word also has the distinctly Falstaffian connotation, meaning 'To cook (meat) by placing it on the fire, or on a gridiron over it; to grill'.[40] Far from offering comic relief from reality, the language of folly, which here is the language of grotesque corporality and of a 'devouring world', is present in Shakespeare's representations of the purposeful world, with its tendency to oxymoronic 'civil butchery' (13), from the outset.

In fact, it is eminently appropriate that the King employs a dynamic image, an image of a body in the process of imbibing, since the grotesque is essentially dynamic. It reminds us that nothing is ever truly finished. After all, *1&2 Henry IV* may start with the King breathing a sigh of relief about the end of the Civil War, but this relief proves to be short-lived. What popular psychology describes as "closure" is possible only within aesthetic semblance, but both history and one's existence within it conspicuously lack a sense of ending. Hal's descriptions of Falstaff make manifest the perennially unfinished and radically imperfect nature of existence, which is exactly what Montaigne's *Essays* so brilliantly record and which an aesthetics order and proportion would discount as ugly, deformed or even, perhaps, degenerate.

4.5 Telling the Truth through Lies

Folly, however, does not simply infiltrate imagery of these plays in the way that, for instance, the Porter's speech in *Macbeth* does. Rather, the paradoxical veracity of folly, a discourse that makes no unequivocal claims to authority, is of central thematic importance. This is because it is through the theme of mendacity that Shakespeare fashions a self-reflexive representation of history, a representation of history, in other words, that makes no claims to tell the truth about the past.

In this respect, *A second and third blast*'s complaint that history plays give the facts 'a newe face, and turn them out like counterfeites to showe themselves on the stage'[41] is true in a way that its author(s) could not possibly have imagined. Questioning the ability of this 'cockpit [to] hold | The vasty fields of France' (*Henry V*, Prologue, 11), *1&2 Henry IV* and *Henry V* recurrently insist upon their counterfeit status. And by acknowledging this, they lie *openly*. Shakespeare, it seems, has little interest in disguising 'falshood in such sort, that he maie passe vnperceaued'.[42] As his wise fool Touchstone reflects: 'the truest poetry is the most feigning' (*As You Like It*, 3. 3. 15–16). These plays reflect upon the intrinsically problematic nature of historical writing and by playing off different accounts of history against one another in the drama, they create a critical space that reflects upon the use and abuse of history.

On the one hand, this attrition between two antithetical accounts of history gives voice to those, like Michael Williams in *Henry V*, who have been silenced by its grand sweep. On the other hand, in *Henry V* particularly, Shakespeare offers a critique of success, a critique of history that shows King Hal as every bit as concerned with how he is remembered as the hapless Richard. History, Shakespeare implies, does not offer us a series of models for present behaviour. Quite the contrary, in fact: these histories imply that an analogical understanding of the past is deeply flawed – just as the comedies, considered in the following chapter, and the tragedies of the final chapter do. Shakespeare's theories about history are not limited to his history plays, since history has a vital role right across his drama.

Shakespeare is, of course, too good a dramatist to simply put a sceptical account about the value of history into the mouth of a foolish character, such as Falstaff or Pistol. In fact, one of the most overt comments about the dangers of viewing the past as pregnant with significance is found in the exchange between Henry IV and Warwick. Henry suggests that Richard's prophecy that "The time shall come that foul sin, gathering head, | Shall break into corruption", which, like Henry's opening soliloquy, uses the image of a grotesque body politic, predicts 'this same time's condition, | And the division of our amity' (*2 Henry IV*, III. 1. 71–74), whereas Warwick argues:

WARWICK: There is history in all men's lives
Figuring the natures of times deceased;
The which observed, a man may prophesy,
With a near aim, of the main chance of things
As yet not come to life, who in their seeds
And weak beginnings lie intreasurèd.
Such things become the hatch and brood of time;
And by the necessary form of this
King Richard might create a perfect guess
That great Northumberland, then false to him,
Would of that seed grow into a greater falseness,
Which should not find a ground to root upon
Unless on you.

(III. 1. 75–87)

Warwick warns the King, imbuing the past with a false significance, based on a retroactively imposed narrative. These plays are not, in the manner that Sidney considered historians to be, 'captivated by the truth of a foolish world'.[43] Instead, Shakespeare's histories display 'humanistic pathos'[44] about the suffering caused by the obsession with how one's life will be remembered. What matters, Shakespeare implies, is not that we learn from the past, but that we learn to criticise the wisdom of the ancients and develop a sceptical understanding of our past, an understanding that eschews the establishment of certainties and is 'capable of being in uncertainties, without any irritable reaching after fact'.[45] Such scepticism about the analogical value of the past is encapsulated in an astonishing reflection of John Donne's: 'Young men mend not their sight by using old men's spectacles; and yet we look upon nature, but with Aristotle's spectacles, and upon the body of man, but with Galen's'.[46] Not only does Donne express in a nutshell the dangers of being beholden to the past, but his comment also betrays an attitude that presages the great mantra of the Enlightenment: *Sapare Aude*!

* * *

Scrutiny of the ostensible act of truth telling, which frames the action of *1 Henry IV*, supports the argument that these plays are deeply preoccupied with mendacity. In his famous soliloquy, the Prince admits that he is playing along with Poins's duping of Falstaff in *1 Henry IV* as part of a wider deception:

> I know you all, and will awhile uphold
> The unyoked humour of your idleness.
> Yet herein will I imitate the sun,
> Who doth permit the base contagious clouds
> To smother up his beauty from the world,
> That when he please again to be himself,
> Being wanted he may be more wondered at,
> By breaking through the foul and ugly mists
> Of vapours that did seem to strangle him.
> If all the year were playing holidays,
> To sport would be as tedious as to work;
> But when they seldom come, they wished-for come,
> And nothing pleaseth but rare accidents.
> So, when this loose behavior I throw off
> And pay the debt I never promisèd,
> By how much better than my word I am,
> By so much shall I falsify men's hopes;
> And like bright metal on a sullen ground,
> My reformation, glitt'ring o'er my fault,
> Shall show more goodly and attract more eyes
> Than that which hath no foil to set it off.
> I'll so offend to make offence a skill,
> Redeeming time when men think least I will.
>
> (I. 2. 173–95)

In contrast to his sources, Shakespeare gives a reason for Hal's degenerate behaviour: it is a piece of politic mendacity. This point is made recurrently throughout the three plays – when, for instance, the English Constable informs the French court that when he cavorted with Falstaff, Hal was merely 'Covering discretion with a coat of folly' (*Henry V*, II. 4. 38). Owing to this instrumental use of folly, the subsequent tavern scenes take on the quality of a dissimulation within the action of the play, an intrinsically dishonest form, which cherry-picks from the dubious truths of the play's sources.

Hal's trickery illustrates how history infiltrates the recesses of one's subjectivity. In this soliloquy, Shakespeare stages the fact that there is no such thing as a subjective space that is wholly free from the sway of the prevailing ideology, there is no space of the sort that Montaigne described as his 'principal place of retreat and solitude [...] [an] *arriereboutique*, a room, just for ourselves, at the back of the shop'.[47] After all, when Hal levels with the audience, confessing his secret motives in soliloquy, these motives merely reflect what is expected of him. In other words, he has what Isabella in *Measure for Measure* calls a 'glassy essence' (*Measure for Measure*, II. 2. 23), an essence – if ever there were such a thing – that reflects back the historical coercion he has undergone. In this respect, at least, he too is duped and, arguably, the biggest fool of the piece.

This act of truth-telling dramatises what Adorno means when he reflects that 'we are preformed by that being-for-others to the very core of our being' (*HF*, p. 71), for although 'Prince Hal [...] thinks he can operate outside of history' and attempts 'to write history to accommodate his personal wishes',[48] these very wishes and hopes are a series of pragmatic choices, which have been scripted for him from birth. The only truth Hal tells in his soliloquy is a negative one: he is deceiving the other characters, both at court and in the tavern. Paradoxically, this liar honestly confesses his mendacity. Yet while the audience may perceive that Hal's innermost desires and hopes are predetermined, this startling realisation is decidedly bittersweet, since it necessarily implies that their innermost desires and hopes are also nothing special.

Hal's piece of mendacity, which frames the comic action of *1 Henry IV*, alludes to Ephesians: 'Take heed therefore that ye walk circumspectly, not as fools, but as wise; Redeeming the season: for the days are evil' (*Geneva*, 5. 15–16). Although our polemicist uses the very same scriptural passage as the epigraph for *A second and third blast*, the contrast between its two invocations could scarcely be more striking. Whereas Hal uses it to justify his use of theatre for the earthly end of falsifying 'men's hopes', it is employed in *A second and third blast* to support the contention that theatregoing is a sinful waste of time – theatre audiences are liable to lose both 'themselues and the time'.[49]

Unwilling to accept the critical capacity of theatre, the polemicist employs sustained metaphors of consumption to describe the London populace's enthralment by the theatre as gluttony:

> Those vnsauerie morsels of vnseemelie sentences passing out of the mouth of a ruffenlie plaier doth more content the hungrie humors of the rude multitude, and carieth better rellish in their mouthes, than the bread of the worde, which is the foode of the soule. They are alwaies eating, & neuer satisfied; euer seeing, and neuer contented; continualie hearing, & neuer wearied; they are greedie of wickednes, and wil let no time, nor spare for anie weather (so great is their deuotion to make their pilgrimage) to offer their penie to the Diuel.[50]

Drawing a similar comparison, Falstaff ironically assumes a position of moral superiority in order to castigate Hal's his 'most unsavoury similes' (*1 Henry IV*. I. 2. 70). Falstaff also suggests that the implicit meaning of Hal's descriptions of him infects his listeners with immorality:

FALSTAFF: An old lord of the council rated me the other day in the street about you [...], but I regarded him not; and yet he talked very wisely, and in the street too.
PRINCE HARRY: Thou didst well, for wisdom cries out in the streets and no man regards it.
FALSTAFF: O, thou hast damnable iteration, and art indeed able to corrupt a saint. Thou hast done much harm upon me, Hal, God forgive thee for it. Before I knew thee, Hal, I knew nothing; and now I am, if a man should speak truly, little better than one of the wicked.
(74–84)

The comic incongruities of this exchange warrant clarification in the context of truth telling. Not without some wisdom, Falstaff confesses to being blind to the moral sense of the Lord Chief Justice's castigations; Hal travesties a misunderstanding of the significance of Proverbs 1. 20. 20–22 that people remain obstinately in 'love' with 'foolishness' when they *should*, in fact, heed what 'Wisdom cries without'. Subsequently, Falstaff disingenuously assumes the role of penitent sinner, hypocritically reprimanding the Prince for his parody of holy writ, before making the outrageous suggestion that Hal has corrupted him. Falstaff's detachment from explicit values undermines even negative, Socratic wisdom – 'Before I knew thee, Hal, I knew nothing' – by travestying it.

Tacitly, Falstaff's mock lament that 'company, villainous company, hath been the spoil of me' (*1 Henry IV*, III. 3. 8–9) ridicules the notion apparent in anti-theatrical polemics that proximity with actors not only made the audience imitate what they saw on stage, but also caused a radical alteration in their identity.[51] The polemic contends that authorities are tarnished by their tolerance of and complicity with the theatres:

> An euil cause maintained is nearetheles euil; &, as pitch defiles the toucher thereof, be he neuer so cleane: so the virtuous bring their life into question either by sufferace, or maintenance of euil.[52]

Shakespeare, however, memorably redeploys the Erasmian adage, which is here evoked to justify his ideas about sin by association (see *CWE*, 33, p. 172). Donning the persona of Henry IV, Falstaff rehearses the castigation the Prince is soon to receive from his father: 'There is a thing, Harry, which thou hast oft heard of, and it is known by many in our land by the name of pitch. This pitch, as ancient writers do report, doth defile. So doth the company thou keepest' (II. 5. 375–78). Falstaff's citation of the wisdom of the ancients humorously subverts the authority of 'ancient writers'. When, in the guise of the King, he comments that 'there is virtue in that Falstaff. Him keep with; the rest banish' (391), he both rescripts the past, suggesting (as he frequently does) that he has not led an errant life, and envisages an alternative future, in which Hal neither 'throw[s] off' his 'loose behaviour', nor gets castigated by his father for his association with *everyone* in the tavern. Whereas history may well happen first as tragedy and then as farce, in *1 Henry IV*'s blissfully counterfactual realm, at least, history happens first as farce and then, perhaps, as tragedy.

Hal's description of Falstaff's mendacious utterances – 'These lies are like the father that begets them – gross as a mountain, open, palpable' (II. 4.189–90) – aptly associates him with a gigantic geological formation. 'The grotesque' writes Neil Rhodes, 'relies upon images which have a physical similarity, but which normal experience classifies quite separately'.[53] Clearly, Falstaff is 'open' in the Bakhtinian sense too, for his body is 'blended with the world'.[54] Indeed, Falstaff is preeminent among Shakespeare's characters for (all too amply) embodying the subversive comic potential of corporeal openness. After the botched robbery, for instance, he 'lards the lean earth as he walks along' (II. 3. 17) and this slippery grossness is even more overt when he confesses: 'I am as subject to heat as butter, a man of continual dissolution and thaw' (*The Merry Wives of Windsor*, III. 5. 98–100).

Insincere as it may be, it is nonetheless crucial that Hal's dispraise of Falstaff in their 'play extempore' is rooted in aesthetic objections to him. Falstaff is disgusting and morally reprehensible because he is grossly disproportioned. He is 'out of all reasonable compass' (*1 Henry IV*, III. 3. 19),[55] not unified. He spectacularly fails to conform to the socially expedient aesthetic/moral ideals of being 'neat and cleanly' (II. 5. 415). During their inspired improvisation, which puts the serious business of history on hold, Falstaff, in the guise of the Prince, sophistically takes exception to these insidious values:

> FALSTAFF: [...] I know of no more harm in him [Falstaff] than in myself were to say more than I know. That he is old, the more the pity, his white hairs do witness it. But that he is, saving your reverence, that I utterly deny. If sack and sugar be a fault, God help the wicked. If to be old and merry be a sin, then many an old host I know is damned. If to be fat be to be hated, than Pharaoh's lean kine are to be loved.
>
> (II. 5. 425–31)

Certainly, when compared with the serious world of betrayal, civil war and regicide, Falstaff's vices are indeed minor and, in comparison with Northumberland, Henry IV and Henry V, he is almost honest. Beneath Falstaff's claim lies a cogent defamation of the idealising aesthetic values implicit in the mock king's tirade. The platonic association of virtue with aesthetic proportion, his speech suggests, merely reflects the dominant values of the reasonable world, which, paradoxically, is characterised by suffering, strife and betrayal. And as his characteristically mangled biblical allusion implies, such Apollonian aesthetics are susceptible to a *reductio ad absurdum*. Are emaciated cows any more pleasing to the eye and, therefore, virtuous than this 'tun of man'?

It is primarily through the discourse of folly that Shakespeare stages the limitations inherent in an aesthetic the values of neatness and cleanliness – an aesthetic, in other words, that attempts to overcome the brute facts of reality by shaving off their rough edges. When he comments about Bardolf's complexion, the protean Falstaff assumes the standpoint of someone who associates virtue with neat proportion. This parodies the idealising aesthetic that he himself confounds: 'I make as good use of it as many a man doth of a death's head, or a *memento mori*. I never see thy face but I think upon hell-fire and Dives that lived in purple – for there he is in his robes burning, burning' (*1 Henry IV*, II. 3. 25–28), a comment that resonates with Salvian's reflection that theatre encourages a hedonistic intoxication, which ultimately causes an utter disregard for the spiritual *telos* of human being: 'we burne, we burne, yet dread we not the fire wherwith we burne'.[56] Needless to say, however, Falstaff embodies this state of spiritual blindness. He not only forgets part of the parable – Dives was rich, whereas Bardolf is not – but also, despite his duplicitous protestations to the contrary, he fails to heed the moral message of his paradoxically incarnate death's head. In *2 Henry IV*, Falstaff attempts to wilfully forget about his mortality, imploring Doll, to whom his physical limitations are manifest, to 'not speak like a death's head; do not bid me remember mine end' (II. 4. 232–33).

4.6 Cretan Historians

The paradoxical wisdom of folly is present in the grotesque language of these plays and the way that they seek only to tell a fool's truth – they honestly admit their own necessary dishonesty by foregrounding their status as aesthetic semblance. But this paradoxical candour is not simply thematic, for it has a vital structural significance within *1&2 Henry*. Before I elucidate what this is, however, it is worth pointing out that a similar logic is present in Erasmus's *Praise of Folly*, which could be read as a skit on the Cretan Liar paradox. In the *Praise*, any serious philosophical insight that is potentially present is ironised by virtue of the fact that it is delivered by an embodiment of folly, engaged in the conspicuously foolish task of praising folly.

For J. M. Coetzee, moreover, this paradox is not simply an essential aspect of the *Praise of Folly*; it is crucial in understanding how Erasmus navigated the dangerous political landscape of early modern Europe, without ending up at the stake:

> The entire project of Erasmus was to create for himself a position from which to speak without being drawn into a dynamic of rivalry (Erasmus adopted Terminus, Roman god of boundaries, as his personal emblem) depends on a massive elaboration of the Cretan Liar paradox.[57]

Not unlike Coetzee, Erasmus's refusal to take sides has long been a source of controversy. Yet, refusing to insist upon the veracity of one's arguments is itself an ethical action, since it involves renouncing any claim to authority. It is to prefer not to foist one's beliefs – or, for that matter, one's interpretation of history – onto anyone else.

In the conclusion of the 'third blast', the polemicist, perhaps propelled by his own hyperbole, describes actors as 'Cretan liers'.[58] Ironically, of course, if Shakespeare's friend and collaborator Munday – an actor, translator and a prolific writer of plays and pageants who worked with practically every significant playwright of the Elizabethan and Jacobean eras – did indeed translate this passionate invective against the theatre and pen its third section, which, analogically, compares the dangers of modern theatre with those that caused the fall of Rome, he must have done so with his tongue in his cheek. An actor and playwright, who denounced his profession as perverse, dishonest and politically subversive, would of course be akin to the Cretan liar.

In any case, the Cretan Liar paradox is not only embodied on stage in Hal's soliloquy, but it is also present in Rumour's Induction and when Falstaff, reflecting upon his first meeting with Shallow, exclaims: 'Lord, lord, how subject are we old men to this vice of lying!' (*2 Henry IV*, III. 2. 275–76). While the hapless Justice of the Peace's reminiscences throw into relief the combination of nostalgia and forgetfulness to which acts of remembrance are prone, Falstaff's comment clearly recalls this paradox. Do we trust a self-confessed liar's confession of his own mendacity? And this question is all the more pressing because Falstaff's candour about his habitual dishonesty echoes Rumour's comparable disclosure.

While confessing her untruthfulness, this remarkable extra-historical figure, Rumour, whose soliloquy frames the action of *2 Henry IV*, accidentally tells the truth. Realising that she was uncharacteristically candid, she then corrects herself: 'But what mean I | To speak so true at first? My office is | To noise abroad that Harry Monmouth fell' (*2 Henry IV*, 'Induction', 27–30). This flagrantly fictional supplement replays an alternative history within *2 Henry IV*, before the "true" account of history has even taken to the stage. Rosalie Colie's observation that the 'essence of paradox is its doubleness, with its concomitant detachment and postponement of commitment',[59] is certainly borne out by the way in which any claim to historical veracity in this play is framed by Rumour's remarkable admission of her mendacity, which cannot but draw attention to the fictional nature of what follows. There is, furthermore, a related paradox at work. It is Rumour's Cretan Lie that takes the audience *para doxa*. Her mendacity, in other words, takes them outside of the very opinions, *doxa* – the 'slanders', 'false reports', 'surmises' and 'conjectures' (6, 8, 16, 16) that continue to baffle humankind – which this personification of dishonesty honestly admits to spreading 'from the orient to the drooping west' (3). This means, however, that the audience must take her avowedly unreliable word as gospel and are left stranded in a state of insoluble contradiction and uncertainty.

Thus when it comes to writing history, Lucian's desire for it to consist of the 'establishment of truth'[60] is exposed as either naive or over-ambitious – those who go to 'History looking for truth [...] shall go away full fraught with falsehood'. Shakespeare's histories, however, lie in the manner of the Cretan Liar. By pointing out their manifestly false nature – not least by using Rumour and the Chorus in *Henry V* – they exploit the negative potential of mimesis to give the lie to reality. Ultimately, these plays use this paradox to expose the intrinsic mendacity of an *orthodox* account of history – an account of history that standardises and orders (as the prefix, *ortho* implies) opinions, *doxa*, and passes them off as facts. However, historical writing, which knows itself to be dishonest and judges this dishonesty, is not altogether untrue.

4.7 The Use and Abuse of History

> At present, while each man looks out for himself, while popes and bishops are preoccupied with power and wealth, while princes are made reckless by ambition or anger, and while everyone else finds it to his advantage to defer to them, we are running headlong into the storm, with folly as our guide.
>
> —Erasmus, *CWE*, 27, p. 287

In *Henry V*, Shakespeare stages how a glorified past can be used instrumentally to justify what is expedient in the present. Indeed, Falstaff has already made a mockery of this tendency when he plays on Shallow's false memories for his personal gain, confessing to the audience: 'If the young dace be a bait for the old pike, I see no reason in the law of nature but I may snap at him' (*2 Henry IV*, III. 2. 295–96). What really seems to preoccupy Shakespeare in the last play of the Second Tetralogy, however, is the abuse of history.

While Falstaff's death is reported early on in the play, folly does not die with him; rather, in *Henry V*, Shakespeare plays the jester at the court of history and uses the paradoxical wisdom of folly to expose the dangerous folly of a sovereign, who uses history to bruise, batter, murder and maim in the present. The abuse of history is apparent from the very first scene: out of pure self-interest, the Archbishop of Canterbury wilfully misreads Numbers 2. 28, providing an obscure genealogy to create Henry's right to the throne of France.[61] The retroactive construction of the past was certainly a key factor in Tudor nation-building and one with which Shakespeare's chronicle sources were complicit: 'Genealogies were constructed to derive the Tudor dynasty directly out of the line of Brutus, come to reunite for ever the divided kingdoms of England, Wales and Ireland'.[62] Yet Shakespeare not only questions the legitimacy of hereditary privilege, but, early in his career, he also travesties this sort of flagrant fabrication of history. In *2 Henry VI*, the manifestly illegitimate Jack Cade constructs a thoroughly mendacious genealogy (see IV. 2. 33–51); through a piece of egregious mendacity, Cade declares his legitimacy: 'My father was a Mortimer', a comment deflated by the Butcher's aside – 'He was an honest man and a good bricklayer' (33–35). And although it could be overlooked as merely a comment calculated to rile the Globe's audience, the Dauphin's petulant, although not exactly inaccurate, description of the British nobility as 'Normans, but bastard Normans, Norman bastards' (*Henry V*, III. 5. 10) debunks the fictions of legitimacy upon which the aristocracy and royalty depend – by the French account, at least, Henry is *sans droict.*

Perhaps it is for this reason that Fluellen's providential analogies are comically vague. They imply that the historical analogues of the *de casibus* tradition, from which the popular *Mirror for Magistrates* developed, reflect the self-interest of victors as much as the fall of great men:

> I tell you, captain, if you look in the maps of the world I warrant you shall find, in the comparisons between Macedon and Monmouth, that the situations, look you, is both alike. There is a river in Macedon, and there is also moreover a river at Monmouth [...]. If you mark Alexander's life well, Harry of Monmouth's life is come after it indifferent well. For there is figures in all things.
>
> (IV. 7. 19–24)

The self-aggrandising Welshman is foolish to the point of absurdity because of his dogmatic adherence to theoretical frameworks, regardless of how they are contradicted by reality.

Fluellen is duped by a providential tradition of historical writing, which suppresses the physical privations and material consequences of war. No doubt the 'pristine wars of the Romans' (III. 3. 25–26), to which he compares present actions, actually caused as much physical suffering, with 'shrill-shrieking' daughters raped and 'naked infants spitted on pikes' (112, 115), as Henry's invasion of France might. Throughout the Second Tetralogy, Shakespeare remains sceptical about the ways one can use history to predict 'main chance of things | As yet not come to life'. In *I Henry IV*, for instance, Glyndwr's comment that he 'can call spirits from the vasty deep' to tell the future or aid him in war is memorably countered by Hotspur's bluntly reductive: 'Why, so can I, or so can any man; | But will they come when you do call for them?' (III. 1. 51–53). Whereas Hollingshead uncritically accepts the mystic portents that allegedly attended Glyndwr's birth (see *NDSS*, 4, p. 184), these portents are vigorously debunked by Hotspur's railing. As in *Macbeth*, prophecies prove to be radically ambiguous. Henry IV, whom even Hollingshead considers 'gave too much credit to foolish prophesies & vaine tales' (*NDSS*, 4, p. 278), does indeed die in 'Jerusalem' as 'hath been prophesied', but this, ironically, turns out to be the name of a room, not the spiritual centre of the 'Holy Land' (IV. 3. 365, 366).

By foregrounding Henry's insecurities and the war's spurious justification, Shakespeare certainly undermines Holinshed's analysis of this miraculous triumph as a particular instance of the universal principle that 'victories for the most part followeth where right leadeth, being advanced forward by justice, and set foorth by equitie' (*NDSS*, 3, p. 382). *Henry V* insists upon the illegitimacy of Henry's claim to France – not to mention his dubious right to the English crown. And after Agincourt, Shakespeare immediately stages the selective amnesia that characterises the writing of history. The names of some of Henry's erstwhile 'band of brothers' (IV. 3. 60) do not warrant being recorded in history: 'Edward duke of York, the Earl of Suffolk, | Sir Richard Keighley, Davy Gam Esquire; | None else of name, and of all other men not five and twenty' (IV. 8. 96–100).

As we have seen, negative truths about the untruth of the received account can be voiced through aesthetic semblance. Nonetheless, writing history necessarily lends aesthetic form to facts and events. Indeed, in *Henry V*, Shakespeare employs the Chorus, another supplement to history, to peddle the authorised account of history, which conveniently forgets inconvenient facts. Only present in the Folio edition of the play, the Chorus frames the action as a whole and each act with a jingoistic and often providential account of the history that the play stages. It offers, amongst other things, the 'point of crystallisation for the complexity of this history',[63] and recurrently evokes art's triumph over, and inevitable separation from, reality. It does so by using Henry's favoured rhetorical tactic, *occupatio*, which he employs in his wooing of Katherine. By saying that it is incapable of describing the action, the Chorus describes it:

> I humbly pray them to admit th'excuse
> Of time, of numbers and due course of things,
> Which cannot in their huge and proper life
> Be here presented.
>
> (5. 0. 2–5)

As Phyllis Rackin puts it, 'Grounded in the contemporary material reality of the playhouse' Shakespeare's histories 'undermined the authority of the imagined historical action, and with it the authority of history'.[64]

Moreover, the disparity between the history that the Chorus imposes on events and what the play's action dramatises is no less great than that between Falstaff's tale of the robbery and what is presented:

> Now all the youth of England are on fire,
> And silken dalliance in the wardrobe lies;
> Now thrive the armourers, and honour's thought
> Reigns solely in the breast of every man.
> They sell the pasture now to buy the horse,
> Following the mirror of all Christian kings,
> With winged heels, as English Mercuries.
>
> (2. 0. 1–7)

The following scene, in which the inept, reluctant and old soldiers illustrate the grotesque reality of 'silken dalliance', incorporates an alternative to the triumphal account of events that the Chorus is attempting to give. But so too does the Chorus's language.

The image of the mirror, which recalls the providential historiography of the *Mirror for Magistrates* and the function of mimesis to 'hold as 'twere the mirror up to nature' (*Hamlet*, III. 2. 20), reworks Holinshed's opinion that Henry was one 'that bothe lived & died a pattene in princehood, a lode-starre in honour, and mirror of magnificince' (*NDSS*, 3, 408). Citing historical precedence, the Chorus implies that Henry's 'Following the mirror of all Christian kings' is self-destructive. His self-evidently unchristian warmongering is damaging to the commonwealth; it betrays the fact that he is interested only in the ephemeral pleasure of worldly glory; prodigally, this 'starre' sells 'the pasture now to buy the horse'.

At the close of the play, Shakespeare also inverts the significance of Holinshed's image of Henry as 'a lode-starre' in the Epilogue, which is spoken by the Chorus:

> Small time, but in that small most greatly lived
> This star of England
> [...]
> Henry the Sixth, in infant bands crowned king
> Of France and England, did this king succeed,
> Whose state so many had the managing
> That they lost France and made his England bleed.
> ('Epilogue', 5–6, 9–11)

At a stroke, the closing lines of the play write off Henry's achievements. The tension between the official account of history and an alternative one premised on the critique of such accounts is even apparent in the Chorus's metaphor of Henry's soldiers as 'English Mercuries'. It implies that Henry's mission is divinely sanctioned. Like Mercury, the English solders are messengers from the gods, and thus agents of their wills, although this allusion is certainly strained by the foregrounding of the trumped-up grounds for going to war. But like Mercury, the trickster, they are also thieves. They are not only invading another country with no real justification, but also certain members of the army are 'sworn brothers in filching' (III. 2. 41–43).

Such ambiguities stand in stark contrast to Samuel Daniel's *First Four Bookes of the Civil War*, which seek to create a national identity based on a shared, unequivocal, memory of this victory. Daniel castigates present 'times': 'Ungrateful times that impiously neglect | That worth that never again times shall show', before invoking the nationalistic potential of poetry: 'O what eternall matter here is found! | Whence new immortal *Illiads* might proceed' (*NDSS*, 3, p. 421 [Book IV, Stanzas, 4–5]). It is easy to see Shakespeare's antagonistic historical practice at work in *Troilus and Cressida*, his disenchanted reworking of one of the founding stories of western civilisation, the myth to which Daniel refers. Shakespeare questions the significance of the fall of Troy, and the bruised malcontent Thersites debases poetry that seeks to unequivocally honour the war caused by Paris's abduction of Helen: 'Here is such patchery, such juggling and such knavery! All the argument is a whore and cuckold' (II. 3. 64–65).

At the start of the fourth act, the Chorus praises how 'a little touch of Harry in the night' inspires the 'ruined band' (IV. 0. 28) with his 'cheerful semblance and sweet majesty' (40). However, this 'little touch' conspicuously fails to make a 'deep impression'.[65] What is noticeable about the scene in which Henry visits the soldiers is that here the imagery of monstrosity reaches its zenith. Given the impending physical annihilation that the 'poor, condemmèd English' (IV. 0. 22) fear, the theoretical niceties of Henry's debate with Bates about the demands the State places on the King seem incongruous. Williams, with characteristic tenacity, makes this abundantly apparent:

BATES: If his cause be wrong, our obedience to the King wipes the crime of it out of us.

WILLIAMS: But if the cause be not good, the King himself hath a heavy reckoning to make, when all those legs and arms and heads chopped off in a battle shall join together at the latter day, and cry all, 'We died at such a place' – some swearing, some crying for a surgeon, some upon their wives left poor behind them, some upon the debts they owe, some upon their children rawly left. I am afeard there are few die well that die in a battle, for how can they charitably dispose of anything when blood is their argument? Now, if these men do not die well, it will be a black matter for the King that led them to it –who to disobey were against all proportion of subjection.

(IV.1. 127–38)

Breaking through the legal quibbling between the King and Bates, he posits a view of history as something eminently physical. History is something that maims, deforms and obliterates living bodies, which is a simple fact that is frequently obscured by the political, legal and economic discourses analysed by historians.

In this scene, Shakespeare counterpoises two distinct models of history. On the one hand, there is Williams's embodied history. This makes it clear that obeying earthly powers can have serious consequences for the soul; the syntactical proximity of 'proportion' and 'subjection' implies that ideas of aesthetic proportion, which both the grotesque imagery of his prose and his very presence violate, are closely related to his historical 'subjection'. On the other hand, Henry would like to tell a providential version of history – it is surely no coincidence that national destiny tends to reflect the desires of the aristocracy for more wealth and political power. Henry's history, however, is characterised by techniques of abstraction and disassociation. He even manages to cancel out the potentially egalitarian idea of man's shared physical vulnerability, which is used to great effect in *The Merchant of Venice*, by employing this idea instrumentally in Henry V's politic humbling.

Henry actually enables and justifies his destruction of the nameless victims of his conquest for personal prestige by appearing to be 'but a man' (IV. 1. 99):

> I think the King is but a man, as I am. The violet smells to him as it doth to me. All his senses have but human conditions. His ceremonies laid by, in his nakedness he appears but a man.
>
> (99–102)

Falstaff, his mentor in excess, has already warned him of the consequences of his politic dissimulations. As the authorities knock on the tavern door, at the end of their curtailed 'play extempore', Falstaff anticipates a crisis of meaning that will arise in *Henry V*: 'Dost thou hear, Hal? Never call a true piece of gold a counterfeit – thou art essentially made without seeming so' (*1 Henry IV*, II. 5. 449–50). What Falstaff means, I think, is that because of all his dissimulation, Hal's essence, which is in any case merely a product of history, takes on the quality of a performance. Even as Henry declares 'the King is but a man', he testifies to the fact that the King is a perpetual performer, a 'counterfeit'. Henry has again come to embody the Cretan Liar paradox, for by confessing the essentially histrionic nature of his political authority, he undermines his own authority as a sovereign. And although he desperately attempts to authorise his own history – 'Chrispin Chrispin shall na'er go by | From this day to the ending of the world | But we in it shall be rememberèd' (*Henry V*, IV. 3. 57–60) – just like Richard, the memory that remains is at odds with the one he attempts to fashion.

Nonetheless, the player-king's encounter with Williams certainly gives him cause for reflection:

> 'Let us our lives, our souls, our debts, our care-full wives,
> Our children, and our sins, lay on the King.'
> We must bear all. O hard condition,
> Twin-born with greatness: subject to the breath
> Of every fool, whose sense no more can feel
> But his own wringing. What infinite heartease
> Must kings neglect that private men enjoy?
> And what have kings that privates have not too,
> Save ceremony, save general ceremony?
> And what art thou, thou idol ceremony?
> What kind of god art thou? That suffer'st more
> Of mortal griefs than do thy worshippers?
> What are thy rents? What are thy comings in?

> O ceremony, show me but thy worth.
> What is thy soul of adoration?
> Art thou aught else but place, degree and form,
> Creating awe and fear in other men?
> Wherein thou art less happy being feared,
> Than they in fearing.
>
> (IV.1.214–51)

This soliloquy betrays an understanding of what I considered earlier in connection with Henry's soliloquy in the tavern: namely, that 'At the very moment when people believe they are most themselves and belong to themselves, they are not only the prey of ideology. We might even go so far as to say that they themselves have turned into ideology (*HF*, p. 78). Here, however, Henry realises there is possibly no remainder, no recess, no 'room, just for ourselves' – 'men', including kings, 'Are as the time is' (*King Lear*, V. 3. 31–32). Kingship is ultimately an aesthetic product, one that is dependent upon 'place, degree and form' and it is built on the uncertain footings of 'opinion', which Henry IV confesses 'did help' him 'to the throne' (*1 Henry IV*, III. 2. 41).

Whereas Erasmus denounces the 'idol ceremony' associated with kingship as meaningless – 'nobility, statues, wax masks, family trees, and all heraldic pomp which makes the common people swell with girlish pride, are only empty gestures' (*CWE*, 27, p. 213) – Henry makes the radical suggestion that these props are all there is to kingship. Yet even in this moment of clarity, this soliloquy betrays the way in which he has now become beholden to a rationality premised on 'reckoning' or measurement.[66] Such an instrumental way of understanding cannot conceive of the excessive, valueless and even idolatrous nature of regal 'ceremony'.

Just as in his first soliloquy, Henry uses what Robert Weimann calls the *platea*,[67] the part of the stage closest to the audience, to estrange the fictions that constitute political sovereignty. It is surely rather more than a coincidence that all the characters that use this space are either lying or reflecting about lying: it is from this location that Falstaff formulates his liar paradox; the Chorus peddles a dubious account of events; Rumour owns up to her dishonesty and Hal performs his soliloquies.

* * *

1&2 Henry IV and *Henry V* make it clear that the world in which they were composed and the minds of the actors and audience alike are mediated by history, yet history's authority is far from genuine. It takes a Cretan Liar to expose the complicity of aesthetic semblance in peddling one account of history and passing it off as gospel. As Heinrich Böll's clown, Hans Schnier, laconically reflects in *Ansichten eines Clowns*: '*Das was andere Non-Fiction nennen, kommt mir sehr fiktiv vor*'.[68] The polemicist's complaint that early modern historians are like dishonest tailors, who use 'shreds' of 'old coate[s]'[69] to create new ones, encapsulates the self-confessed plurality of Holinshed's *Chronicles* and Shakespeare's treatment of his source materials.

In other words, from the fragments of what has been, these plays work to elucidate the inadequacies of the world in which they were written. They offer thought that is not bound into its objective circumstances, but goes beyond them through critical reflection – 'A good wit', reflects Falstaff, 'will make use of anything. I will turn diseases to commodity' (*2 Henry IV*, I. 2. 227). In these histories, the crucial function is that the discourse of folly, which is built into their language, themes and structure, is to enable a space for critical reflection, which uses aesthetic semblance to mind 'true things by what their mock'ries be' (*Henry V*, IV, 0, 53). Yet what vitiates such critical reflection is the principal paradox with which I have been concerned: namely, that to guard against mendacity, one must employ the openly dishonest form of theatrical representation. One must, in other words, learn to lie like a Cretan.

Notes

1. *Memory in Shakespeare's Histories: Stages of Forgetting in Early Modern England* (London: Routledge, 2012), p. 16.
2. *An Apology for Poetry: or the Defense of Poetry*, ed. by R. W. Maslen (Manchester: Manchester University Press, 2002), p. 103.
3. Frederic Jameson, *Late Marxism: Adorno, or, the Persistence of the Dialectic* (London: Verso, 1990), p. 166.
4. *Shakespeare and Impure Aesthetics* (Cambridge: Cambridge University Press, 2009), p. 5 ff.
5. See Robert Bell, *Shakespeare's Great Stage of Fools* (Basingstoke: Palgrave, 2011), pp. 20–35; Andrew McCulloch, '"Events Borrowed from History": the Real Life Drama of *Henry IV*', *The English Review*, 16 (2006), 2–5. David Wiles contends that 'Falstaff is the clown of *Henry IV*' and that his part was written for Kemp in *Shakespeare's Clown: Actor and Text in the Elizabethan Playhouse* (Cambridge: Cambridge University Press, 1987), pp. 116–35 (p. 116).
6. See Walter Kaiser, *Praisers of Folly: Erasmus, Rabelais, Shakespeare* (London: Victor Gollancz, 1964), pp. 195–267. Enid Welsford distances Falstaff from tricksters like Eulenspiegel, because he is a 'typical buffoon, understood and interpreted by Shakespeare': he is not like opportunist tricksters, since 'Like Quixote [...], Falstaff tilts against reality and loses'; see *The Fool: His Social and Literary History* (London: Faber and Faber, 1935; rept. 1968), p. 52. Cathleen T. McLaughlin argues for strong similarities between Rabelais's *Gargantua and Pantagruel* and *1&2 Henry IV* and the possible influence of the former on the latter. She argues that the Silenic Socrates (as transmitted through Lucian) accounts for the fascination with folly that Erasmus, Rabelais and Shakespeare share (*Shakespeare, Rabelais, and the Comical Historical*, Currents in Comparative Romance Languages and Literatures, 80 (New York: Peter Lang, 2000), esp. pp. 137–48). Examining the various ways in which Shakespeare combines traditions and types of fool in his construction of Falstaff

is another popular critical move, which goes back as far as Karl Friedrich Flögel at the close of the eighteenth century, who dubs Falstaff 'the king of clowns' and provides a detailed taxonomy of Falstaff's lineage (*Geschichte des Grotesk-Komischen: ein Beitrag zur Geschichte der Menschheit*, ed. by Max Bauer, 2 vols (Munich: Georg Müller, 1913 [1788]), I, pp. 154–160 [p. 155]).

7. See Grady, 'Falstaff: Subjectivity between the Carnival and the Aesthetic', *MLR*, 96 (2001), 609–623; this was reprinted in a revised form in *Shakespeare, Machiavelli and Montaigne*, pp. 143–162). David Rutter argues that 'festivity is, both structurally and politically, the tie that binds the four plays of Shakespeare's Second Henriad together' in *Shakespeare's Festive History: Feasting, Festivity, Fasting and Lent in the Second Henriad* (Aldershot: Ashgate, 2003), p. 169; Focusing on the idea of carnival, Tim Prenki examines Falstaff's relationship with the 'dominant ideology in the world of the play' (*The Fool in European Theatre: Stages of Folly* (Basingstoke: Palgrave, 2012), pp. 50–68). Applying Bakhtin, Graham Holderness considers Falstaff a 'collective rather than individual being' (*Shakespeare Recycled: The Making of Historical Drama* (Hemel Hempstead: Harvester, 1992), p. 139). Joachim Frenk views him as essentially a carnival figure, but points out the important 'dialectic' between the way in which Falstaff is shown and how he is narrated; see 'Falstaff erzählen und zeigen', Deutsche Shakespeare-Gesellschaft: *Wissenschaftliches Seminar* 3 (2005), 16–23 (p. 16 ff).
8. David Ellis provides a cogent attack on this tendency, which is apparent from Johnson to L. C. Knights; indeed, even Grady adopts a character-centred approach in 'Between the Carnival and the Aesthetic'. However, despite his protestations to the contrary, Ellis also considers Falstaff in isolation. See 'Falstaff and the Problems of Comedy', *Cambridge Quarterly*, 34 (2005), 95–108.
9. *Civil Idolatry: Desacralizing and Monarchy in Spenser, Shakespeare and Milton* (London and Toronto: Associated University Presses, 1992), p. 130.
10. *Shakespeare, Machiavelli and Montaigne: Power and Subjectivity from Richard III to Hamlet* (Oxford: Oxford University Press, 2002), p. 175.
11. For a more detailed reading of the role of mendacity in these plays see Sam Hall, '*In Mendacio Veritas*: Telling the Truth through Lies in *1&2 Henry IV* and *Henry V*', *Cahiers Élisabéthains*, 90 (2016) [forthcoming].
12. 'How to Write History', in *The Works of Lucian of Samosata*, trans. by H. W. and F. G. Fowler, 4 vols (Oxford: Clarendon Press, 1905), II, pp. 110–137 (p. 136).
13. See *OED*, definitions nos. 1a, c, 2a, b.
14. *OED.*, definition no. 1.
15. *OED.*, definition, no. 1.
16. In the play's main dramatic source, the anonymous *Thomas of Woodstock*, Lancaster (John of Gaunt) employs this word to describe Richard: 'A heavy charge good Woodstoke hast thou had | To be protector to soe wyld a prince, | Soe far degenerate from his noble father' (*NDSS*, 3, p. 461 [I.1.34–7]).
17. Roy Rosenstein, 'Richard the Redless: Representations of Richard II from Boccaccio and Polydore to Holinshed and Shakespeare', in Michael Pincombe ed. *International Conference on Travels and Translations in the Sixteenth Century: Selected Papers from the Second International Conference of the Tudor Symposium* (Aldershot: Ashgate, 2004), pp. 137–148 (p. 143). As Phyllis Rackin shows at length, the 1587 version of Holinshed's chronicles, which Shakespeare used, is a text characterised by its plurality both in terms of the multitude of sources

it drew on and in the number of augmentations and glosses that other writers added to it; see *Stages of History: Shakespeare's English Chronicles* (Ithaca: Cornell University Press, 1990), esp. pp. 22–26.

18. *Being and Having in Shakespeare: Oxford Wells Shakespeare Lectures* (Oxford: Oxford University Press, 2013), p. 26.
19. *Ibid.*, p. 2.
20. Grady writes: 'The references here and elsewhere in the play to farming, weeds, and caterpillars, however, suggest a connection to another form of reification investigated by Shakespeare in other plays: the social context for this language, as a number of recent works have understood, is the enclosure movement which was proceeding apace as Shakespeare wrote in the 1590s, a slow economic process in which once customarily half lands which had existed largely outside the money economy were alienated by their legal possessors and turned over from farming to sheep-raising for the wool trade – all in the interest of the money to be made from such transactions' (*Shakespeare, Machiavelli and Montaigne*, p. 74). Ralph Robinson's 1551 English translation of More's *Utopia* renders the Latin '*helluo*', which signifies 'glutton' (*CWM*, 4, pp. 64–68), as 'cormorant' (*Three Early Modern Utopias: Utopia, The New Atlantis and The Isle of Pines*, ed. by Susan Bruce (Oxford: Oxford University Press, 1999; repr. 2008), p. 22). This word is used in Hythloday's attack on the Tudor enclosures to describe the voracious sheep eating away the livelihoods of the poor, all in the name of the production of a profitable luxury good, wool.
21. *Idols of the Marketplace: Idolatry and Commodity Fetishism in English Literature, 1580–1680* (New York: Palgrave, 2001), p. 58.
22. Maus, p. 17 ff.
23. Benjamin, 'Theses on the Philosophy of History', p. 258.
24. For a cogent examination of 'The Lucianic Use of the Metaphor by Erasmus and Robert Burton', see Lynda G. Christian, *Theatrum Mundi: The History of an Idea* (London: Garland, 1987), pp. 144–150.
25. 'How to Write History', p. 132.
26. As Richard Hillman shows, this word is initially employed in *Woodstock* to describe Richard's flatterers; see *Shakespeare, Marlowe and the Politics of France* (Basingstoke: Ashgate, 2002), p. 178). 'According to *OED*, the word "caterpillar" had been applied for roughly a century to social parasites; playwrights may have especially relished the term, given Stephen Gosson's 1579 polemic, *The Schoole of Abuse, Conteining a plesent inuectiue against Poets, Pipers, Plaiers, Iesters, and such like Caterpillers of a Commonwealth*' (*Ibid.*, p. 223, n.7); my thanks to Prof. Hillman for drawing my attention to this fact.
27. Anthony Munday [?],*A second and third blast of retrait from plaies and theaters the one whereof was sounded by a reuerend byshop dead long since; the other by a worshipful and zealous gentleman now aliue: one showing the filthines of plaies in times past; the other the abhomination of theaters in the time present: both expresly prouing that that common-weale is nigh vnto the cursse of God, wherein either plaiers be made of, or theaters maintained. Set forth by Anglophile Eutheo* (London: Henrie Denham, 1580), p. 25.
28. *Ibid.*, p. 14.
29. *Ibid.*, p. 74.
30. Hardin, p. 133.
31. *The Origin of German Tragic Drama*, trans. by John Osborne (London: Verso, 1998; repr. 2009), p. 156.

32. This line is presented as a fragment in the Oxford/Norton edition.
33. Bristol, p. 150.
34. See Geoffrey Bullough, 'Introduction' in *NDSS*, 3, pp. 353–383 (p. 380); Richard F. Hardin, *Civil Idolatry: Desacralizing and Monarchy in Spenser, Shakespeare and Milton* (London and Toronto: Associated University Presses, 1992), pp. 127–33; Grady, *Shakespeare, Machiavelli and Montaigne*, p. 66.
35. Zenón Luis-Martínez, 'Shakespeare's Historical Drama as *Trauerspiel*: *Richard II*—and After', *ELH*, 75 (2008), 673–704 (p. 690).
36. See Paul Budra, *A Mirror for Magistrates and the de Casibus Tradition* (Toronto and Buffalo: University of Toronto Press, 2000), pp. 85–95.
37. "Eyed awry'—*Richard II* and the Shapes of History', *Shakespeare Jahrbuch*, 147 (2011), 145–154 (p. 153).
38. Bakhtin, p. 165.
39. *Rabelais and His World*, p. 221.
40. OED, definitions nos. 1 and 4; the OED cites Hollinshed's *Chronicles* as coining the idea of 'the grieuous daunger of setting things in broyle' in connection with starting a civil war.
41. *A second and third blast*, p. 106.
42. *A second and third blast*, p. 16.
43. *An Apology for Poetry*, p. 94.
44. Gerhard Schweppenhäuser, 'Narrenschelte und Pathos der Vernunft. Zum Narrenmotiv bei Sebastian Brandt und Erasmus von Rotterdam', *Neophilologus*, 71 (1987), 559–574 (p. 570).
45. 'To George and Tom Keats, 21 Dec. 1817', in *The Selected Letters of John Keats*, ed. by Grant F. Scott (Cambridge: Harvard University Press, 1959; repr. 1983), pp. 59–61 (p. 60).
46. 'Sermon Preached at the funeral of Sir William Cokayne', in *The Sermons of John Donne*, VII, pp. 257–278 (p. 260).
47. *Essays*, trans. by M. A. Screech in *Montaigne and Melancholy: The Wisdom of the Essays* (London: Duckworth, 1980; repr. 2000), p. 68 (Book, 1, Chapter, 39).
48. Ivo Kamps, *Historiography and Ideology in Stuart Drama* (Cambridge: Cambridge University Press, 1996), p. 95.
49. Munday, p. 96.
50. *Ibid*, pp. 69–71.
51. For instance, William Prynne, in a typically hysterical tone, describes theatrical transvestism as 'a despicable effeminacie, for men, for Christians, thus to adulterate, emasculate, metamorphose, and debase their noble sexe. Thus purposely, yea, affectedly, to vnman, vnchristian, vncreate themselves, if I may so speake, and to make themselves, as it were, neither men nor women, but Monsters'; (*Histrio-mastix The players scourge, or, actors tragaedie, divided into two parts* [...] (London: E.A. and W.I. for Michael Sparke, 1633), p. 35).
52. A second and third blast, p. 45.
53. *Elizabethan Grotesque* (London: Routledge, 1980), p. 14.
54. *Rabelais and His World*, trans. by Helene Iswolsky (Bloomington, IA: Indiana University Press, 1984), p. 26.
55. In the period, the word 'compass' was polysemous. It signified the mariner's compass and thus the instrumental rationality that sought to control and calibrate nature; the 'circuit' or 'revolution' of time, so clearly a concern of these plays; man's limitations; and 'a crafty artifice or design'. In this usage, its primary

significance is something within a reasonable measure, something of 'proper proportion', (see *OED*: definitions nos. 4a; 3a, b; 9a; 2a, b).

56. *A second and third blast of retrait from plaies and theatres*, p. 24.
57. Coetzee, J. M., Erasmus: Madness and Rivalry' in *Giving Offence: Essays on Censorship* (Chicago: University of Chicago Press, 1996), pp. 83–103 (p. 98).
58. *Ibid.*, p. 124.
59. *Paradoxica Epidemica: The Renaissance Tradition of Paradox* (Princeton: Princeton University Press, 1966), p. 408.
60. 'How to Write History', p. 105.
61. *Shakespeare's Festive History: Feasting, Festivity, Fasting and Lent in the Second Henriad* (Aldershot: Ashgate, 2003), p. 145.
62. Phillip Edwards, quoted in Baldo, p. 117. As Rackin argues, Tudor genealogies were, in essence, reactionary: 'A major impetus for the Tudor fascination with history was to defend against the forces of modernity, to deny change, and to rationalize a bewildering world in fictions of hereditary privilege' (*Stages of History*, p. 22).
63. Uwe Baumann, 'Der Nationalheld im Spannungsfeld von Panegyrik und Dekonstruktion: *Henry V*', in Baumann, ed., *William Shakespeare: Historien und Tragödien: Neue Wege der Forschung* (Darmstadt:Wissenschaftliche Buchgesellschaft, 2007), pp. 49–55 (p. 50).
64. *Stages of History*, p. 206.
65. Andrew Gurr, '*Henry V* and the Bees' Commonwealth', *SS*, 30 (1977), 61–72 (p. 66).
66. *OED*, definitions, nos. 3a, b, c and d.
67. See *Shakespeare and the Popular Tradition in the Theatre*, ed. and trans. Robert Schwartz (Baltimore, NJ: Johns Hopkins University Press, 1979), p. 74.
68. *Ansichten eines Clowns* (Munich: Deutscher Taschenbuch Verlag, 1991 [1963]), p. 185. That which other people call nonfiction appears to me to be very fictive.
69. *A second and third blast of retrait from plaies and theatres*, p. 105.

5 Love's Fools

5.1 Introduction

> Hope refresheth, as much as misery depresseth; hard beginnings have many times prosperous events, and that may happen at last, which never was yet.
>
> —Robert Burton[1]

That love makes a fool of everyone is something of a commonplace. Indeed, in *The hospitall of incurable fooles* (1586), Thomaso Garzoni goes so far as to argue that the folly of love is perhaps the most beguiling peculiarity of the human race:

> Now woulde it be requisite that we had the knowledge and practise togither of as many amorous accidents, as haue fallen out both in the old, and this our present age, that we might describe with conuenient solemnitie, all the fopperies of louers, they being manifest causes of a thousand other follies, which from this stock as from their beginning, drawing their originall and essence, cause their life not onely to appeere, but really and in effect to be the strangest and maddest race, that may be imagined.[2]

This view, it would seem, is shared by Shakespeare, who reflects upon it primarily through the discourse of folly. As Touchstone observes: 'We that are true lovers run into strange capers. But as all is mortal in nature, so is all nature in love mortal in folly' (*As You Like It*, II. 4. 48–49).

Unsurprisingly, the relationship between love and folly has not escaped critical attention. In *The Fool in European Theatre*, Tim Prentki devotes a chapter to Shakespeare's comedies, arguing that they 'take as their theme the discrepancies between the ideal view of love and the reality of the workings of desire within the human animal';[3] Robert Bell shows how in Shakespeare love is persistently characterised as a necessary folly,[4] whereas Andy Mousley argues that 'in Shakespeare's comedies [...] love is foolish and proves the "only human" ridiculousness of human beings'.[5] Examining the 'influence of liturgical, Pauline and Erasmian paradoxes concerning faith and folly', Chris Hassel argues for the centrality of holy folly – 'the great love where with He loved us' (*KJV*, Ephesians 2. 5) – to Shakespeare's 'comic vision and comic form'.[6] And Donald Wehrs develops these arguments in a more theoretically informed direction, providing a nuanced reading of Shakespearean comedy through the prism of Erasmus's theories of grace and Levinasian ethics.[7]

This chapter, however, contends that in *As You Like It*, *Twelfth Night* and *The Winter's Tale* love and folly are connected in a twofold way that has not hitherto been considered. On the one hand, Shakespeare suggests that the *promesse de bonheur* ultimately lies in the acceptance of the folly of love, the acceptance that 'Love is wise in folly, foolish witty' (*Venus and Adonis*, 838). On the other, he critiques the distorted, ideologically mediated, form in which it manifests itself in the everyday world. Crucially, however, he does not straightforwardly dismiss the possibilities latent in the concept of love. Indeed, these plays suggest that to be wholly outside of love's sway means taking a conceited satisfaction in one's own wisdom. And, paradoxically, such conceit is itself a form of self-love, a perverse form of affection, which is considered at length in this chapter. Not least because it represses the libidinal drives that make everybody tick, Stultitia reminds us that scoffing at love is disingenuous:

> Consider now (I praie you) how muche more Affection, than Reason, Iupiter hath put in man, to the end theyr lyfe should not althogethers be heauy, and vnpleasant. [...] he shutte vp Reason within the narowe compasse of mans head, leauyng all the rest of the bodie to affections. (*PF*, p. 23)

By Stultitia's estimation, 'cool reason' (*A Midsummer Night's Dream*, V. 1. 6) has little sway over us; it is the 'affection' we feel for others that makes life bearable.

Moreover, whereas it may be true that 'Wishers were ever fools' (*Anthony and Cleopatra*, IV. 16. 38), it is in the very nature of thought to be discontented with what is and to foolishly grasp for what is not – quite in the manner of an infatuated lover. The great philosopher of hope, Ernst Bloch, formulates this with great clarity, when he writes that 'Thinking means going beyond [*Überschreiten*]'.[8] And commenting along similar lines to Shakespeare's archetypal lover, Cleopatra, Montaigne associates certainty with intellectual complacency. For Montaigne, yearning for something other is characteristic of genuinely insightful thinking: 'if you grant follie what it desireth, it will no-whit be satisfied', whereas seeming 'wisdome [is] content with that which is present, and never displeased with it selfe' (*E*, Book I, Chapter 3, p. 5). Owing, however, to his Erasmian techniques of ironic distortion, Shakespeare goes one step further than Montaigne. As we have seen, the wisdom of the fools could be said to lie in the way that whatever they utter is immediately qualified by the fact that, owing to their profession, they make no claims to certainty. And not only does this curious logic inform Shakespeare's "Cretan" representation of history, but it is also present in *As You Like It*, *Twelfth Night* and *The Winter's Tale*, which disavow their own capacity to create the absolute convictions upon which conceited wisdom is based. In other words, they even suggest that the negative wisdom that, in one way or another, love dupes everyone might itself be mere nonsense.

As You Like It and *Twelfth Night* contain two of Shakespeare's most esteemed wise fools, Touchstone and Feste, but while my readings of these plays emphasise the thematic and structural integrity of these jesters, it is by no means limited to the professional jesters of these plays. Rather, folly possesses as vital a thematic, structural and conceptual significance as it does in the histories. Like the histories, these comedies employ the discourse of folly to promulgate a critical philosophy, which reflects on the ways in which aesthetic semblance has a hand in perpetrating discourses that prevent people from loving as they wish. Simultaneously, however, these comedies also suggest it is through play that staid poetic conceits about the nature of *Eros* may be ridiculed. Like the histories, then, there is a self-critical tension at the heart of these plays. In other words, Shakespeare uses representation to criticise representational thought. Shakespeare's critique of representation, by which I mean how humankind makes sense of the world, is perhaps most apparent in the ways that the discourse of folly offers a caustic critique of allegorical ways of understanding. This critique is grounded in the fact that those who understand the world in this way automatically foreclose the possibility of experiencing the radically new. Instead, they seek to incorporate every transient experience into a set framework, unconsciously transforming the remarkable and the astonishing into a fixed component of an inert world-*picture*. The play to which I turn first, *As You Like It*, offers one of Shakespeare's most sustained critiques of allegorical thought.

Furthermore, *As You Like It* illustrates the curious irrationality at the heart of three other key ways of making sense of the world. First, because 'there's no clock in the forest' (III. 2. 275), the spacialisation and calibration of time is shown to be an abstraction, which is as wholly at odds with lived experience as Jaques's melancholic allegories. Second, the labile comic universe of the play is governed by a peculiar logic that defies the rule of non-contradiction. This is the logic of the wise fool, who is cannily at home in the logical impossibility of being simultaneously wise and foolish, true and false. Finally, by re-scripting some of the narratives that continue to form the cultural bedrock of conceptions of human nature, *As You Like It* attempts to work through what Fredric Jameson describes as the 'vivid guilt' of aesthetic semblance. This play is at pains to show that even the oldest story can be given a new spin.

5.2 Inhuman Allegories

> The more pity that fools may not speak wisely what wise men do foolishly.
>
> (*As You Like It*, I. 2. 72–73)

For G. K. Chesterton, the very title of *As You Like It* is 'an expression of utter carelessness, but it is not the bitter carelessness which Mr. Bernard Shaw reads into it; it is the god-like and inexhaustible carelessness of a happy man'.[9] Of course, Chesterton does not mean that the comedy is careless in the sense that it is badly constructed or slapdash in the way that Stultitia's citations sometimes are.[10] Rather, the 'inexhaustible carelessness' Chesterton perceives designates a playful attitude towards life, the sort of attitude that is apparent in Montaigne's wry comment: 'Our life consisteth partly in folly and partly in wisedome. Hee that writes of it but reverently and regularly, omits the better moitie of it' (*E*, Book III, Chapter 5, p. 498).

Such wisdom is apparent in Rosalind's opening dialogue with Celia, who enjoins her disenfranchised cousin to 'be merry' (I. 2. 15):

ROSALIND: From henceforth I will, coz, and devise sports. Let
me see, what think you of falling in love?
CELIA: Marry, I prithee do, to make sport withal; but
love no man in good earnest, nor no further in sport
neither than with safety of a pure blush thou mayst
in honour come off again.
ROSALIND: What shall be our sport, then?
CELIA: Let us sit and mock the good housewife Fortune from
her wheel, that her gifts may henceforth be bestowed equally.
ROSALIND: I would we could do so, for her benefits are
mightily misplaced; and the bountiful blind woman
doth most mistake in her gifts to women.
CELIA: 'Tis true; for those that she makes fair she scarce
makes honest, and those that she makes honest she
makes very ill-favouredly.
ROSALIND: Nay, now thou goest from Fortune's office to
Nature's. Fortune reigns in gifts of the world, not in the
lineaments of Nature.

(20–36)

At this moment, love, the emotion around which the events of the comedy revolve, is not taken at all sincerely – not least because, as Rosalind later comments, 'Men have died from time to time and worms have eaten them, but not for love' (IV. 1. 91–92). Love, in other words, becomes a provisional proposition, a 'sport', which seems to reflect her counterpart's attitude towards love in the play's chief source, in which she considers it 'a toye, and fancie a momentary passion, that as it was taken with a gaze, might be shaken off with a winck' (*NDSS*, 2, p. 172). This badinage reduces the grand concepts of 'Love', 'Fortune' and 'Nature' to mere playthings. Not only does this mockery of the 'good housewife Fortune' voice a longing for the 'benefits of fortune' to be 'bestowed equally', but it also demands a detached perspective, a perspective that entails a refusal to resign oneself to the idea that one 'must be circumstanced' (*Othello*, III. 4. 196) or hopelessly immured in the world as it is – in the manner of the prostitute Bianca in *Othello*.

Rosalind and Celia's pseudo-scholastic quibbling about the auspices of 'Nature' and 'Fortune' gestures towards the tension at the heart of *As You Like It*. This is the tension between sincerity and insincerity or between perceiving the world in prefabricated allegorical categories and the parody of such wisdom, which writes of life all too 'reverently and regularly'. The main problem with an allegorical understanding of the world, which is that it generalises and thereby stultifies, was not lost on John Donne, who suggests that such a way of understanding shoehorns the diversity of human behaviour and relationships into predetermined categories, regardless of whether they fit or not:

> When thou knowest a wife, a sonne, a servant, a friend no better, but that that wife betrayes thy bed, and that sonne thy estate, and that servant your credit, and that friend thy secret, what canst thou say thou knowest?[11]

Donne implies that such an understanding of the world actually bars any possibility of experiencing a new or unusual relationship with a person or the world. As Shakespeare's sceptical treatment of providential history's allegories attests, allegory both supports the status quo and interprets new events and ideas in the terms of the past. Ultimately, the allegorist remains, like Lot's wife, paralysed by the past.

From the very first scene of *As You Like It*, the danger of perceiving the present in the terms of the past is apparent. When Oliver uses the stock example of folly, the parable of the prodigal son, to justify his denial of Orlando's inheritance, his younger brother rightly questions the analogy. Echoing Luke 15, 16 – 'Shall I keep your hogs and eat husks with them? What prodigal portion have I spent, that I should come to such penury?' (*Geneva*, I. 1. 29–32) – Oliver evidently misses the point of the parable, which is used to explain God's foolishly gratuitous love for every human. But when Orlando rescues Oliver from the lion, it is just this sort of unwarranted, irrational love that he extends to his brother. In the parable, the elder son is angered by his father's joyous welcoming of his erring son with 'melody, and dancing' (Luke 15. 25), for he has 'done thee service, neither brake I at anytime thy commandment' (*Geneva*, Luke 15. 29). Oliver, however, has done his father a disservice by ignoring his behest to bequeath Orlando 'a thousand crowns' (I. 1. 2). In contrast to the prodigal son, Orlando is innately good: 'he's gentle; never schooled, and yet learned; full of noble device; of all sorts enchantingly beloved' (141–42), and it is partly for this reason that his Canaanite brother despises him.

This mockery of allegory continues when the audience meets the lachrymose Jaques, albeit via a report of his passionate reaction to the injured animal. Here Shakespeare critiques allegory even as he employs one:

FIRST LORD: [...] The wretched animal heaved forth such groans
That their discharge did stretch his leathern coat
Almost to bursting, and the big round tears
Coursed one another down his innocent nose
In piteous chase. And thus the hairy fool,
Much markèd of the melancholy Jaques,
Stood on th'extremest verge of the swift brook,
Augmenting it with tears.
DUKE SENIOR: But what said Jaques?
Did he not moralize this spectacle?
FIRST LORD: O yes, into a thousand similes.
First, for his weeping into the needless stream;
'Poor deer,' quoth he, 'thou makst a testament
As worldlings do, giving thy sum of more
To that which had too much.' Then being there alone,
Left and abandoned of his velvet friend,
'Tis right,' quoth he, 'thus misery doth part
The flux of company.' Anon a careless herd,
Full of the pasture jumps along by him
And never stays to greet him. 'Ay,' quoth Jaques,
'Sweep on, you fat and greasy citizens,
'Tis just the fashion. Wherefore do you look
Upon that poor and broken bankrupt there?'
Thus most invectively he pierceth through
The body of the country, city, court,
Yea, and of this our life, swearing that we
Are mere usurpers, tyrants, and what's worse,
To fright the animals and to kill them up
In their assigned and native dwelling place.

(II. 1. 36–63)

Jaques's sustained prosopopoeia turns the Duke's earlier assumption that nature is insensible on its head. For Jaques, it is civilised men – especially the enfranchised 'citizens' of cities – who are insensible. They are content to cold-shoulder the suffering around them, with which they are complicit, so long as they can cram themselves with 'greasy' commodities.

Yet, this, like the rest of Jaques's sententious wisdom, is hardly insightful. Shakespeare clearly does not endow Jaques with the powers of divination associated with melancholia by Ficino and Agrippa; Jaques appears to be the very opposite of 'a common type of Renaissance utopianist or Arcadian, who out of his own medically aberrant consciousness spins a tale of a better world'.[12] Because he shares the Duke's tendency to allegorise, his wisdom is decidedly short-sighted: even in the radically new or unusual, he can only ever see more of the same – his thought conspicuously fails to go 'beyond'. In fact, he does not so much 'moralize' as *allegorise* the spectacle of the deer, reducing it to yet another example of man's innate cruelty and even characterising it as a fellow melancholic, thereby muting physical suffering of this 'poor dappled fool' (II. 1. 22).

This is not altogether surprising, since this image of the weeping deer 'is the closest approximation we have in Shakespeare of an actual emblem',[13] and emblems were the primary way through which allegories were peddled in the Renaissance. This particular emblem hails from Ovid's *Metamorphoses* and recalls the famous moment when Actaeon glimpses his reflection after he has been transformed into a stag:

> But when he saw his face
> And hornèd temples in the brook, he would have cried, 'Alas!'
> But as for then no kind of speech out of his lips could pass,
> He sighed and brayed; for that was then the speech that did
> remain.
> And down the eyes that were not his, his bitter tears did rain.
> No part remained (save his mind) of what he erst had been'.[14]

But Shakespeare employs this image to evoke Jaques's alienation from society rather than the alienation from personal identity apparent in Ovid. Moving in a heartbeat from sympathy to an aggressive attack on society – 'invectively he *pierceth through* | *The body* of the country, city, court' – Jaques is not passive in the manner of Actaeon; rather, this extended metaphor links the scoffing satirist's actions unequivocally to those of the hunters. He turns the 'native burghers of this desert city' (II. 1. 24) to his own uses.

5.3 Temporality and Allegory

In his first encounter with Jaques, Touchstone, who is absent from the play's sources, makes a mockery of the seriousness associated with this allegorical habit of mind. This mockery, however, is clearly lost on Jaques, who is simply delighted to find a fellow outsider, a homeless philosopher:

> JAQUES: A fool, a fool, I met a fool i'th' forest,
> A motley fool – a miserable world! –
> As I do live by food, I met a fool,
> Who laid him down and basked him in the sun,
> And railed on Lady Fortune in good terms,
> In good set terms, and yet a motley fool.

> 'Good morrow, fool,' quoth I. 'No, sir,' quoth he,
> 'Call me not fool till heaven hath sent me fortune.'
> And then he drew a dial from his poke,
> And looking on it with lack-lustre eye
> Says very wisely, 'It is ten o'clock.'
> Thus we may see,' quoth he, 'how the world wags.
> 'Tis but an hour ago since it was nine,
> And after one hour more 'twill be eleven;
> And so from hour to hour we ripe and ripe,
> And then from hour to hour we rot and rot;
> And thereby hangs a tale.' When I did hear
> The motley fool thus moral on the time
> My lungs began to crow like chanticleer,
> That fools should be so deep-contemplative,
> And I did laugh sans intermission
> An hour by his dial. O noble fool,
> A worthy fool–motley's the only wear.
>
> (II. 7. 12–34)

In a play otherwise characterised by logic chopping, role-playing, parody and disguise, Jaques remains unchanged by the bizarre course of events, remaining to the last a melancholic. Even when he laughs, crowing 'like chanticleer', his laughter does not distance him from the rigid identities of the sublunary world. It recalls the case of the melancholic in Galen,[15] who, in Garzoni's words, 'imitate[s] the crowing and noise the cocke made with his winges'.[16] And because he takes the fool's Janus-faced discourse at face value, the paradoxical wisdom or 'moral' implicit in Touchstone's meditation on time and decay is lost on Jaques. The fool, spread-eagled in the sun, travesties the behaviour of the depressive's fixation on lost time, on what could have been.

Touchstone implies that the spacialisation and calibration of time, which made modernity possible, is not without an irrational element. Comparable attitudes towards the time in the 'working-day-world' are apparent elsewhere in the play. For instance, when she chastises Orlando's tardiness, Rosalind contends that such an account of time is an abstraction, wholly at odds with lived experience, in which 'Time travels in divers paces with divers persons' (III. 2. 282–83):

> Break an hour's promise in love! He that will divide a minute into a thousand parts and break but a part of the thousand part of a minute in the affairs of love, it may be said of him that Cupid hath clapped him o'th'shoulder, but I'll warrant him heartwhole.
>
> (IV. 1. 39–44)

Precisely because 'There's no clock in the forest' (III. 2. 275), a temporality not based on the clock time of the quotidian world is possible – Celia, for one, likes Arden and 'willingly could *waste* [her] time in it' (II. 4. 90) [my emphasis].

Allegory is a fragile thing, not least because, as Walter Benjamin contends, 'the parody of a form proclaims its end'.[17] This is apparent in the complex parody at work in Jaques's on-stage report of Touchstone's famous theatrical allegory:

> All the world's a stage,
> And all the men and women merely players.
> They have their exits and their entrances,
> And one man in his time plays many parts,
> His acts being seven ages. At first the infant,
> Mewling and puking in the nurse's arms.
> And then the whining schoolboy with his satchel
> And shining morning face, creeping like snail
> Unwillingly to school. And then the lover,
> Sighing like furnace, with a woeful ballad
> Made to his mistress' eyebrow. Then, a soldier,
> Full of strange oaths, and bearded like the pard,
> Jealous in honour, sudden, and quick in quarrel,
> Seeking the bubble reputation
> Even in the cannon's mouth. And then the justice,
> In fair round belly with good capon lined,
> With eyes severe and beard of formal cut,
> Full of wise saws and modern instances;
> And so he plays his part. The sixth age shifts
> Into the lean and slippered pantaloon,
> With spectacles on nose and pouch on side,
> His youthful hose, well saved, a world too wide
> For his shrunk shank, and his big manly voice,
> Turning again toward childish treble, pipes
> And whistles in his sound. Last scene of all,
> That ends this strange, eventful history,
> Is second childishness and mere oblivion,
> Sans teeth, sans eyes, sans taste, sans everything.
>
> (II. 7. 135–65)

On the face of it, this account of man's inexorable decline into senility seems to echo Stultitia's famous description of the innate foolishness of each age of man. Crucially, however, Jaques's melancholy skews her descriptions. For Stultitia, 'the first age of man' is 'most gracious and acceptable vnto all folks' (*PF*, p. 16). People delight in babies because of the 'allurement of Folie; all men put to theyr helpyng handes' to assist youths (*PF*, p. 16), whereas in the serious part of his life, 'Manhode', 'the floure of his beautie decaieth, his myrth fadethe, his grace waketh colde', and in 'Eld' man becomes 'not only vrksome to others, but hatefull also to himselfe'. But, at 'deaths dore', he reverts 'back againe vnto childhode' (*PF*, p. 17). As a 'wasshying awaie [of] all the troubles and carefullnesses of the mynde', this sort of 'Obliuion' (*PF*, p. 17) is far from the abysmal state of non-being to which Jaques alludes. Instead, it is a gift that helps man to die well, maintaining his hope in the face of the brute facts of physical finitude. It could be said, therefore, that the essential difference between Stultitia's understanding of the Seven Ages of Man and Jaques's is that the former conceives it in essentially comic terms, whereas the latter regards life, aging and death with a sense of tragic inevitability.

Yet such a generalisation is at risk of ignoring the multiple layers of parody operating in this speech, layers through which Shakespeare makes a mockery of clear-cut standpoints. It is not insignificant that Erasmus puts his speech into the mouth of an unreliable narrator, the high priestess of folly, Stultitia. And her invocation of this allegorical conception of human development, itself based on the notion of linear progression of time, of which *As You Like It* is so suspicious, is very far from serious. Sincerely peddling the wisdom of both Touchstone and Stultitia, Jaques not only foolishly takes their word for gospel, but he also misunderstands it – his conception of the universality of folly is more akin to Sebastian Brandt's remorseless didactic satire than the vertiginous ironies of the *Praise*. As with the death of the stag, he understands the *theatrum mundi* topos, which is insistently invoked by Stultitia, in his own melancholic terms, in which it epitomises a world drained of meaning. Ironically, however, the world appears in this way to him precisely because he is certain about his own wisdom, which for the most part is sententious drivel – Orlando points out that this melancholic has 'studied' his 'questions' from a cheap wall hanging, 'a painted cloth' (III. 2. 251–52). Since he places his faith in the wisdom of the past, he is unwilling to take part in the possibilities afforded by the redeemed world that opens up at the close of the play – 'I am for other than for dancing measures' (V. 4. 182).

Jaques – like Leontes in *The Winter's Tale* – obstinately views the world through the lens of the past. He not only attempts to reduce every person's existence to an allegory of progressive disintegration, but also indulges in narcissistic reflection about his melancholy, which the rapier wit of Rosalind cuts down to size immediately:

JAQUES: Why 'tis good to be sad and say nothing.
ROSALIND: Why then, 'tis good to be a post.
JAQUES: I have neither the scholar's melancholy, which is emulation, nor the musician's, which is fantastical, nor the courtier's, which is proud, nor the soldier's, which is ambitious, nor the lawyer's, which is politic, nor the lady's, which is nice, nor the lover's, which is all these; but it is a melancholy of mine own, compounded of many simples, extracted from many objects, and indeed the sundry contemplation of my travels, in which my often rumination wraps me in a most humorous sadness.

ROSALIND: A traveller! By my faith, you have great reason to be sad. I fear you have sold your own lands to see other men's.

(IV. 1. 8–20)

It transpires that Jaques's almost Burtonian attempt at defining his melancholy is no less absurd then the relativism that Touchstone parodies in his extemporisation on the phrase 'in respect that' (III. 2. 13 ff).

5.4 True, False, Other: The Logic of Folly

In contrast to its source, *As You Like It* sets the static wisdom of the serious world into motion. The play's dazzling ironies subject positive knowledge, allegorical worldviews and any sincere endorsement of a particular standpoint or system of values to ridicule. For this reason, this chapter takes a very dim view of sincerity indeed – not least because those who are captive to sincerity equate seriousness with veracity, whereas all three of the plays considered imply that the opposite is true. Paradoxically, their philosophical seriousness lies in their artful playfulness.

When Touchstone deflates the rustic William's self-satisfied assertion – 'I have a pretty wit' – with his comment 'Why, thou sayst well. I do now remember a saying: "The fool doth think he is wise, but the wise man knows himself to be a fool"' (V. 1. 27–29), any kind of self-admiration, the *philautia* that Stultitia decries –and (since she is praising herself) simultaneously embodies – is debunked. Crucially, however, William's opinion of himself is not simply disproved and replaced with another fact. Rather, arguing along the same lines as Socrates, the fool suggests that any estimation of one's wisdom is an act of folly. Yet this insight itself oscillates in a state of ironic indeterminacy because the baffled rustic, William, shares his name with the creator of the play.

In eschewing the logical law of the excluded middle, which holds that either a proposition is true or the negation of it is true, Touchstone embodies a mindset that does not attempt to understand by creating universally valid categories and rigid identities. Early on in the play, this mercurial jester extemporises on a knight, who, contrary to what he avows to be the truth, claims that certain pancakes 'were good pancakes, and swore "by his honour" the mustard was naught' (I. 2. 54–55), but is not 'foresworn', 'for he never had any [honour]' (64) to lose in the first place, from which Kiernan Ryan concludes: 'Truth-claims are only as secure as the assumptions on which they rest.[18]

It was not lost on either Shakespeare or Erasmus, therefore, that the very notion of a wise fool gives the lie to the law of the excluded middle. He is a creature who is neither wholly wise nor essentially foolish, a creature that, by being wise in his folly, confounds any straightforward distinction between wisdom and folly, between being correct and being wrong. This resonates with the philosophical procedure of the play as a whole, which is far less concerned with questions of truth and falsehood than with examining the ways in which such certainties are formed.

5.5 Love's 'Strange Capers'

Throughout his oeuvre, Shakespeare is critical of the aesthetic conceits commonly employed in the representation of love; such staid commonplaces are, for instance, memorably satirised in 'Sonnet 130': 'My mistress' eyes are nothing like the sun; | Coral is far more red than her lips' red' (1–2). And early on in his career, Shakespeare has Dromio of Syracuse debase the clichéd geographical analogies, commonly employed in the amorous verse of the early modern period. Of Nell, the kitchen wench, Dromio observes:

> She is spherical, like a globe. I could find out countries in her.
>
> [...]
>
> ANTIPHOLUS OF SYRACUSE: Where is her America, the Indies?
>
> DROMIO OF SYRACUSE: O, sir, upon her nose, all o'er embellished With rubies, carbuncles, sapphires, declining their rich aspect to the hot breath of Spain, who sent whole armadas of carracks to be ballast at her nose.
>
> ANTIPHOLUS OF SYRACUSE: Where stood Belgia, the Netherlands?
>
> DROMIO OF SYRACUSE: Oh, sir, I did not look so low.
>
> (*The Comedy of Errors*, III. 2. 113–14, 131–37)

In this bout of repartee, the 'Comparisons' are indeed 'odorous' (*Much Ado about Nothing*, III. 5. 14), as Dogberry's memorable malapropism has it.

In *Twelfth Night*, when Viola professes Olivia's singularity in thoroughly conventional terms and asks her not to 'leave the world no copy', Olivia mocks such Petrarchan posturing:

> O sir, I will not be so hard-hearted. I will give out divers schedules of my beauty. It shall be inventoried and every particular utensil labelled to my will, as, *item*, two lips, indifferent red; *item*, to grey eyes with lids to them; *item*, one neck, one chin, and so forth.
>
> (I. 5. 213, 214–18)

Her comment travesties the conventional descriptive techniques of amorous poetry by reducing them to a grotesque list of isolated body parts; the effect of this travesty is to show how an allegorical – or analogical – understanding of the world fails to inquire into the particular features of its object of discourse.

In *As You Like It* the self-regard latent in writing sonnets to one's lover is overcome through parody. Yet this parody eventually turns out to be a sincere attempt at a relationship based on a kind of reciprocity impossible for self-infatuated creator-lovers from Pygmalion onwards. While he refuses to be 'cured' (III. 2. 380) of his love melancholy, Orlando is more than prepared to woo Ganymede in the guise of what he already is, a fool for love. Undercutting expectations of how a lover might appear, Ganymede catalogues the 'marks' of a true lover; a lover, s/he contends, must have 'A lean cheek, which you have not; a blue eye and sunken, which you have not; an unquestionable spirit, which you have not' (357, 337–40). This tension between performing and satisfying one's desires is also apparent in the way that the weddings at the end are structurally presaged by the travesties of the marriage ceremony performed by both Touchstone and Audrey and Ganymede and Orlando.

When Touchstone parodies Orlando's verses – "Sweetest nut hath sourest rind", | Such a nut is Rosalind' (III. 2. 98–99) – the fool's primary objection to them is not that they are hopelessly mannered, but that they lack technical skill. They are the 'very false gallop of verses' (102) and fail to display any mastery of poetic techniques. Playing the role of a literary critic, the fool reflects that such poetry is prone to be copious – 'I'll rhyme you so eight years together, dinners and suppers, and sleeping-hours excepted. It is the right butter women's rank to market' (85–87) – but, like the proverbially garrulous chitchat of milkmaids, it is ultimately vacuous. As with Rosalind's infatuated comment – 'my affection hath an unknown bottom, like the bay of Portugal', which Celia inverts: 'Or rather bottomless, that as fast as you pour your affection in, it runs out' (IV. 1. 177–81). Linguistic plenitude is often a cover for conceptual paucity.

In her parody of what someone outside love's sway might say, Rosalind contends, very much in the manner of Garzoni, that love is a universal folly: 'Love is merely a madness, and I tell you, deserves as well a dark house and a whip as madmen do; and the reason they are not so punished and cured is that the lunacy is so ordinary that the whippers are in love too' (III. 3. 359–63). But in contrast to Theseus's disenchanted comment that 'The lunatic, the lover, and the poet | Are of imagination all compact' (*A Midsummer Night's Dream*, V. 1. 7–8), Rosalind is not peddling the kind of wisdom that removes her from the other 'country copulatives' (*As You Like It*, V. 4. 53). Rather, she parodies the attitude of a disenchanted scoffer at the folly of lovers. Yet her treatment of Orlando's love melancholy through playful substitution, which turns out to be no substitution at all, is in turn debunked by Touchstone: when he describes the time when he was in 'love' (II. 4. 41) with 'Jane Smile' (43), he offers a grotesque replay of the self-dramatisations, substitutions and role-playing that lovers employ – be it carving poetry on trees, the wooing of Ganymede, or the token of the blood stained cloth:

> [...] I remember the kissing of her batlet, and the cow's dugs that her pretty chapped hands had milked; and I remember the wooing of a peascod instead of her from whom I took two cods, and giving her them again, said with weeping tears, 'Wear these for my sake'. We that are true lovers run into strange capers. But as all is mortal in nature, so is all nature in love mortal in folly.
>
> (43–49)

As in Rabelais, the production and consumption of food and human reproduction are gleefully and grotesquely conflated. The tautology of 'weeping tears' invokes the tears of 'true' lovers like Orlando, but this is wholly undercut by the fact that the gift to his beloved, a 'peascod', possesses overt phallic connotations.

Touchstone's detachment from explicit values inflects the sincerity of the marriage scene, with which the comedy concludes – even Jaques is wise enough to realise that this Jester's marriage, his 'Loving voyage', 'Is but for two months victualled' (V. 4. 180–81). It is no coincidence that Touchstone's extemporal travesty of duelling codes defers the crucial moment of recognition at the end of the comedy by discussing the 'degrees of the lie' (V. 4. 80):

> O sir, we quarrel in print, by the book, as you have books for good manners. I will name for you the degrees. The first, the Retort Courteous; the second, the Quip Modest; the third, the Reply Churlish; the fourth, the Reproof Valiant; the fifth, the Countercheck Quarrelsome; the sixth, the lie with Circumstance; the seventh, the Lie Direct. All these you may avoid but the Lie Direct; and you may avoid that too with an 'if' [...]. Your 'if' is the only peacemaker, much virtue in 'if'.
>
> (81–92)

Be it the hair-splitting of philosophical discourse, the details of love poetry or duelling etiquette, this professional fool has a remarkable command of the otiose systems of the serious world. In this respect, Touchstone could be said to speak 'wisely what wise men do foolishly'.

Moreover, Touchstone's praise of 'if' imbues the final scene with a sense of provisionality, emphasising how unlikely – even patently fictional – the events on stage are:

> ROSALIND [*to the* DUKE]: To you I give myself, for I am yours.
> [*to* ORLANDO] To you I give myself, for I am yours.
> DUKE: *If* there be truth in sight, you are my daughter.
> ORLANDO: *If* there by truth in sight, you are my Rosalind.
> PHOEBE: *If* sight and shape be true,
> Why then my love adieu!
>
> (V. 4. 105–10; [my emphasis])

'To you I give myself', evokes self-surrender, although, as Ryan contends, this is not simply submission to 'patriarchal conventions, since the premises on which these conventions rest have been kicked away in the course of the play'.[19] The conditional clause in '*If* there be truth in sight' estranges the audience; it reminds them that they are watching 'improbable fiction' (*Twelfth Night*, III. 4. 115) unfold upon the stage. What they see in the theatre is, by definition, not straightforwardly 'true', a point emphasised moments later, when the god Hymen introduces a note of uncertainty: he will join the characters in marriage, '*If* truth holds true contents' (V. 4. 119). In Arden, it seems, even the gods are uncertain. Perhaps they too are under the sway of that magical conditional, "if", which is anathema to the serious, sincere and dogmatic, and is also the conditional with which we describe the relationship between events of the present and future possibilities.

As You Like It avoids being a 'Lie Direct', which avows things to be true, when they are manifestly untrue, by using 'if'. By not insisting upon the veracity of its own claims, the play renders the world conditional, deftly submitting any sincere worldview to parody. Perhaps the most significant moment of the play occurs when Oliver wakes up in the forest as his brother wrestles with a lion: 'in which hurtling | From miserable slumber I awakened' (IV. 3. 130–31). In saving his brother, albeit after some understandable hesitation, Orlando confounds the logic of self-preservation, of getting by in the world. In an inversion of what occurs in *A Midsummer Night's Dream*, which suggests that the forest outside Athens was a mere dream, a theatrical illusion – 'If we shadows have offended, | Think but this, and all is mended: that you have but slumbered here' ('Epilogue', 1–3) – Oliver awakens from a nightmarish reality into a realm of fictional possibility. This realm is characterised by the possibility of generosity and reciprocity, a model of which is offered by servant Adam's gift to Orlando of 'five hundred crowns | The thrifty hire I saved' (II. 4. 39–40), rather than the 'bubble reputation' that motivates both the tyrant Duke's banishment of Rosalind, who thinks Celia 'wilt show more bright and seem more virtuous | When she is gone' (I. 3. 75–76), and Oliver's jealousy of Orlando.

In fact, *As You Like It* rehearses alternative endings to the two biblical tales that form the bedrock of common conceptions of fallen human nature. Adam does not transgress. Cain does not murder Abel. When Oliver wakes in the forest it signifies neither the nadir of his insanity, as it does in Chrétien de Troyes's *Yvain,* nor a period of spiritual anguish as in Dante. The wise fool's paradoxical comment to Audrey that 'the truest poetry is the most feigning' (III. 3. 15–16) resonates far beyond its immediate context. In this most manifestly fictional of plays, with its fragments from Ovid, romances, parables and the *Praise of Folly*, the injustices of the world as it is can be rendered visible and, concomitantly, risible.

In this respect, *As You Like It* epitomises a fact that Adorno formulates with great clarity in his essay 'Is Art Lighthearted':

> [A]rt is a critique of the brute seriousness that reality imposes on human beings. Art imagines that by naming this fateful state of affairs it is loosening its hold. That is what is lighthearted in it; as a change in the existing mode of consciousness, that is also, to be sure, its seriousness. (*NL*, 2, p. 248)

To indulge, for a moment, in a paradox almost worthy of a wise fool: the serious point of *As You Like It* lies in its playful exposure of the insincerity at the heart of the serious world. The play's ironies clear the way for amazement – both in the modern sense of astonishment and in the early modern sense of confusion. Although the resolution of this comedy is so incredible that it is compared to the art of a 'magician' (V. 2. 54), the fact that the play fragments and rewrites the fictions that shape reality suggests that it is not wholly constrained by the ways of the world. Shakespeare's comic art is prepared to speculate in the conditional, adumbrate alternatives and embrace the hypothetical liberties of 'if'.

5.6 The World Turned Upside-Down

> Since, therefore, laughter is the principal sign of this frisky pleasure that we like so much, which counteracts old age, is common to all, and proper to man, I am most astonished that the diligent ancients, scrutinisers of causes, have omitted the investigation of its origin, working a great deal more to find the reasons behind the things which touch us less and in less far regard. Why do we not stop to consider the familiar, common miracles that we carry about, and are able to examine them closely and at leisure?
>
> —Laurent Joubert[20]

For August Wilhelm Schlegel, folly is central to the implicit philosophical vision of *Twelfth Night*. In his *Lectures on Dramatic Art and Literature*, he contends that this play is structured around the contrast between the 'idealistic follies' of Orsino, Olivia and Viola, who are duped by the prevalent notion of what love is, with the 'naked follies [...] of the risible persons of the piece, [who are] likewise acting under the pretext of love'.[21] Far from being a theme, folly is of considerable structural significance to this play. Sir Toby, Maria and the other merry-makers not only embody the spirit of celebration alluded to by the first of the play's titles, which is the feast of the Epiphany, a 'brief, licensed period of festive release and frivolity on the last eve of the holiday season',[22] but they also suggest that the performance of the stereotypes, in which the more serious-minded citizens of Illyria indulge, is patently absurd. Unlike the Duke, Olivia and Malvolio, these revellers are not in thrall to an allegorical – or analogical – mindset. This analysis examines *Twelfth Night*'s representation of inappropriate festivity, arguing that it serves to unfix the constants from the seemingly sensible world; I then offer an analysis of Shakespeare's mockery of modish melancholy, before finally illustrating the structural integrity of mutability to this play. In fact, perhaps the most significant facet of *Twelfth Night*'s implicit philosophical vision is the way in which – much like a wise fool – its form, themes and structure serve to insist upon the provisionality and relativity of its insights.

Schlegel's analysis neither wrests the main action from the backstairs world, nor dismisses the overtly festive scenes as comic relief as Barber and Laroque's discussions of festivity do; rather, Schlegel suggests that 'These scenes are as exquisite and significant as they are delightfully and humorously organized'.[23] Not least because festivity can create, for a moment, an alternative world that comes far closer to what the characters (and audience) will than the serious world, even the antics of the play's tosspot and gull cannot be discounted as insignificant. In fact, the labile, grotesque world of carnival is a realm that operates according to the rules of 'if'. But it does not operate according to Barber's rather proscriptive rubric of 'through release to clarification',[24] since the festivity in this play is unlicensed, and refuses to remain within appropriate calendrical bounds.

Indeed, on his first entrance, Sir Toby is asked by Maria to 'confine' himself 'within the modest limits of order' (I. 3. 6–7). In his quibble on the word 'confine', he evokes his unruly body, a socially useless body undeterred by the self-discipline characteristic of the burgeoning bourgeois age: 'Confine? I'll confine myself no finer than I am. These clothes are good enough to drink in, and so be these boots too' (8–9). And at the close of the play, when one might expect clarification, the wounded braggarts cannot be treated by the doctor, because he has chosen drunken torpor over facing up to the everyday reality of Illyria: 'Dick Surgeon' is 'drunk [...] an hour ago. His eyes were set at eight i'th' morning' (V. 1. 190, 191–92). Likewise, the disguised Viola describes her persistent courtship of Olivia on behalf of Orsino in terms of a violation of decorum. She will encamp herself at Olivia's gate and 'Write loyal cantons of contemnèd love, | And sing them loud *even in the dead of night*' (I. 5. 239–40) [my emphasis].

The thoroughly instrumental Malvolio famously attacks the backstairs revellers precisely on the grounds that their levity is out of control:

> My masters, are you mad? Or what are you? Have you no wit, manners nor honesty, but to gabble like tinkers at this time of night? Do ye make an alehouse of my lady's house, that ye squeak out coziers' catches without any mitigation or remorse of voice? Is there no respect of place, persons, nor time in you?
>
> (II. 3. 78–83)

For the steward, who, according to Maria, is nothing 'but a time-pleaser' (131–32), this 'uncivil rule' (111) threatens to turn the world on its head, upsetting what he considers the immutable hierarchy of 'place', 'persons' and 'time'. Needless to say, however, the play points out that these ostensibly watertight concepts are scarcely more stable than the festivity that unsettles them. Earlier in this scene, for instance, Sir Toby solipsistically invokes the topsy-turvy temporality of festivity, an 'uneven element', which does not see time as a 'measurable quantity or a simple factor in observable physical phenomena':[25] 'To be up after midnight and to go to bed then is early; so that to go to bed after midnight is to go to bed betimes' (5–7).

Sir Toby's utterances are not always mere bluster; when he asks: 'What the plague means my niece to take the death of her brother thus? I am sure care's an enemy to life' (I. 3. 1–2), he is not only an evangelist for the 'God-like carelessness of the happy man', which includes a healthy indifference to the workaday world's edicts of time, place and persons, but he also recalls the primary medical purpose of the fool: namely, to prolong and enrich his master's life by 'making his or her liege laugh'.[26] Since 'there was no way conceptually or discursively to separate the psychological from the physiological' in Renaissance medical discourses,[27] the laughter arising from folly and the notoriously 'ambivalent' laughter of the carnival had physical consequences; 'Mirth', Burton writes, '*purgeth the blood, confirms health, causeth a fresh, pleasing, and fine colour*, prolongues life, whets the wit, makes the body young, lively, and fit for any manner of employment'.[28]

Malvolio, however, is receptive neither to Sir Toby's 'Saturnalian creed',[29] nor Feste's foolery. And when Olivia praises the potential inherent in folly to belittle the privations of a hostile reality, she reproves her steward:

> O, you are sick of self-love, Malvolio, and taste with a distempered appetite. To be generous, guiltless, and of free disposition is to take those things for birdbolts that you deem cannon bullets. There is no slander in an allowed fool, though he do nothing but rail.
>
> (I. 5. 77–81)

By her account, the paradoxical wisdom of folly, later alluded to in Viola's comment 'This fellow is wise enough to play the fool; | And to do that well craves a kind of wit' (III. 1. 1–2), is a 'careless' or indifferent wisdom. What is more, it is 'free' insofar as it is neither swayed by dominant ideas, nor given to mendacity; it is 'generous' in that the fool gives without being motivated by the desire for personal preferment.

Indeed, it is Malvolio's sanctimonious lack of humour – 'I marvel your ladyship takes such delight in such a barren rascal' (I. 5. 71) – that occasions Feste's involvement in his humiliation. The fool downplays this by making it the consequence of an abstract entity and simultaneously evokes the restorations, recognitions and reprisals that conclude comedies: 'thus the whirligig of time brings in his revenges' (V. 1. 364). But immuring Malvolio in 'hideous darkness (IV. 2. 27) is the central example of how jokes turn sour in this play. Crucially, this seriocomic pseudo-treatment fails to cure Malvolio of his illness, his self-love – like Jaques and Leontes, he remains ultimately unenlightened by the miraculous resurrections and unlikely matches of his comedy. Malvolio's self-estimation is perhaps most apparent in his fantasy of leaving a sexually exhausted Olivia asleep on a 'daybed' (II. 5. 43), while he castigates her dissolute kinsmen. His virtue, such as it is, becomes the object of his own desire. He does not simply yearn for coitus with Olivia. Rather, he primarily desires the power his sexual possession of her will give him to enforce his moral authority on others. Whereas he may seem at a remove from Oliva's excessive mourning and Toby and Andrew's gormandising, he too is excessive: he has a surfeit of 'Self-love', a kind of love that, for Thomas Wright, is an 'infected love' from which 'sprung all the evils, welnie that pester the world'.[30]

For Joost Daalder, *Twelfth Night* is a play concerned with 'questions of reality versus the imagination, though in the case of illusion the imagination is a positive force, while delusion is negative', because the latter 'depends on a serious distortion produced by the individual's own mind, whereas illusion depends on what others do to us'.[31] It is illusion that Erasmus' Stultitia praises and delusion that she attacks; similarly, the play exposes the absurdities of deluded melancholia, excessive mourning and self-love, while exulting in the capacity of illusion, of aesthetic semblance, to debunk these delusions and rehearse the possibilities latent in the hope for a very different world. In much the same way as the forest in *As You Like It* offers a realm of fictional possibility far preferable to the social realities vividly illustrated in the opening scenes, *Twelfth Night*'s Sebastian desperately hopes that his illusion is not a delusion: 'Let fancy still my sense in Lethe steep | If it be thus to dream, still let me sleep' (IV. 1. 61–62).

Yet *Twelfth Night* frustrates any neat dichotomy between reality and imagination. In fact, the tension between two types of folly – *illusion*, in which one is, as at a magician's act, eventually aware that one is being duped, and *delusion*, in which one is convinced by one's own fancy – becomes most acute in the gulling scene, which 'satirises' the serious contemporary concern with 'demonic possession':[32]

> FESTE: *Bonos dies*, Sir Toby, for, as the old hermit of Prague, that never saw pen and ink, very wittily said to a niece of King Gorboduc, 'That that is, is.' So I, being Master Parson, am Master Parson; for what is 'that' but 'that', and 'is' but 'is'?
> [...]
> *MALVOLIO within*
> MALVOLIO: Who calls there?
> FESTE: Sir Topas the curate, who comes to visit Malvolio the lunatic.
> MALVOLIO: Sir Topas, Sir Topas, good Sir Topas, go to my lady.
> FESTE: Out, hyperbolical fiend, how vexest thou this man! Talkest thou nothing but of ladies?
>
> (IV. 2. 11–14, 17–20)

Feste's catechising of the madman is the climax of a game staged by Maria and the others; and because it is a game within a play, it is doubly distanced from the spectators. Feste's nonsensical citation of a spurious scholastic authority to justify his blasphemous impersonation deftly parodies the dogmatic platitudes of naive realism, which denies the possibility that things might be other than they seem. 'That that is, is' is an inversion of Feste's comment, after a discussion at cross-purposes with Sebastian, 'Nothing that is so, is so' (IV. 1. 6). Both of these comments use anadiplosis to gesture to the inherent instability of what 'is'. Viola also employs this sort of repetition when she hopes for a future radically different from the one she had hitherto envisaged, a future that includes her brother: 'Prove true, imagination, O prove true, | That I, dear brother, be now ta'en for you!' (III. 4. 340–41).

Whereas Burton observes that '*Jacinth* and *Topaz,* they allay anger, grief, diminish madness, much delight and exhilarate the mind',[33] the fictional parson, Sir Topas, who shares his name with a gem thought to cure melancholy, merely entangles Malvolio further in the web of Maria's illusion, delighting on-stage and off-stage spectators alike. Feste, however, is no absolutist monarch of misrule, since his persona's name alludes to Chaucer's ironic, self-effacing authorial persona in the *Canterbury Tales*. The 'elvyssh' Sir Topas contributes an inept and clichéd doggerel romance to the story-telling game, but is stopped in his tracks by the Host: 'Thy drasty rymyng is nat worth a toord! | Thou doost noght elles but despendest tyme' (*Canterbury Tales*, VII, 703, 929–30).[34] Feste's simulated religious authority is, not unlike the authority of the daft 'hermit' he pedantically cites, no authority at all. But it is a dizzyingly complex piece of parodic intertextuality, which illustrates the epistemological consequences of a jester citing an authority, one that in this case turns out to be spurious. The 'wisdom' Feste cites is a fragment from a bogus authority, travestied by the professional fool, disguised as a parson, whose name refers to the most risible character in the *Canterbury Tales*. Sir Topas' presence serves to discredit the *auctoritee* of the speaker, and it thereby makes a mockery of authorial pretentions to certainty.

5.7 Modalities of Melancholy

Olivia and Orsino find themselves in a festive space, insofar as they must neither work for their survival nor submit to the inflexible will of parents, the tragic consequences of which Shakespeare dramatises in *Romeo and Juliet*. In fact, *Twelfth Night* omits the fathers who appear in its probable source, *The Deceived* (see *NDSS*, 3, pp. 286–342). Perhaps it is for this reason that, like Portia in *The Merchant of Venice*, these bright young things fashion their own pseudo-problems.

The carnival imagery of 'cakes and ale' (II. 3. 104), of gluttony, and 'excess' (I. 1. 2) runs disconcertingly throughout Orsino's descriptions of his love melancholy, attesting to the difficulty of separating the serious action from the light-hearted interludes of Sir Toby and Co. But far from furnishing us with perceptive insights into his subjective state such as one might expect from a creative, melancholic genius, the Duke's self-indulgent meditations about his *ennui*, although protracted, are at best superficial and at worst vacuous. Recalling his first sight of Olivia, he reflects, invoking Ovid's tale of Actaeon:

> Methought she purged the air of pestilence;
> That instant was I turned into a hart,
> And my desires, like fell and cruel hounds,
> E'er since pursue me.
>
> (I. 1. 19–22)

His avowed adoration of Olivia is ideologically mediated in a twofold way. First, he cannot express his ostensibly unique love without drawing a mythological analogy. Second, as I shall show, Orsino's love initially has more to do with him fashioning a socially recognisable identity – that of the modish melancholy lover – than with either affection or physical desire.

His narcissism is especially apparent in his sententious reflections to Cesario on the nature of women's love:

> There's no woman's sides
> Can bide the beating of so strong a passion
> As love doth give my heart; no woman's heart
> So big, to hold so much. They lack retention.
>
> (II. 4. 91–94)

Not only is the 'hunter turned hunted' an archetypal trope of the *mundus inversus* associated with folly and festivity,[35] but also, in this particular story, Ovid makes much of how it might feel to be trapped in a vulnerable, alien body. In the moments before the hounds tear their transformed master to pieces, Actaeon

> strainèd often times to speak, and was about to say,
> 'I am Actaeon. Know your master, sirs, I pray'.
> But use of words and speech did want to utter forth his mind.
> Their cry did ring though all the wood, redoubled with the
> wind.
>
> (Book III, 276–80)

In that she is forced to play the role of wooer when she would herself be wooed, Viola finds herself in a comparable, albeit less lethal, situation. She is unhappy because she must play the role her assumed identity dictates.

Orsino's supposed infatuation certainly enables the clichéd posturing as an unrequited lover that he so excels at. He advises Cesario:

> ORSINO: If ever thou shalt love,
> In the sweet pangs of it remember me;
> For such as I am, all true lovers are,
> Unstaid and skittish in all motions else
> Save in the constant image of the creature
> That is beloved.
>
> (II. 4. 14–19)

Orsino cannot help but take pride in how exemplary his suffering is. And he plays his socially sanctioned role of unrequited lover as perfectly as the shepherd Silvius in *As You Like It* – as Schlegel astutely observes, love in *Twelfth Night* has much more to do with 'the imagination than with the heart'.[36]

Because it objectifies his lover, Orsino's affection might also be said to be fetishistic – Olivia refers to the 'heresy' (I. 5. 201) in his poetry, implying that his love is idolatrous. Such captivation of a lover by the remembrance of a mental image of their beloved is explicitly compared to idolatry in *All's Well That Ends Well*. Helen reflects: 'But now he's gone, and my idolatrous fancy | Must sanctify his relics' (I. 1. 92–93). The very same emotion is manifest in Orsino's castigation of Olivia for her faithlessness:

> You uncivil lady,
> To whose ingrate and unauspicious alters
> My soul the faithfull'st off'rings hath breathed out
> That e'er devotion tendered.
>
> (V. 1. 107–10)

Although Orsino's brand of melancholy is brilliantly mocked by Olivia's list of body parts praised in conventional love poetry, it is nonetheless significant; he fails to regard Olivia as a *person*. He misapprehends her. Like Bassinio at the end of the casket test in *The Merchant of Venice*, he venerates an 'image' of his lover: Orsino's implication that he is more worthy of grace because he has made 'off'rings' – an assumption tainted by the mercantile connotations of the word 'tendered' that further characterises him as a pagan idolater.

The mercurial Feste, however, emphasises the mutability of all things, especially thought, upbraiding Orsino thus:

> Now the melancholy god protect thee, and the tailor make thy doublet of changeable taffeta, for thy mind is a very opal. I would have men of such constancy put to sea, that their business might be everything, and their intent everywhere, for that's it that always makes a good voyage of nothing.
>
> (II. 4. 72–76)

Orsino's *idée fixe* 'constancy' is hopelessly at odds with a world characterised by constant flux. Saturn must protect it. So long as one unlearns the fictions of certainty, Feste argues, a receptive mind may have its preconceptions and expectations transformed at every turn.

What sends Malvolio mad, after all, is his determination to believe that the letter from Olivia is true. Sir Toby comments to Maria in at the end of the gulling scene: 'Why thou hadst put him in such a dream that when the image of it leaves him, he must be mad' (II. 5. 168–69) – he is bound to be bowled over by her fiction. But illusion is inevitable: 'Folly's reference to the extreme unlikelihood of anyone unmasking actors introduces the argument that just as everyone accepts illusion as the substance of theatre, so one should likewise accept that illusion and uncertainty are the condition of man's existence'.[37] The wisdom of Feste's comment to Orsino is borne out by the rest of the play.

Olivia is similarly deluded. As Feste points out when he 'proves' her a 'fool' (I. 5. 50), she is held captive by the past, or rather, a static image projected onto the past from the present, one that almost prevents her from being receptive to the possibilities of an astonishing future. For 'A brother's dead love' (I. 1. 30), she will deny herself the pleasures of the flesh; this is emphasised by Orsino's peculiar syntax, since the adjective 'dead' qualifies her 'love' rather than the brother himself. Her mourning focuses on another polarity of the word 'if': it is fixated on what could have been different in the past, rather than how different things could be in the future. Sir Andrew's propensity to regret – 'O, had I but followed the arts!' (I. 3. 80) – displays a regressive tendency to regret possibilities of the past that have been thwarted, as does his poignant reflection on his own 'dead love': 'I was adored once too' (II. 4. 160). The problem with perceiving the world in pre-determined and immutable categories is that it is at odds with the nature of existence and, more significantly perhaps, that it makes one unhappy. Indeed, all of the melancholics considered in this chapter share this tendency to categorise new experiences in inflexible terms.

It comes as little surprise, then, that Feste, a self-professed 'corrupter of words' (III. 1. 32), has already underscored the instability of the words upon which fixed identities are predicated: he points out the incoherence of fixed ways of understanding. In a bout of repartee between Cesario and Feste about the fluidity of words, Feste assumes the identity of someone nostalgic for a time in which word and matter corresponded, lamenting with his tongue in his cheek: 'To see this age! – A sentence is but a cheverel glove to a good wit, how quickly the wrong side may be turned outward' (10–12). Although the metaphor of the 'cheverel glove' was proverbial,[38] it might not be altogether fanciful to detect an echo of Erasmus's Stultitia in this comment.

In her attack on the ignorance of theologians, more interested in Scholastic authority than textual interpretation, she inveighs against the perverse interpretations that these wise men project onto scripture: 'all doctours [of Divinity] take it commenly for theyr priuilege, to stretche out heauen (that is to saie) holy writte lyke a *cheuerell skynne*'; they wrest 'the woordes of scripture fare as if they were of contary senses, whereas being set in their right places, they do varie neuer a dele' (*PF*, p. 111). In contrast to the received wisdom that words themselves are intrinsically deceptive or that language *per se* has fallen into confusion, Feste and Stultitia suggest that it is man's use of words that has debased them. Dropping his nostalgic persona, Feste contends that 'words are very rascals since bonds disgraced them' (18–19). Appropriately enough, he refuses to give Cesario the 'reason' (20) he demands: 'Troth, sir, I can yield you none without words, and words are grown so false I am loath to prove reason with them' (21–22). With a passing reference to Stultitia, Feste points out the impossibility of certainty; in fact, the whole play is tuned into Feste's scepticism, for it makes no claim to uphold certainties and is concerned with the capacity of art to liberate people and things from petrified identities.

Feste's interest in the mutability of all human certainties has a structural significance too, since *Twelfth Night* is framed by two reflections that perhaps imply what Adorno was later to formulate explicitly: namely, that art's 'content could be its own transitoriness [*Vergänglichkeit*]' (*AT*, p. 4). In other words, both the *content* of the play and its *structure* give the lie to static identities. The play, after all, opens *in medias res*, halfway through a performance; Orsino desires his musicians to continue playing a song, but then changes his mind:

ORSINO: If music be the food of love, play on,
Give me excess of it that, surfeiting,
The appetite may sicken and so die.
That strain again, it had a dying fall.
O, it came o'er my ear like the sweet sound
That breathes upon a bank of violets,
Stealing and giving odour. Enough, no more,
'Tis not so sweet now as it was before.

(I. 1. 1–8)

The first lines evoke the mutability of art's affective significance, suspending what follows in a space of semantic indeterminacy. Orsino's reflections echo the scornful estimation of man's achievements in Psalm 103, which the *Geneva Bible* renders thus: 'The days of man are as grass: as a flower of the field, so flourisheth he. | For the wind goeth over it, and it is gone, and the place thereof shall know it no more' (15–16). That the significance of a piece of music or the equivocal wisdom offered by a work of dramatic art is intimately connected to the sensibility of the audience is clear: it is as fleeting as the wind on a bank of flowers on a spring day. Whatever *Twelfth Night* says, it asserts but for a moment, a moment that is replayed with a different emphasis in each performance.

Crucially, the play does not conclude with marriages, but with Feste's plangent song, a fragment of which is later echoed and replayed in a demonic key in *King Lear*. In this song, the wryly detached, even 'transcendent',[39] perspective that Feste has espoused all along comes to the fore:

A great while ago the world begun,
With hey, ho, the wind and the rain,
But that's all one, our play is done,
And we'll strive to please you every day.

(V. 1. 392–96)

Appended to the final festivities, the Jester steps out of the world of aesthetic semblance, the world in which what you will is fulfilled no matter how unlikely it seems, and addresses the audience directly. He suggests that the provisional wisdom of the play is but a moment in history in an eternity of physical suffering and reminds us that the 'wind and rain' of a cold, indifferent universe ultimately 'pities neither wise man nor fools' (*King Lear*, III. 2. 12). But although his song serves a relativising function, like that of Orsino's meditation on music, it also suggests that such material facts become irrelevant, 'all one', to those captivated in a moment of illusion, a fleeting glimpse of a world worthy of hope that Shakespearean comedy offers.

5.8 What a Fool Honesty Is

> To bathe in the Waters of Life, to wash off the Not Human,
> I am come in Self-annihilation & the grandeur of Inspiration.
> —William Blake[40]

In *The Winter's Tale,* Camillo describes the self-begetting nature of Leontes's jealousy, which is compared to an 'infectious soare' (*NDSS*, 8, p. 156) in the play's principal source, thus:

> The fabric of his folly, whose foundation
> Is piled upon his faith, and will continue
> The standing of his body.
> (I. 2. 429–31)

Here Camillo neatly describes how ideas can become ossified. Leontes's ideas about the nature of women are based on socially embedded assumptions, *doxa*, rather than his own experience. The King's misapprehension attests to the way in which 'the custome and vse of common life overbeareth us' (*E*, Book III, Chapter 5, p. 477). Indeed, it is because the King is beholden to the customary obsession with posterity and legitimacy that he commits the outrageous action of abandoning his baby, an action that ironically makes him less humane than the savage 'creatures' to which he refused to compare Hermione – as Antigonus observes: 'Wolves and bears, they say, | Casting their savageness aside, have done | Like offices of pity' (II. 3. 187–89). Clearly, a rational creature can be cruel, whereas an animal bereft of reason cannot.

In a nutshell, *The Winter's Tale* offers a dramatization of the consequences of a tendency of thought in which particular objects, persons and discourses are reified or denuded of their particular features. Perhaps the main problem with this type of thinking is that it forgets the simple fact that nothing – no custom, discourse institution or value – lasts forever. Time admits that he can 'o'erthrow law, and in one self-born hour | Plant and o'erwhelm custom' (IV. 1. 5–9). In what follows, I illustrate the play's critique of how aesthetic semblance has a hand in perpetuating assumptions that thwart the possibilities inherent in love and argue that even in the miraculous final scene Leontes remains hoodwinked by an inhuman set of aesthetic expectations. What the play implies about the distinction between art and nature is closely connected with the process Camillo describes.[41] I say "distinction" rather than "opposition" because these terms are far from the binary opposites they might at first seem – in fact, such oppositions prove to be part of the problem. Contrary to Laroque's contention that in this play festive 'cycles of nature win over the forces of anti-nature and perversion',[42] I believe that the play confronts the concepts of art and nature, with themselves and with their customary opposites. The manner in which socially embedded assumptions pervert relationships remains, in the final analysis, a moot point. There is certainly no outright victory of an honest, pre-social "nature" over a perverse "anti-nature". The play, in fact, debunks the assumption that we inhabit a fallen present and implies that what we call nature is always already mediated by aesthetic form.

Through that most patently fictional of events, Hermione's resurrection, *The Winter's Tale* rehearses the possibility of a world no longer governed by obsolete ideas, a world freed from the stultifying grip of the prevailing wisdom. The resurrection of this berated 'thing' is astonishing. As Frank Kermode observes, it 'seems not a theatrical trick but an epiphany, such that those who experienced it might well seem silent, aghast'.[43] Strikingly, Leontes's simple words of wonder – 'O, she's warm! | If this be magic, let it be an art | Lawful as eating' (V. 3. 109–11) – reverse both the negative connotations of his earlier imagery associated with bodily warmth – 'Too hot, too hot: | To mingle friendship far is mingling bloods' (I. 2. 110–11) – and the positive connotations of proverbially "cold" chastity.

Since it lies in art's power to strip away everyday assumptions about women, enabling Leontes to experience the warmth of human contact, a perfectly ordinary yet strangely uncanny experience, the 'magic' of this piece of 'art' is to be found in how it furnishes the reader with a negative image of a reformed nature. A nature, in other words, that will perhaps one day be possible. Leontes has washed off what Blake calls the 'Not Human' – the commonplaces of popular wisdom. And for the first time, he does not perceive his wife as an example of a pre-ordained category. She is neither one of history's numerous wronged women, nor as yet another example of an unfaithful wife, but a particular being, some*one* warm to the touch.

Hermione's resurrection, absent from the main source, *Pandosto: The Triumph of Time* by Robert Greene, is not a foreseeable outcome of events. But far from being one in which, as Laroque argues, 'The festivity which was rendered impotent or destroyed in the no man's land of tragedy, miraculously re-emerges here in an atmosphere of freshness and innocence',[44] it still retains traces of darkness. There is both the pressing memory of the time lost and people killed by Leontes's folly and the lurking implication that aesthetic semblance is partly responsible for the misery caused by the inhuman demands humans place on themselves. This is most apparent in the debate about nature and art between the disguised Polixenes and Perdita. In the midst of a festive celebration of nature's plenitude, these characters discuss the capacity of aesthetic semblance to uncover a nature truer than that manifested in the quotidian world, an 'art' that 'itself is nature' (IV. 4.

97). Although Perdita advises Florizel that, because their love is 'Opposed, as it must be, by th' power of the King,' she 'must change this purpose, | Or I my life' (IV. 4. 27, 39–40), it is her life – or at least her social position – that is transformed in the course of the play. In the realm of fictional possibility, characteristically opened up by Shakespearean comedy, this young man's unlikely hope of marriage is neither thwarted nor brought down to earth.

Polixenes contends that the grafting of wild flowers onto cultivated ones is 'an art | Which does mend nature – change it rather; but | The art itself is nature' (IV. 4. 95–97). He suggests that human creations are dependent upon 'great creating nature' (87), and that the inner workings of this sort of 'nature' can be fathomed only through something as manifestly unnatural as 'art'. Perdita, in contrast, insists on unadulterated art. Her aesthetic product, the floral 'garlands' (IV. 4. 128) for the sheep-shearing festival, excludes impure flowers, 'carnations and streaked gillyvors [...] nature's bastards' (82–83). This form, an idealisation based on the exclusion of impurities, is at odds with the nature of the play in which it finds expression, since *The Winter's Tale* is the quintessential 'mongrel tragi-comedy'.[45]

Hermione's idealisation also raises a problem about aesthetic form that remains unresolved at the end of the play: namely, the tendency for aesthetic semblance to skate over the suffering inflicted on people by seriousness. The potentially destructive drive for purity and perfection is as apparent in Othello's murder of Desdemona as it is in Leontes's insanity, when he considers Hermione to 'Sully the purity and whiteness of' his marital 'sheets' (I. 2. 329). Leontes evokes the subversive 'openness' of the human body – in contrast to the completed, pure form possible in, for instance, sculpture – when he reflects that there is 'No barricado for a belly. Know't, | It will let in and out the enemy' (205–206). Even at the end of the play, he displays a desire for a perfectly proportioned aesthetic form, rather than a breathing being – 'Hermione was not so much wrinkled, nothing | So agèd as this seems' (V. 3. 27–28).

In other words, Leontes remains blind to the fact that the concept of the ideal human exceeds the bounds of possibility; but in the myth of Pygmalion, the chief classical antecedent of Hermione's resurrection, Ovid emphasises how art can create the ideal in a way that nature simply cannot:

> Now in the while by wonderous art an image he did grave
> Of such proportion, shape and grace as nature never gave
> Nor can to any woman give. In his work he took
> A certain love.
>
> (Book 10, 265–68)

Crucially, rather than giving expression to his beloved's 'proportion, shape and grace', Pygmalion creates it. *The Winter's Tale* stages a tension between the complicity of mimesis in perpetuating discourses that figuratively and literally reduce the likes of Hermione and Desdemona to objects, and representation's capacity to bring to life a state of affairs in which those destroyed by such discourses can return to life. Hermione's resurrection is tempered not only by the fact that it is shown to be extraordinary and possible only in a play, but also by the implication that Leontes's idealising aesthetics have not been reformed. And Shakespeare's masterstroke is, of course, that he *stages* Leontes's captivation by the aesthetics of purity and completeness, which collude in sustaining the ossified opinions that threaten to plunge the spectacular events of this romance into the realm of tragedy.

5.9 Losing Eden

> For we wrestle not against flesh and blood, but against principalities, against powers, against the rulers of the darkness of the world, against spiritual wickedness in high *places*.
>
> —*KJV*, Ephesians 6., 12

The source makes clear its intention to provide a moral edification and prove an adage to be correct. *Pandosto* is a 'pleasant Historie, that although by the meanes of sinister fortune Truth may be concealed, yet by Time in spight of fortune it is most manifestly reuealed [...] *Temporis filia veritas*' (*NDSS*, 8, p. 156). But *The Winter's Tale* debunks this providential account of history. It contrasts a regressive present with one that is transformed by hope. After he has been persuaded to stay in Sicily a little longer, Polixenes recounts to Hermione his and Leontes's fall from grace:

POLIXENES: We were as twinned lambs that did frisk i'th' sun,
And bleat the one at th'other. What we changed
Was innocence for innocence. We knew not
The doctrine of ill-doing, nor dreamed
That any did. Had we pursued that life,
And our weak spirits ne'er been higher reared
With stronger blood, we should have answered heaven
Boldly 'not guilty', the imposition cleared,
Hereditary ours.

(I. 2. 69–77)

Polixenes recalls a pre-pubescent state, without the 'temptations' of desire. Because such innocence can only ever be reflected upon in a fallen world, *post factum*, the state of immaculate innocence, which he considers to have had the potential to wipe the slate clean for humanity, is essentially a state of ignorance. The association of his awakening sexual desire with fallen nature is theologically dubious, for Adam and Eve loved shamelessly in Eden. It was knowledge that undid them. Moreover, this comment replicates the King of Sicily's embedded beliefs about the debasing influence of women on men. In fact, the myth of the loss of Eden, so tantalisingly re-imagined in *As You Like It*, could be partly responsible for the rearward-gazing, melancholic disposition that Shakespeare is so critical of in these comedies. However, as his rendering of the Cain and Abel trope in *As You Like It* and his reworking and refocusing of the myth of Troy in *Troilus and Cressida* attest, even the foundational myths of western culture can be reconfigured.

Given what Polixenes misremembers about their shared childhood, it is perhaps surprising that sexual imagery pervades Leontes's exchange with his son, Mamillius:

LEONTES: [...] Art thou my boy?
MAMILLIUS: Ay, my good lord.
LEONTES: I' fecks,
Why, that's my bawcock. What? Hast smutched thy nose?
They say it is a copy out of mine. Come, captain,
We must be neat – not neat, but cleanly, captain.
And yet the steer, the heifer, and the calf
Are all called neat. – Still virginalling
Upon his palm? – How now, you wanton calf!
Art thou my calf?
MAMILLIUS: Yes, if you will, my lord.

(I. 2. 121–29)

In this double-edged exchange, Leontes is an advocate of the virtue of being 'cleanly', a virtue that is rendered absurd by the double meaning of 'neat', which, as a noun rather than an adjective, signifies castrated cattle.[46] This prompts his Menippean reduction of all of the inhabitants of this 'bawdy planet' to the bestial, substituting the 'hyper-sexuality'[47] associated with the fool for the notion that all humans are driven by an insatiable lust. His insistence on 'cleanly' deportment contrasts sharply with his narrative of the cuckolded husband holding 'his wife by th'arm, | That little thinks she has been sluiced in's absence, | And his pond fished by Sir Smile, his neighbour' (194–97). Leontes's only consolation lies in the obvious legitimacy of his son, whose features, like those of the daughter he denies, reflect his.

Hermione's alleged actions 'Give scandal to the blood o'th' prince, my son, | Who I do think is mine and love as mine' (I. 2. 332–33). The three possessive pronouns make it clear that his affection for Mamillius springs from the self-love so characteristic of the Shakespearean melancholic. The love of a parent for a child is exposed, in this instance, as an unnatural infatuation with himself. And it is no coincidence, then, that the 'chief mythic source for Leontes's derangement' is 'Ovid's tale of Narcissus'.[48] Contrary to Erasmus's injunction in *Institutio Principis Christiani* that the 'glory' of a King 'cannot be more truly illuminated than by being overshadowed' (*CWE*, 27, p. 207) by his son, this King's hopes for the future are an inauthentic projection of the present, a projection of his power.

Thus Kermode is not wrong to point out that 'Leontes's language is always tyrannical'.[49] After all, Erasmus advises that the 'tyrannical slogans "I desire this, I command this, let my will be the reason"', so characteristic of Leontes's utterance, should 'be far removed from the mind of a prince' (*CWE*, 27, p. 243). The Sicilian King's conviction that he is 'blest' in his 'true opinion' (II. 1. 38, 39) is undercut by the fact that it is clearly an oxymoron – by definition, an 'opinion' cannot be 'true'. The absurdity of this conviction is compounded by his statement that 'There is no truth at all i'th' oracle' (138). Oracles cannot be dishonest. Moreover, although they can sometimes utter cryptic prophecies, which cannot be understood in the ignorance of the present moment, this particular prophecy is pretty unambiguous.

Polixenes, Leontes's double, is scarcely less tyrannical. Both men are characterised by their nostalgia. Polixenes's tyrannical nature is apparent in the contrast between his horticultural and his social theories; upon discovering his son's betrothal to Perdita, he views his son as degenerate, threatening to 'bar' him 'from succession, | Not hold thee of our blood, no, not our kin' (IV. 4. 418–19). He is just as concerned with his family tree as his counterpart. Presumably for fear that it will threaten the legitimacy of other noble lineages, he threatens to deface Perdita's beauty, the source of her 'witchcraft' (411): 'I'll have thy beauty scratched with briars and made | More homely than thy state' (412–13). In *Pandosto*, not only has the prince been betrothed by his father 'vpon reasonable conditions' (*NDSS*, 8, p. 176) to the Princess of Denmark, but he has also already married without his father's permission, whereas in *The Winter's Tale* Florizel has not actually married Perdita at this stage and insists, contrary to his father's assumption that this 'royal fool' has copulated with the shepherdess, that his 'desires | Run not before mine honour, nor my lusts | Burn hotter than my faith' (33–34). In *Pandosto*, although Dorastus's father becomes 'somewhat chollericke' (*NDSS*, 8, p. 177), he at least attempts to dissuade his son (see *NDSS*, 8, p. 177). The explosive response of Polixenes, in contrast, emphasises the irrationality of the reified opinions by which even kings are governed.

After Leontes has realised that the events of the first half of the play were 'All mine own folly' (V. 1. 134), he remains in thrall to a nostalgic mode of thought; inverting the notion that 'melancholy is the nurse of frenzy' (*The Taming of the Shrew*, 'Induction 2', 128), his jealous frenzy has caused his melancholy. Under the influence of Paulina, he has 'performed | A saint-like sorrow' and 'paid down | More penitence than done trespass' (V. 1. 1–2, 3–4). The imagery of performance is employed throughout the play and is apparent in the King's sustained and public mourning. This comment continues the imagery of finance and exchange associated with personal relationships from the very first scene: 'the King of Sicilia means to pay Bohemia the visitation which he justly owes him' (I. 1. 6).[50] For Cleomenes, at least, the king has 'paid' his dues. By the end, Hermione has become an object of nostalgic veneration, a totem object of an idealised past. 'There is none worthy | Respecting her that's gone' (34–35), says Paulina, while Leontes pities 'not the state nor the remembrance | Of his most sovereign name' (25–26), the desire for posterity, which motivated him in the first half of the play. Not unlike the courts in the *Trauerspiele* that Benjamin analyses, the King of Sicily's court of mourning represents a life paralysed by the past; drained of all vitality and significance, the present is obliterated along with any hope for the future. The eyes of the dead Queen appear to him as 'Stars, stars', whereas those of the living, 'All eyes else', are but 'dead coals!' (68–69) – just as when Henry VI sees Gloucester's corpse: 'seeing him, I see my life in death' (*2 Henry VI*, III. 2. 151). Since Leontes's comments arrive at a definitive judgement of the world in much the same way as when he meditates on the universality of cuckoldry, they drain singular lives and experiences of any potential significance – in much the same way as Donne considers allegories to do.

It is no coincidence that in the scene in which the play begins to morph from a tragedy into a comedy, while the Clown laments about Antigonus being eaten by the bear and 'the most piteous cry of the poor souls!' (III. 3. 84–5) of the shipwreck, the Shepherd responds with a concern for the future: 'Heavy matters, heavy matters. But look thee here, boy. Now bless thyself. Thou mettest with things dying, I with things newborn' (103–105). This openness to the future entails an awareness that something radically new might at any moment invade the present, opening up the possibility of an alternative, genuinely unpredictable, future – as, for instance, when Hermione's statue returns to life. It is the utopian impulse behind truly philosophical thought, which goes beyond existing categories and identities, rather than being constrained by them. Indeed, the final section of the *Praise of Folly* argues that it is this sort of hope – rather than the inauthentic, nostalgic projections onto the future of the sort Leontes and Polixenes indulge in – that characterises Paul's 'fools for Christ's sake' (*KJV*, I Corinthians, 4, 10):

> [T]he life of good Christians is naught els than a continuall meditacion or certaine shadow as it were of that life to come, it chanceth, that they yet living have for theyr coumforte permission at sometimes to discerne a taste or savour of that hieghest rewarde behight vnto them. (*PF*, p. 127)

Here Erasmus's seriocomic lauding of folly and his serious theories about the nature of grace, which he views as unexpected and utterly surprising (see *CWE*, 47, pp. 50–60, *et passim*), correspond: 'Erasmus follows Paul in casting the relation of God to humanity in terms of unmotivated kindness',[51] kindness that is conspicuously different from the calculating generosity of the two kings.

But Leontes even construes the silence of the statue as an accurate representation of his wife's nature: 'thou art she | In thy not chiding, for she was as tender | As infancy and grace' (V. 3. 25–27). The stultifying discourses to which he still adheres distort his understanding of 'grace'. Even his experience of wonder remains manacled to the past and mediated by quotidian wisdom. In striking contrast, however, even momentary contact with the oracle, an embodiment of the 'grandeur of inspiration', occasions an unlearning akin to Blakean 'Self-annihilation' – what the Orthodox church calls *kenosis*:

CLEOMENES: But of all, the burst
And the ear-deaf'ning voice o'th' oracle,
Kin to Jove's thunder, so surprised my sense
That I was nothing.

(III. 1. 8–11)

This baffling of 'sense', of the assumption that 'I' am something, offers a model of a humbled consciousness, astonished, and liberated to a certain extent, from the mind-forged manacles that continue to make people unhappy.

As Montaigne argues, consciousness is innately orientated towards the future. Because consciousness is all but consumed by anxieties about the future, one never inhabits a unitary identity in the present:

> We are never in our selves, but beyond. Feare, desire, and hope, draw us ever towards that which is to come, and remove our sense and consideration from that which is, to amuse us on that which shall be, yea when we shall be no more.
>
> (*E*, Book I, Chapter 3, p. 5)

On the one hand, *The Winter's Tale* dramatises the dangers of being captive to nostalgia, a subjective inclination that relies on a consciousness that is drawn to what has been or what could have been, rather than what could be. On the other hand, in its *coup de théâtre*, this play suggests that it is at least possible for authentic, utterly unexpected, futures to come to fruition. But *The Winter's Tale* does so unreliably. It is – as *Twelfth Night*, *As You Like It* and the Second Tetralogy are – self-conscious about its fictional nature. Not unlike Feste's disguise as Sir Topas, the authority of this text is improvised, and this frustrates the establishment of any unequivocal standpoint – even if such a standpoint were 'an invitation to accept the openness or, in more recent critical terms, indeterminacy of both art and life'.[52]

Moreover, *The Winter's Tale* concedes that the wonderful events of the ending are possible only in the make-believe realm of play; as Paulina comments: 'That she is living, | Were it but told you, should be hooted at | Like an old tale. But it *appears* she lives' (V. 3. 115–17) [my emphasis]. For Anne Barton, this comment displays a 'desperate artistic honesty which could admit, now, to creating fictions, while making us understand why and how much we should like these fictions to be real'.[53] After all, the very name of the play, *The Winter's Tale*, like Erasmus's *Praise of Folly*, is a title that 'itselfe semeth to set foorth no wisedome' ('Introduction', *PF*, pp. 3–6 [p. 3]), a Cretan title. As Catherine Belsey reminds us: 'Among the terms in circulation in the period for far-fetched narratives and improbable fables, one favourite was "a winter's tale"[54] and young Mamillius unwittingly alludes to this popular tradition in his comment, 'A sad tale's best for winter | Of sprites and goblins' (*The Winter's Tale*, II. 1. 25–26). The play's implication that it is necessary to unlearn the wisdom of the world so as to be open to the wonders of an incredible future is qualified by the suggestion that even this negative wisdom might not be true. The play thereby refuses to commit to an unequivocal epistemological standpoint. This radical scepticism, which is justly sceptical of its own suspicions about the possibility of any sincere, universal or certain way of knowing, finds its most sustained expression in the play to which I now turn, *Hamlet*.

Notes

1. *The Anatomy of Melancholy*, ed. by Thomas C. Faulkner, Nicholas K. Kiessling and Rhonda L. Blair, 3 vols (Oxford: Oxford University Press, 1989–1994), II, p. 167. Subsequent references are to this edition and are given in the text.
2. *The hospitall of incurable fooles: erected in English, as neer the first Italian modell and platforme, as the vnskilfull hand of an ignorant architect could deuise* [...], trans. by anon (London: Edm[und] Bollifant, 1600 [1586]), p. 81.
3. *The Fool in European Theatre: Stages of Folly* (Basingstoke: Palgrave, 2012), pp. 69–96 (p. 69).
4. *Shakespeare's Great Stage of Fools* (Basingstoke: Palgrave, 2011), esp. pp. 49–77.
5. *Re-Humanising Shakespeare: Literary Humanism, Wisdom and Modernity* (Edinburgh: Edinburgh University Press, 2007), p. 135.
6. *Faith and Folly in Shakespeare's Romantic Comedies* (Athens, GA: University of Georgia Press, 1980; repr. 2000), p. i.
7. See 'Touching Words: Embodying Ethics in Erasmus, Shakespearean Comedy, and Contemporary Theory', *MP*, 104 (2006), 1–33.
8. *Das Prinzip Hoffnung*, 3 vols (Frankfurt: Suhrkamp, 1959; repr, 1985), I, p. 3.
9. '*A Midsummer's Night's Dream*', in *On Lying in Bed and Other Essays by G. K. Chesterton*, ed. by Alberto Manguel (Calgary: Bayeux Arts, 2000), pp. 193–203 (p. 194).
10. See Jon Haarberg, *Parody and the Praise of Folly*, Acta Humaniora, 42 (Cambridge, MA: Scandinavian University Press, 1998) pp. 137–175.
11. 'Sermon Preached at the funeral of Sir William Cokayne Knight, Alderman of London, December 12. 1626', in *The Sermons of John Donne*, ed. by George R. Porter and Evelyn M. Simpson, 10 vols (Berkeley: University of California Press, 1953–62), VII, pp. 257–278 (p. 157).
12. Winfried Schleiner, *Melancholy, Genius, and Utopia in the Renaissance*, Wolfenbütteler Abhandlung zur Renaissanceforschung, 10 (Wiesbaden: Otto Harrassowitz, 1991), p. 16.
13. Michael Bath, 'Weeping Stags and Melancholy Lovers: The Iconography of *As You Like It*, II. I', *Emblematica* 1 (1986), 13–42 (p. 14).
14. *Metamorphoses*, ed. by Madeleine Forey, trans. by Arthur Golding (Harmondsworth: Penguin, 2002 [1567]) p. 100 (Book III, 235–247).

15. Schleiner, p. 239; the eponymous, melancholic hero of Belleforest's *Amleth* – a possible source for *Hamlet*—employs this tactic 'when he suspects an ambush in his mother's chamber' (p. 240).
16. Galen, quoted in Garzoni, p. 17.
17. *The Origins of German Tragic Drama*, trans. by John Osborne (London: Verso, 1998; repr. 2009), p. 113.
18. *Shakespeare's Comedies*, p. 214.
19. *Ibid.*, p. 230.
20. *Treatise on Laughter*, trans. by Gregory David De Rocher (Tuscaloosa, AL: University of Alabama Press, 1980), p. 17.
21. *Kritische Schriften und Briefe*, ed. by Edgar Lohner, 7 vols (Stuttgart: W. Kohlhammer, 1967–1975), VI, p. 158 [My translation].
22. Ryan, *Shakespeare's Comedies*, p. 244.
23. Schlegel, p. 158.
24. *Shakespeare's Festive Comedy: A Study of Dramatic Form and its Relation to Social Custom* (Princeton, NJ: Princeton University Press, 1959; repr. 1990), p. 5ff.
25. Laroque, p. 29.
26. Tiller, p. 43.
27. Gail Kern Paster, *Humoring the Body: Emotions and the Shakespearean Stage* (Chicago: The University of Chicago Press, 2004), p. 12.
28. *The Anatomy of Melancholy*, II. p. 116. This argument goes at least as far back as Quintilian (see Joubert, p. 16).
29. Ryan, p. 238.
30. *Passions of the Minde in Generall* (London: Valintine Simmes, 1601), p. 8.
31. 'Perspectives of Madness in *Twelfth Night*', *ES*, 78 (1997), 105–110 (p. 107).
32. *Ibid.*, p. 9.
33. *The Anatomy of Melancholy*, II, p. 19.
34. *The Riverside Chaucer*, ed. by Larry D. Benson and others (Oxford: Oxford University Press, 1987).
35. Jean Klene, 'The Fool, Folly, and the World Upside-Down in *Measure for Measure*', *Upstart Crow*, 3 (1980), 1–10 (p. 3).
36. Schlegel, p. 157.
37. Catherine Birkinshaw, '"Past the Wit of Man": *A Midsummer Night's Dream*'s Debt to *Praise of Folly*', *Shakespeare in Southern Africa*, 5 (1992), 43–58, p. 51.
38. Clarence Miller cites Tilley's collections of proverbs (see 'Explanatory Notes', *PF*, pp. 131–202 [p. 193]); 'cheuerell skynne' is Thomas Chaloner's rendering of the Latin, '*Pellem*' (*PF*, p. 193).
39. *Shakespeare's Comedies,* p. 277.
40. 'Milton', in *Blake: Complete Writings with Variant Readings*, ed. by Geoffrey Keynes (Oxford: Oxford University Press, 1969), pp. 480–535 (p. 533) (Book 2, Section, 42); [the irregular capitalisation is Blake's].
41. See 'Touching Words', pp. 2 ff.
42. Laroque, p. 199.
43. *Shakespeare's Language* (Harmondsworth: Penguin, 2000), p. 272.
44. Laroque, p. 199.
45. Philip Sidney, *An Apology for Poetry: or the Defence of Poesy*, ed. by R. W. Maslen (Manchester: Manchester University Press, 2002), p. 112.
46. Compare *OED*, definition nos. 1 and 2.

47. Laroque, p. 126.
48. David Houston Wood, "He Something Seems Unsettled": Melancholy, Jealousy, and Subjective Temporality in *The Winter's Tale*', *Renaissance Drama*, 31 (2002), 185–210 (p. 186).
49. *Shakespeare's Language*, p. 280.
50. Money, the play makes clear, is ambivalent to terms of 'mannerly distinguishment'; it mediates between kings and beggars alike. This is apparent in the Clown's association of romance with considerable personal expenditure: 'If I were not in love with Mopsa, thou shouldst take no money of me, but being enthralled as I am, it will also be the bondage of certain ribbons and gloves' (IV. 4. 226–28). Autolycus provides a disenchanted reflection on this fact in one of his songs, which are themselves commodities: 'Come to the pedlar, | Money's a meddler, | That doth utter all men's ware-a' (307–310) – even this idea cannot escape the market. In the report of the first scene of recognition, however, the Second Gentleman suggests that 'such a deal of wonder is broken out that ballad-makers cannot be able to express it' (V. 2. 23–25), a comment which transforms wonder into a commodity to be sold in broadsheets or at playhouse doors. In fact, *The Winter's Tale* as a whole could be said to cash in on wonder.
51. 'Embodying Ethics', p. 12.
52. Knapp, p. 161.
53. 'Leontes and the Spider' in Kiernan Ryan, ed., *Shakespeare: The Last Plays* (Basingstoke: Routledge, 1999), 22–42 (p. 41).
54. 'Shakespeare's Sad Tale for Winter: *Hamlet* and the Tradition of Fireside Ghost Stories', *SQ*, 61 (2010), 1–27 (p. 4).

6 Folly and Aesthetic Judgement

6.1 Pitiful Ambition in the Fool

> KNAPP VORM DRITTEN HAHNENSCHREI ZERREISST EIN NARR DAS SCHELLENKLEID DES PHILOSOPHEN.
>
> —Heiner Müller, 'Die Hamletmaschine'[1]

While Robert Bell is quite correct to argue that in 'Shakespearean tragedy, fooling matters seriously and fools take centre stage',[2] *Hamlet*'s engagement with the discourse of folly is unique. Because the discourse of folly is omnipresent in the play's language, *Hamlet* does not simply engage with folly, but is constituted by it. The play's recurrent rhetorical tics are 'foolish figure[s]' (II. 2. 198) of speech. Shakespeare's philosophical masterpiece abounds in the circumlocutions, puns, riddles, paradoxes and oxymora characteristic of the loquacious patter of the wise fool.

Indeed, the play's near obsession with such rhetorical figures is manifest from the outset. In the first exchange between Claudius and Hamlet, the King employs an oxymoron – 'But now, my cousin Hamlet, and my son' (I. 2. 64) – a figure of speech that means 'pointedly foolish'[3] in Greek and baffles us by negating both the meanings it evokes: Hamlet cannot be the 'son' and 'cousin' of the same man. The Prince responds with his famous opening pun; his 'uncle father' (II. 2. 323) is 'A little more than kin, and less than kind' (I. 2. 65). For Catherine Bates, puns embody in miniature what is special about art: namely, its removal from the purposeful world. Bates writes:

> As the smallest unit of linguistic deviation the pun was a microcosm of literariness, since it contained ambiguity, polysemy, and frequently metaphor all within a single word. A pun is literariness writ small, and its supposed difference from 'ordinary words' explains why it's traditionally been branded as illegitimate and treated as a barbarian – a foreign element or exotic intruder.[4]

Because it tempts him from the high road of instrumental utterance, speech with a clear-cut purpose, Hamlet's pun, which implies that Claudius is an unkind schemer, departs from what is acceptable to say in the new King's 'rotten' (I. 4. 90) state.

Elsewhere in the play, the Prince uses quibbles and puns, 'indirections', to discover his mother's thoroughly dishonourable intentions, her 'directions' (II. 1. 63):

HAMLET: Now, mother, what's the matter?
QUEEN GERTRUDE: Hamlet, thou hast thy father much offended.
HAMLET: Mother, you have my father much offended.
QUEEN GERTRUDE: Come, come, you answer with an idle tongue.
HAMLET: Go, go, you question with a wicked tongue.
QUEEN GERTRUDE: Why, how now, Hamlet!
HAMLET: What's the matter now?
QUEEN GERTRUDE: Have you forgot me?
HAMLET: No, by the rood, not so.
You are the Queen, your husband's brother's wife,
And, would it were not so, you are my mother.

(III. 4. 7–15)

This terse stichomythia, which is a rhetorical technique that has been in the fool's linguistic armoury from Aristophanes onwards, attests to Hamlet's propensity for 'punning equivocation'. It connects him, as Jacques Lacan writes in his famous essay about the play, with 'those characters called fools [or] court jesters' and, ultimately, allows him 'to uncover the most hidden of motives'.[5] The non-authoritative discourse of folly furnishes Hamlet with a position from which to question the values of what is commonly accepted as reasonable or natural.

It is no coincidence, then, that the tragic hero's very name in the *Historiae Danicae*, Amleth, 'probably means fool or weakling'.[6] And Livy's *Roman History*, a possible source for the play and one with which Shakespeare was certainly familiar, relates the story of Brutus, who resolves to 'save himself' by 'counterfeit[ing] a noddie and a verie innocent' (*NDSS*, 7, p. 80). At the Temple of Apollo at Delphi, where Socrates was considered the wisest of men for knowing nothing, Brutus presents Apollo with a silenic offering, 'a 'golden rod within a staffe of cornell wood' (*NDSS*, 7, p. 80), an offering that symbolises his hidden wisdom. Not only does Hamlet, like Brutus, disguise 'his long hid wits' out of 'deep policy' (*The Rape of Lucrece*, 1815–1816), but he also assumes his 'antic disposition' (I. 5. 170) in order to penetrate the façade of the serious world. The Prince's feigned folly or madness offers a position outside the serious world, from which he can examine the opinions, the *doxa*, that constitute it. For Richard Wilson, Hamlet's response to his father's death is nothing other than Shakespeare's 'meta-dramatizing [of] his own evasion of absolutism's neoclassical aesthetic, with its imperious demand for decorum, transparency, and order'.[7]

Moreover, folly's digressive tendencies are intrinsic to the play's dramatic structure as a whole as well as its language. Between the Ghost's injunction – 'remember me' (I. 5. 91) – and the fencing match at the conclusion, the play's action is hardly action at all. Hamlet postpones his revenge, evading the role history has scripted him to play. Whereas, in *1&2 Henry IV*, the digressions in the tavern enable Shakespeare to hold the purposeful world on hold and question its assumptions, in *Hamlet* digression – both at a linguistic and a structural level – pushes the serious action or 'necessary question' of the play to the margins: *Hamlet* is nothing other than a set piece in the fool's favourite art of narrative dilation. Its circumlocutions, diversions and digressions give the lie to the idea that the 'structure' of a play must run in 'a satisfactorily linear, sequential course';[8] this play is one long farcical digression, which is full of quibbling, role-playing and logic chopping.

While creative responses to the play are attuned to its digressive kernel,[9] critical analyses have, for the most part, either viewed folly as an isolated phenomenon and examined it in terms of its generic implications[10] or considered it in connection with the play's main protagonist.[11] They have generally stuck to the ostensibly solid categories of character and genre. However, as the previous chapters of this study have shown, playful digression is of crucial significance to Shakespeare's philosophy of folly. Kiernan Ryan contends that the play's peculiar structure and language are, in fact, the keys to its elusive *philosophical* vision:

> [When] we find *Hamlet* scuppering its own plot and deranging its own discourse to baffle and confound generations of critics, what we are feeling is nothing less than the tidal pull of the possible, of the as-yet-unrealized, twisting the script into this unique convolution of language and form that continues to hold us spellbound.[12]

Precisely because of its ostensible purposelessness, digression – even the momentary digression of the pun – puts the serious world on hold and such moments of purposelessness within the play work to stage the dangers inherent in an inflexible, purposeful seriousness, a seriousness that has led to *Hamlet* being interpreted as a sober philosophical essay, which is merely interrupted by the occasional scurrility.

The Graveyard Scene is calculated to confound the expectations brought to bear on it by a 'neat and cleanly' (*1 Henry IV*, II. 5. 417) aesthetics. When he inveighs against the tendency of clowns to extemporise, Hamlet endorses such neo-classical aesthetics:

> [...] let not those that play your clowns speak more than is set down for them. For there be of them that will themselves laugh to set on some quality of barren spectators to laugh too, though in the meantime some necessary question of the play be then to be considered.
>
> (III. 2. 36–41)

Ironically, however, Hamlet not only plays the fool, but his foolery is also what occludes the 'necessary question of the play', its serious *purpose*.

By reading the main action out of the play's inbuilt creative interpretation of itself, the Graveyard Scene, this chapter's analysis turns such decorous interpretations of the play topsy-turvy. Paradoxically, it is the interruptions of the tragic action that are important. Lacan contends that the key question posed by *Hamlet* is: 'what happens in the Graveyard scene'?[13] While this is something of an exaggeration, like all exaggerations, perhaps, it has a grain of truth. To paraphrase Adorno's comments about art in general, this play's seriousness lies in its light-heartedness. Yet this is not the cruelly incurious light-heartedness of blithe optimists; rather, it is a darker laughter, a laughter that acts against 'what we fear might take control of us'.[14]

6.2 Your Sovereignty of Reason

Hamlet is full of disorientating moments of doubling, which offer indecorous replays of what is supposed to happen. This play does not simply 'hold as 'twere the mirror up to nature' (III. 2. 20); instead, it holds a distorting fairground mirror up to itself. For instance, Hamlet and the Gravedigger's quibbling equivocation about who 'liest' (V. 2. 11) in the grave travesties the figure of the ghost and the revenge plot: this is neither the first time that the prince has been spoken to from a grave, nor will it be the last – this comic exchange precludes the presence of the 'quick' (114) in Ophelia's grave.

Like *The Winter's Tale*, *Hamlet* hinges on an event that is absent from the sources and only possible in the manifest 'illusion' (I. 1. 126) offered by drama. Stalking the battlements of Elsinore, the Ghost fractures the linear notion of time upon which the sensible world and its systems depend – 'The time is out of joint' (I. 5. 186). Its histrionic presence as an absence, something that is neither living nor dead, disrupts the fundamental distinction between the 'quick' (V. 1. 114) and the 'dead' (119), about which Hamlet and the Gravedigger quibble. By definition, a Ghost is a non-identical element in any epistemological system or ontology:

GHOST: Swear by his sword.
HAMLET: Well said, old mole, canst work i'th' earth so fast?
A worthy pioneer! Once more remove good friends.
HORATIO: O day and night, but this is wondrous strange.
HAMLET: And therefore as a stranger give it welcome:
There are more things in heaven and earth, Horatio,
Than are dreamt of in your [F, *our*] philosophy.

(I. 5. 160–66)

Not least because it straddles two supposedly separate philosophical disciplines, challenging the division between natural philosophy and metaphysics, Hamlet encourages Horatio to embrace the challenge this 'strange' addendum poses to existing knowledge. This is all the more pronounced in the Folio's use of the second person personal pronoun 'our', since this means

Hamlet extols the virtues of learned ignorance rather than merely questioning Horatio's stoic standpoint.

Referring to his father's ghost as an 'old mole' and a 'fellow in the cellarage' (151), Hamlet does not take the 'necessary question' of his own play wholly seriously: the Ghost, an absolute challenge to our existing epistemic systems, is not taken without a pinch of salt. By comically undercutting the seriousness of this uncanny figure, which 'bodes some strange eruption' (I. 1. 68) to Denmark, Hamlet refuses to incorporate this absolute challenge to reason's conceptual categories into the cold language of reason. Moreover, the remarkable way that Hamlet philosophises through irony, holding up any unequivocal standpoint to playful mockery, epitomises the seriously playful, philosophically anti-philosophical movement of this tragedy.

Although *Hamlet* has been commonly held to be Shakespeare's most philosophical play, it is at pains to point out that the reasonable world is far less reasonable than one might imagine. The play is not only full of ineluctable complexities, curtailments, and elaborate theoretical connivances, most of which go disastrously wrong, but, just like the Henriad, it memorably evokes the insane self-destructiveness of the purposeful world:

> How stand I then
> That have a father killed, a mother stained,
> Excitements of my reason and my blood,
> And let all sleep; while to my shame I see
> The imminent death of twenty thousand men
> That for a fantasy and trick of fame
> Go to their graves like beds, fight for a plot
> Whereon the numbers cannot try the cause,
> Which is not tomb enough and continent
> To hide the slain? O, from this time forth,
> My thoughts be bloody or be nothing worth!
>
> (IV. 4. 55–65)

Hamlet, paradoxically, is compelled to revenge his father by the foolish example of men caught up in an Hobbesian war of all against all, fighting for the sake of that most fickle of things, fame.

Reason's self-destructive tendencies are further emphasised by Laertes's peculiar response to Hamlet's apology; this apology is itself incongruous because the Prince claims diminished responsibility, despite the fact that his 'madness' (see V. 2. 215, 217) has been a performance:

> I am satisfied in nature,
> Whose motive in this case should stir me most
> To my revenge. But in my terms of honour
> I stand aloof and will no reconcilement
> Till by some elder masters of known honour
> I have the voice and precedent of peace

To keep my name ungored. But all that time
I do receive your offered love like love
And will not wrong it.

(221–28)

On the one hand, Laertes must, to an extent, accept the prince's apology in order to justify the fencing match, a game, rather than have an outright duel; Hamlet's oxymoron – they will 'frankly play' (230) in their bout – is not only accidentally ironic, since Laertes fully intends to cheat, but it also evokes a key concern of the play: namely, how representation can get to the truth of things. On the other, it seems to me that the statesman's son's equivocating answer, alongside Hamlet's reflections on the war, shows how these characters frequently act in bad faith. Laertes knows that what he is doing is thoroughly dishonourable and admits that cheating 'is almost against my conscience' (279) and Hamlet follows an example of pointless self-destructiveness, even as he perceives its futility. Both characters adhere to a system of historically ratified values and beliefs that they judge to be wrong.

Furthermore, in *Hamlet*, Shakespeare insistently points out – as More seems to imply in *Utopia* – that the theoretical knowledge that has the possibility to liberate humankind frequently has the opposite effect. Laertes describes himself as 'a woodcock to mine own springe' (291) and points out that: 'The foul practice | Hath turned itself on me' (301–302), whereas Hamlet comments on Polonius's demise: ''tis the sport to have the engineer | Hoist with his own petard' (III. 4. 204–205).[15] As in a farce, there is 'sport' or comic satisfaction to be had in seeing man's *ingenium* – that is, his unique capacity to think and to systematise – destroyed by its own connivance. And at the end of the play, Horatio promises to relate a senseless tale of

carnal, bloody and unnatural acts,
Of accidental judgements, casual slaughters,
Of deaths put on my cunning, and for no cause,
And in this upshot the purposes mistook
Fallen on th'inventors' heads.

(V. 2. 365–68)

Although *Hamlet* makes no claims to be a tragedy of high seriousness, it eloquently illustrates the incoherence of the everyday world's systems and modes of speculation.

In his ostensibly inept love letter, with its 'ill phrase' (II. 2. 109) of 'beautified Ophelia' (109), Hamlet describes his body as a 'machine' (121) – an idea that Heiner Müller borrows for the title of his astonishing adaptation of the play. Because it imbues a human being with a mechanical inflexibility, this phrase is incongruous – as Henri Bergson observes in his famous study of laughter: 'automatism makes us laugh'.[16] Hamlet's comment implies that, far from possessing the mysterious subjective depths, which critics from Coleridge to Bloom have attributed to him, people are, like Prince Hal in the tavern, mere functions of the historical situation and society in which they find themselves. This idea is apparent in modern medical parlance: a functioning depressive or alcoholic still operates as a cog in the social system – he goes to work and buys things. Hamlet, of course, focuses on its protagonist's disinclination to function, his hesitancy to play the socially scripted role of the avenger. Instead, he wastes time, resolving to 'be idle' (III. 2. 87). And it is no coincidence that one of the fragments of a play within this play offers a powerful vignette of a man caught between 'desire' and 'performance' (*Macbeth*, II. 3. 27, 28): '*So as a painted tyrant Pyrrhus stood | Like a neutral to his will and matter, | Did nothing* (II. 2. 418–21). This *mise en abyme* vividly evokes Hamlet's situation: he is an avenger who cannot quite bring himself to avenge.

The Prince may claim to possess a mysterious essence – 'that within which passes show' (I. 2. 85) – but since he takes on a dizzying number of discrete identities, this profession of integrity is decidedly disingenuous. Aside from the fool, he plays a lover, a sailor, a duellist and a playwright. And as Tim Prenki observes, Hamlet's essence is innately histrionic: he 'sees himself from his first appearance as an actor', opts for 'the suppression of any fixed identity',[17] which is perhaps the only course of action open to someone in a thoroughly 'rotten' social totality. While Hamlet reflects critically on such values through play, like Hal, he ultimately does what is expected of him. Thus, because it reflects a realisation that one is not autonomous, the comedy of automatism is dark. The 'pregnant' (II. 2. 206) nonsense of Müller's remarkable rewrite is sensitive to the frustration of one who is forced to play out a role accepted only in bad faith. Müller's Hamlet exclaims:

> WIE EINEN BUCKEL SCHLEPP ICH MEIN SCHWERES
> GEHIRN
> ZWEITER CLOWN IM KOMMUNISTISCHEN FRÜHLING
> SOMETHING IS ROTTEN IN THIS AGE OF HOPE.[18]

The visionary intelligence of the Renaissance melancholic is comically physicalised as a clown's insufferable burden. For Müller, Hamlet's foray into the depths of his own psyche is clearly quixotic. By refusing to take itself seriously, exposing the self-destructive tendencies inherent in a purely instrumental, purposeful form of reason, and by foregrounding the limitations of human knowledge, *Hamlet* clears the way for the radically new modes of understanding furnished by folly. In this play, thought liberates itself from *doxa*, from the received account of what is rational, through a discourse that is located on the extreme edge of the reasonable world: namely, the discourse of folly.

6.3 Here's Fine Revolution

With the possible exception of the balcony scene in *Romeo and Juliet*, the Graveyard scene is the most frequently invoked and commonly parodied scene in the whole of Shakespeare.[19] Because it offers an interlude in which plebeian characters reflect on the dominant values of society, includes the skull of a dead jester and quite probably employs images drawn from *Praise of Folly*,[20] folly takes centre stage in this culturally ubiquitous scene. If the Ghost might be said to act as a Chorus, or 'a retributory voice of conscience' ('Introduction', *NDSS*, 7, p. 26) – one that peddles an account of what should happen – here, workers provide an alternative history, which is rooted in time-wasting discourse.

This scene, in particular, stages the question that Ernesto Grassi and Marisella Lorch consider to be one of the key questions posed by fool-literature from Erasmus to Cervantes: namely, is not 'the formal thought of analytical philosophy nothing but insanity [...] since it involves an absolute removal from objective reality'?[21] *Hamlet* clearly casts a critical gaze over everyday conceptions of rationality; in this scene – and, indeed, in the play as a whole – time-wasting discourse offers a deft parody of the language of intention. Foregrounding the similarities between comical quibbling and philosophical disputation, between the serious and the comic, Hamlet exclaims 'How absolute the knave is!' (V. 1. 129–34), after his disputation with the Gravedigger, who turns out to be something of a Socratic questioner:

> We must speak by the card or equivocation will undo us. By the Lord, Horatio, this three years I have took note of it, the age is grown so picked that the toe of the peasant comes so near the courtier he galls his kibe.
>
> (129–34)

Voltaire's pious categorisation of *Hamlet* as one of literary history's 'monstrous farces' on the grounds that '[A] grave is dug on the stage; some grave-diggers, holding skulls in their hands, make bad puns worthy of their sort; to their abominable scurrilities, Prince Hamlet makes nonsensical replies that are no less disgusting' is inaccurate in one crucial respect.[22] Although there are certainly plenty of puns and scurrilities in this scene, these peasants, Hamlet implies, use hair-splitting distinctions and detect evasive ambiguities of utterance just as well as any 'courtier'.

In fact, the patter between the two workmen, a mock-philosophical dialogue, makes the paradox of reason's desire for clear-cut analytical truths manifest; such definitions, they imply, are at odds with the messiness of reality:

SECOND MAN: The crowner hath sat on her and finds it Christian burial

GRAVEDIGGER: How can that be unless she drowned herself in her own defence?

SECOND MAN: Why 'tis found so.

GRAVEDIGGER: It must be *se offendendo*. It cannot be else. For here lies the point: if I drown myself wittingly, it argues an act, and an act hath three branches – it is to act, to do, to perform. Argal, she drowned herself wittingly.

(V. 1. 4–12)

As in a revenge tragedy, in which the act of revenge is delayed, the facts of the matter do not correspond with the official version of events. 'Is this [the] Law?' (21), asks the Straight Man, evidently unconvinced by the Gravedigger's mock-legal disputation, to which the latter knowingly replies: 'Ay, marry is't. Crowner's 'quest law' (22). The only 'truth' to be extrapolated from this corrupt version of the law is the fact that the rich have the privilege or 'countenance' (27) to do what they will. The Gravedigger inappropriately appropriates both legalistic discourse and its formal 'quiddities' (V. 1. 94) – the play, after all, blurs any possible distinction between acting, doing and performing. He makes divisions where there are none. His malapropisms – '*se offendendo*' and 'Argal' (for *se defendendo* [self-defence] and *ergo*, respectively) – make a mockery of what George Puttenham calls the legal profession's 'peevish affectation of words'.[23] And so too, of course, does the grotesque implication that the coroner has literally sat 'on' Ophelia's corpse.

Shakespeare puts the rhetorical tendency to divide the world into conceptually palatable chunks into the mouths of 'good man delver' (14) and his mate; these plebeian characters 'gall' the 'kibe' of the great humanist rhetoricians as well as the courtiers. As Walter Kaiser contends, what 'the humanist spirit hated most was divisions and distinctions'; 'partition', he continues, 'was most commonly attacked or avoided in humanist oratory'.[24] But rather than refusing to follow 'common sophmisters and rhetoritians' and 'shew by definition what I am' (*PF*, p. 10), as Stultitia does, Shakespeare subverts the authority of otiose divisions and distinctions by travestying them.

Hamlet, after all, furnishes us with the most famous mockery of partition in Renaissance literature. Polonius comments that the players are:

> The best actors in the world, either for tragedy, comedy, history, pastoral, pastoral-comical, historical-pastoral, scene indivisible or poem unlimited. Seneca cannot be too heavy nor Plautus too light for the law of writ and the liberty.
>
> (II. 2. 333–36)

Although uttered with the punctilious earnestness that has become synonymous with this character, these divisions are every bit as absurd as Touchstone's. What Polonius is attempting to say – that the actors are very capable – is obscured by his very attempt at precise definition. The idea that they can adeptly play both classical tragedy and comedy emphasises the fluidity of acting, which contrasts with the pointless formalism of his partition, while the inclusion of the unclassifiable forms – 'poem unlimited' and 'scene indivisible' – further undermines his attempts at classification.

Yet Polonius problematises the paradoxical wisdom of folly, which is so integral to the play. After Hamlet informs him of the content of the satirical work he is reading,[25] which says that 'old men have grey beards, that their faces are wrinkled, their eyes purging amber and plumtree gum, and that they have a plentiful lack of wit' (II. 2. 193–96), he riddles: 'I hold it not honesty to have it thus set down. For yourself, sir, shall grow old as I am – if, like a crab, you could go backward' (298–301), Polonius comments in an aside: 'Though this be madness yet there is method in't' (201–202). He discerns 'a happiness that often madness hits on, which reason and sanity could not so prosperously be delivered of' (207–208). Because he takes a profound pride in his own sententious wisdom, Polonius is himself a fool in a pejorative sense, but it is he who utters this perfectly reasonable insight about the paradoxical wisdom of folly.

Hamlet's alienation from (and *of*) sensible values undermines the wisdom that the only thing one can know is that one knows nothing. As A. D. Nuttall writes of Hamlet and Polonius's digression on the imagined shapes of a certain cloud, which is one of the numerous 'tiny fool's plays' in the play, a production that Bell entitles '*The Clown Prince and Foolonius*':[26]

> Hamlet cruelly draws Polonius into warm, positive agreement and then hits him with the emergent truth that a cloud can be made to resemble anything we like. […] So Polonius is made a fool of, as the play *Hamlet* makes a fool of any critic who offers a single positive interpretation.[27]

The play suggests neither that folly provides a straightforward alternative to wisdom nor that all philosophical ideas are void from the outset. Rather, as Ryan writes:

> To grasp a Shakespeare play as fully as possible at any point in time is to recognize that its gaze is bent upon a vanishing point at which no reader or spectator can hope to arrive. Like the hat that the circus clown kicks out of reach every time he steps forward to pick it up, final comprehension of the play is indefinitely postponed by each act of interpretation.[28]

Due to the way in which *Hamlet* makes a mockery of any unequivocal standpoint, including the view that folly harbours a paradoxical wisdom, it audaciously implies that the serious world is nothing other than a game. And yet, like *The Winter's Tale*, it prefers not to endorse even this wisdom too seriously.

Like the rituals of quotidian life, games are time-limited and dependent upon repetition, which is 'one of the defining characteristics of play'.[29] Because they conspicuously refuse to play by the rules – murdering the rightful king; proceeding 'To post | with such dexterity to incestuous sheets' (I. 2. 156–57); transgressing the rules of primogeniture; and interring Polonius in a 'hugger-mugger' (IV. 5. 84) fashion – Gertrude and Claudius are outrageous. Hamlet contends that his stepfather's authority is assumed by comparing him to a mock king. Claudius is an actor in a pageant, 'A vice of kings' (96) and 'A king of shreds and patches' (99), who has stolen a prop;

he is 'A cutpurse of the empire and the rule | That from a shelf the precious diadem stole | And put it in his pocket' (96–99). The Prince's mother has been duped. Her 'hasty marriage' (II. 2. 57) to someone inferior is akin to an amateur gambler being deceived by a card counter: 'What devil was't | That thus hath cozened you at hoodman blind? (III. 4. 74–75), he asks Gertrude.

This imagery of card-play continues when Claudius says to Laertes that 'with a little shuffling, you may choose | A sword unbated and in a pass of practice | Requite him for your father' (IV. 7. 134–37). As with the related concern about the sort of veracity mimesis can create, the ironies generated by Claudius's attempts to literally 'poison in jest' (III. 2. 228) are as ambivalent as they are paradoxical. Shakespeare *dramatises* the transgression of the rules of a game. Every player or performer of a game must have knowledge of the game's limits and what is at stake. He thereby implies that it is desirable to play by the rules, while, simultaneously, estranging the everyday world by laying bare the fact that everyday life consists in the performance of certain roles. Perhaps with the Globe's motto in mind, Nietzsche writes: 'We have to improvise – all the world improvises its day. Let us proceed today as all the world does'.[30]

6.4 Your Fat King and Your Lean Beggar

Hamlet juxtaposes two models of human relations, one instrumental, one fanciful. The first sort consists of knowing one's place. In their prolix and grovelling acquiescence in the betrayal of their erstwhile friend, Rosencrantz and Guildenstern invoke the body politic, a notion that was already central to the Elizabethan World Picture and the burgeoning theories of absolutism:

GUILDENSTERN: We will ourselves provide.
Most holy and religious fear it is
To keep those many bodies safe
That live and feed upon your majesty.
ROSENCRANTZ: The single and peculiar life is bound
With all the strength and armour of the mind
To keep itself from noyance; but much more
That spirit upon whose weal depends and rests
The lives of many. The cess of majesty
Dies not alone, but like a gulf doth draw
What's near it with it; or it is a massy wheel
Fixed on the summit of the highest mount
To whose huge spokes ten thousand lesser things
Are mortised and adjoined, which when it falls
Each small annexment, petty consequence,
Attends the boisterous ruin. Never alone
Did the king sigh but with a general groan.

(III. 3. 6–23)

The assumption that those in authority have a natural, physical relation to their subjects is reconceived to imply that such a relationship is parasitical. The flatly conventional sentiment of this verse illustrates the dishonesty of decorous language. The allegorical figure of Fortune, scurrilously debased in Rosencrantz and Guildernstern's opening repartee with Hamlet, is invoked insincerely with ostensible sincerity; under the (unconvincing) guise of concern for their fellow subjects – they wish to 'keep those many bodies safe | That live and feed upon your majesty' –Rosencrantz and Guildenstern simply pursue their own advancement.

The second model of relations is based on the fact that death is a radical leveller, a fact not lost on the medieval painters and sculptors of *Totentanzen*.[31] Shakespeare's Richard II invokes this tradition when he realises, aghast, that

> [...] within the hollow crown
> That rounds the mortal temples of a king
> Keeps death his court, and there the antic sits,
> Scoffing at his state and grinning at his pomp.
>
> (III. 2. 160–63)

All creations, systems, people and societies end up as just as they start out. As the Anglican funeral service curtly puts it, they progress from 'earth to earth, ashes to ashes, dust to dust'. 'But age with his stealing steps', intones the Gravedigger in his cheerful appropriation of a courtly lyric,[32] '[...] hath shipped me into the land | As if I had never been such' (67, 69–70). Here, his language is not only without an instrumental *purpose*, but it is also *pointless* in the strongest sense of the word: it registers that all identity is transient. Since it suggests that all the systems, discourses and institutions that mould man's innermost desires and hopes are mutable, this cheerful lyric harbours a potentially revolutionary realisation.

Since it articulates an alternative to the logic of inheritance that governs Hamlet's actions in favour of a shared or common root, the earth, the Gravedigger's boast – 'There is no ancient gentlemen but gardeners, ditchers, and gravemakers; they hold up Adam's profession' (V. 1. 28–29) – is perhaps the most explicit formulation of the revolutionary conception of human relations. It alludes to John Ball's question: 'When Adam delved and Eve span | Who was then the gentleman'? And it seems that man comes from dust as well as returning to it; in the face of this fact, social divisions and class distinctions are absurd. Indeed, this sort of cyclical relationship between humans and matter, between worm and man, is already evident in Livy. The oracle predicts: 'which of you [...] shall first kisse your mother, he shal beare chiefe and soveraigne rule in Rome' (*NDSS*, 7, p. 81). Despite his foolish appearance, Brutus interprets this comment correctly and 'kiss[es] the earth, thinking with himself, that she was the common mother of all mortall men' (*NDSS*, 7, p. 81). It is he who later rules Rome.

Hamlet is astonished that, for all their decisive action, the military heroes of yesteryear have been reduced to earth: 'Why may not imagination trace the noble dust of Alexander till 'a find it stopping a bung-hole?' (192–93), to which Horatio replies: ''Twere to consider too curiously to consider so' (195). Hamlet then rephrases his realisation in seriocomic couplets:

> Imperious Caesar, dead and turned to clay,
> Might stop a hole to keep the wind away
> O, that that earth which kept the world in awe
> Should patch a wall t'expel the winter's flaw.
>
> (V. 1. 201–205)

By repeating his philosophical considerations in nonsensical rhymes, to a certain extent, Hamlet makes a mockery of death; for Indira Ghose, this sort of laughter is characteristic of 'the medieval mind', for which it 'marked one's triumph over the specious threat of evil and the illusion of death. It was a defence strategy against the human fear of dying, intended to expose its absurdity'.[33] Ironically, the supposed harbinger of modern subjectivity has a decidedly old-fashioned theory of laughter. Yet it is precisely this sort of humour that furnishes him with the estranged perspective required for truly philosophical speculation, for thought that 'goes beyond'.[34]

Discussing Hamlet's comment in the graveyard – 'And now my Lady Worm's – chapless and knocked about the mazard with a sexton's spade. Here's fine revolution an we had the trick to see't' (V. 1. 83–86) – Ryan contends:

> The strict historicist scholar will hasten to point out that the word 'revolution' must be construed here as a reference to the wheel of fortune or the whirligig of time, and that to impute our modern political meaning to it would be anachronistic. It would indeed, but it would also be perfectly in keeping with Shakespeare's profoundly anachronistic imagination.[35]

This type of future-orientated thought about the revolution of the times already has traces of the modern understanding of revolution in it; it acknowledges that all the structures, values and systems of the serious world, such as law, lordship and politics, are not set in stone, but rather are embodied in that most perishable of things, human flesh.

This is apparent in Hamlet's subversion of the King's straightforward questions about the location of Polonius's corpse:

KING: Now, Hamlet, where's Polonius?
HAMLET: At supper.
KING: At Supper! Where?

HAMLET: Not where he eats but where 'a is eaten. A certain convocation of politic worms are e'en at him. Your worm is your only emperor for diet. We fat all creatures else to fat us, and we fat ourselves for maggots. Your fat king and your lean beggar is but variable service, two dishes but to one table. That's the end!

KING: Alas, alas.

HAMLET: A man may fish with the worm that hath eat of a king and eat of the fish that hath fed of that worm.

KING: What dost thou mean by this?

HAMLET: Nothing but to show you how a king may go a progress through the guts of a beggar.

(IV. 3. 26–31)

Hamlet's outlandish image of politically savvy worms eating the verbose statesman is humorous precisely because of its absurdity. It perhaps inverts an analogous image in Montaigne: 'the heart and life of a mighty and triumphant emperor is but the break-fast of a *seely* little worme' (*E*, Book II, Chapter 8, p. 258). Through the pun on 'progress', Hamlet compares the elaborate ritual of a monarch's movement around the country houses of the nobility to the digestion and excreting of a fish by a beggar, while another pun serves to conflate the archaic sense of 'diet', which meant a meeting frequently of national importance between members of the aristocracy and royalty, with the familiar sense of 'diet' meaning the type of food one eats.[36] In his explanation of his riddle, he parodies syllogistic thought, a logical mode that is employed ironically by many of Shakespeare's wise fools.[37]

Hamlet's attempts at individuating the skulls – 'This might be the pate of a politician' (73–74) / 'This might be my Lord Such-a-One' (78) – are a little more than the 'pompous platitudes' based on 'the fear of the negation of identity in death' that Ghose considers them to be.[38] As the use of the indefinite article and the mock-title, 'Lord Such-a-One', implies, Hamlet's experience among the skulls involves a *reductio ad absurdum* – or, possibly, *ad nauseam* ('Dost thou think Alexander looked o'this fashion i'th' earth? [...] And smelt so? Pah!' [187–88, 190]) – of the compulsion to create clear-cut identities. Even when he is faced with something literally faceless, a skull conspicuously bereft of any distinguishing features, Hamlet assigns an identity and a profession to it.

Of course, the character that Hamlet fleshes out most vividly is the former Court Jester, Yorick. While the countless appropriations and parodies may have numbed the effect of this moment, its sheer strangeness should be emphasised:

HAMLET: Alas, poor Yorick. I knew him, Horatio. A fellow of infinite jest, of most excellent fancy. He hath bore me on his back a thousand times, and now how abhorred in my imagination it is. My gorge rises at it. Here hung those lips that I have kissed I know not how oft. Where be your jibes now – your gambols, your songs, your

> flashes of merriment, that were wont to set the table on a roar?
> Not one now to mock your own grinning, quite chapfallen.
>
> (V. 1. 174–84)

This astonishing moment, in which the ever-dead Yorick is vividly resurrected, offers an antic pastiche of the dramatist's profession of fleshing out historical or imaginary figures. Bates contends that in his tragedies, Shakespeare 'brings characters on to the stage who speculate on the denial of death that is implicit in any representation of it and on the fact that tragedy's consolatory power rests upon a falsification of life's grim realities'.[39] Put another way, what is so disarming about Shakespeare's tragedies is their mimetic impurity: they refuse to forget that they are fictions, which impart meaning and coherence to a confusing and, quite possibly, meaningless reality.

When he 'abjures' his 'potent art' (50), Prospero observes that 'graves at my command | Have waked their sleepers' (*The Tempest*, V. 1. 49). *Hamlet*, however, admits its own lack of mastery over its material; the play's admission of representation's impotence is expressed indeterminately, through its digressive, riddling seriocomic idiom, so that even *Hamlet*'s awareness of art's inability to affect the brute facts of existence is rendered light-hearted. This moment of mimetic vulnerability, in which an actor holds a skull by an open grave, has become iconic: paradoxically, it has endured.

6.5 Terrible Eloquence

> We assume unto our selves imaginarie and fantasticall goods, future and absent goods, which humane capacitie can no way warrant unto her selfe; or some other, which by the overweening of our owne opinion we falsely ascribe unto our selves; as reason, honour, and knowledge.
>
> —Montaigne (*E*, Book II, Chapter 7, p. 270)

In contrast to many of the plays so far considered, folly has been central to the critical afterlife of *King Lear*. On the one hand, absurdist readings and productions employ the pervasive presence of folly to bolster their argument that the play prefigures the meaningless universe of existentialism. And although this line of argument is most dominant in Cold War readings and performances of the play,[40] it is hardly new – as early as 1811, August Wilhelm Schlegel describes the play as wiping 'away all of humanity's outer and inner virtues, exposing its naked helplessness'.[41] On the other hand, redemptive readings are underpinned by a grander theological conception of folly.[42] When Lear becomes aware of his own folly and Cordelia's immense sacrifice – in the final count, it is she who gives him 'all' (II. 2. 248) – he is humbled; as R. V. Young writes:

> Interpreters have generally sought to show either that the tragic close evinces a redemptive possibility, notwithstanding its horror, or that

> Tate was right, that *King Lear* in facts subverts a Christian or even Enlightenment world view and anticipates the absurd universe of existentialism or postmodern materialism.[43]

Both readings, however, fail to perceive that *Lear* is, more any other Shakespearean tragedy, a play concerned with how meaning is generated – or, perhaps, fabricated.

The central paradox at work in the play, I contend, is that the very institutions, discourses and ideas that have the potential to liberate humankind from its 'naked helplessness' can also reduce them to a 'poor, bare, forked animal' (III. 4. 105–106). Indeed, part of what Frank Kermode terms the play's 'authorial savagery',[44] or what Jan Kott describes as its 'philosophical cruelty'[45] is surely connected with the realisation that, as Marlowe's Mephistopheles puts it, 'this is hell, nor am I out of it':[46] Shakespeare does not allow the reader the luxury of forgetting that evil is a direct consequence of social interactions, discourses and institutions.[47] Shakespeare does not allow the reader the luxury of forgetting that evil is a direct consequence of social values, discourses and institutions.

Edgar, after all, is not possessed by devils because of a malign, supernatural agent. Rather, because of his bastard brother's Machiavellian guile, this 'good, but dull boy' is forced to play the role of a possessed man, a 'bedlam' beggar (II. 2. 185). It is characteristic of *Lear's* bleak irony that Edgar simulates demonic possession in order to escape human evil. Yet his haunting lament, 'Tom's a-cold' (III. 4. 57, 81, 143, 169; IV. 1. 55),[48] is true, insofar as it voices the physical suffering of the insane who were 'whipped from tithing to tithing, and stocked, punished, and imprisoned' (III. 4. 129–30). This garbled utterance chillingly evokes the mad brutality of the serious, supposedly reasonable, world.

As Jonathan Bate shows, in part, at least, the play stages Montaigne's sceptical attack on the stoic denial of human suffering and its concomitant belief that 'reason is our highest faculty and a sign of the power of the human [...] subject'.[49] After all, the monsters in *Lear* are human, and the 'vast universal powers working in the world of individual fates and passions' that A. C. Bradley discerns are wholly absent,[50] while Jan Kott's argument that 'The theme of *King Lear* is the decay and the fall of the world'[51] misses the point too, for it tacitly assumes that the 'world' corresponds to what humankind wants the world to be. Rather, *Lear* exposes the 'decay and fall' of the systems with which humans explain and control the world. This analysis illustrates Shakespeare's seriocomic attack on the structures of calculation, philosophy and law. Moreover, by staging the futility of that all-too-human aspiration to possess 'imaginarie and fantasticall goods', I suggest that the play's profoundly uncomfortable "comedy of the grotesque" frustrates any assessment of the tragedy as offering a sublime aesthetic response to human suffering.

6.6 Reason in Madness

Deformity, Thomas Hobbes and Laurent Joubert agree,[52] is funny. But what the former calls the 'sudden glory'[53] of laughter occasioned by the realisation of one's superiority to someone or something deformed cannot be said to apply to the darker humour of *Lear*. For in this play, as Adorno writes of Beckett's *Endgame*, 'humour is salvaged [...] because [it] infect[s] the spectator with laughter about the absurdity of laughter and laughter about despair' (*NL*, 2, p. 253). And as G. Wilson Knight observes, 'there is humour that treads the brink of tears, and tragedy which needs but an infinitesimal shift of perspective to disclose the varied riches of comedy';[54] such is the laughter when, after his blinded father staggers on stage, Edgar finds stoic consolation in the fact that 'worse I may be yet; the worst is not | So long as we can say "This is the worst"' (IV. 1. 29–30). This black humour frustrates any assessment of the play that might consider it beautiful or sublime – not least because, if '*Sublime* carries in it such a noble vigour, such a resistless strength, which ravishes away the hearer's soul against his consent',[55] then the language of *Lear* is the language of earth-bound weakness. In this play, grand style is at best absurd and at worst grotesque.

In a chapter in *Aesthetic Theory* entitled 'On the Categories of the Ugly, the Beautiful and Technique', Adorno echoes a sentiment not entirely dissimilar to Edgar's pyrrhic self-consolation, suggesting that people view images of 'starving children [...] as documents of that beneficent heart that beats even in the face of the worst [*Ärgsten*], thereby promising that it is not the worst [*Ärgste*]' (*AT*, p. 64; ÄT, p. 79). And shortly before his punning on the superlative "worst", Adorno argues:

> Art must take up the cause of what is proscribed as ugly, though no longer in order to instigate it, mitigate it, or to reconcile it with its own existence through humour that is more offensive than anything repulsive. Rather, in the ugly, art must denounce the world that creates and reproduces the ugly in its own image, even if in this too the possibility persists that sympathy with the degraded will reverse the concurrence with degradation. (*AT*, p. 64)

Lear is concerned with the paradoxical way in which man can generate evils that go far beyond his capacity to explain or express them; but far from attesting to Shakespeare's inhumanity, his "authorial savagery", the play's ugliness displays to a proleptic sort of humanity: ugly art becomes a way of denouncing rather than forgetting an ugly reality. The problem with a redemptive conception of representation is that it implies that life can always 'be embellished, straightened or improved by art', which risks inculcating 'an invidious irresponsibility if not a callously *laissez faire* attitude towards suffering'.[56] In this respect, poetry is silenic: grand style, untouched by the agonies of existence, is ugly, whereas *Lear's* tortured nonsense and demotic discourse may neither be perfectly proportioned, nor sublime, but they are at least humane.

Lear is ugly mainly because of its refusal to pass pain off as anything other than pain. 'The grotesque', writes Kott, 'is a criticism of the absolute in the name of frail human experience'.[57] Consider Lear's encounter with Poor Tom, an encounter that epitomises the fact that, as Bate puts it, 'biology is an affront to rationalising philosophy':[58]

KING LEAR: Why, thou wert better in a grave than to answer with thy uncovered body this extremity of the skies. Is man no more than this? Consider him well. Thou ow'st the worm no silk, the beast no hide, the sheep no wool, the cat no perfume. Ha? Here's three on's are sophisticated; thou art the thing itself: unaccommodated man is no more but such a poor bare, forked animal as thou art. Off, off, you lendings: come unbutton here.
[*Tearing at his clothes, he is restrained by Kent and the Fool*]
Enter GLOUCESTER, with a torch

FOOL: Prithee, nuncle, be contented; 'tis a naughty night to swim in. Now a little fire in a wild field were like an old lecher's heart; a small spark, all the rest on's body cold: look, here comes a walking fire.

(III. 4. 99–107)

Although Lear's insight that man's mastery of the world is a consequence of his physical vulnerability is a fine example of how 'true things' may be conceived 'by what their mock'ries be' (*Henry V*, IV. 0. 53), that Edgar is only playing at being the 'thing itself' – not to mention, that he is playing this role within a drama – should not be forgotten.

Lear's realisation of the ostensibly authentic nature of 'unaccommodated man', the universal corporal vulnerability of humankind, is a consequence of an artful deception, which Edgar, doing his histrionic skills a disservice, later compares to a poorly executed painting, a 'daub' (IV. 1. 55). The crucial paradox is that even in this realisation Lear remains, to a certain degree, in error. His error is to assume that 'something must lie beneath the surface of appearance when surface was all there ever was'.[59] For this reason – and others that shall become apparent – the discourse of folly in this play cannot be wholly reduced to the comment that '*King Lear* states the basic ontological distinction of Erasmus's two follies: folly as true, genuine perception of the inner nature of human things, and madness as the false, distorted perception of it'.[60]

Rephrasing Stultitia contention that man is endowed with infinitely more 'Affection, than reason' (*PF*, p. 23) in a demonic key, the Fool counters Lear's comment with the suggestion that people are sustained by carnality alone; he 'presents an extraordinary image of the world as a dead body and of the life that survives as feebly posthumous flickerings of lust'.[61] The notion that suffering enables insight – 'When the mind's free, | The body's delicate' (III. 4. 11–12) – may be reassuring in a world characterised by plainly intolerable physical conditions, but, for two reasons, it is wrong. First, it skates over the fact that all ratiocination is contingent upon bodily needs, which is something that even Lear realises when he reflects: 'they are not men o'their words: they told me I was everything; 'tis a lie, I am not ague-proof' (IV. 6. 103–105). Second, it implies that man is animated by reason rather than the animal drives that the Fool believes to govern human behaviour.

Poor Tom's nonsense appeals to the King more than the reasonable advice of the Fool, Kent and Gloucester. To Lear's mind, he is a 'good Athenian' (III. 4. 176) and a 'Noble philosopher' (168):

KING LEAR: First let me talk with this philosopher:[*To Edgar*] What is the cause of thunder?
KENT: Good my lord,
Take his offer, go into the house.
KING LEAR: I'll talk a word with this same learned Theban: What is your study?
EDGAR: How to prevent the fiend, and to kill vermin.

(150–55)

A recurrent humanist criticism of scholastic philosophy was that it pursued pointless pseudo-problems; rather than attempting to fathom the 'common miracles' of life, such as the cause of 'laughter',[62] men of theory, as Erasmus's Stultitia seriocomically puts it, vainly seek to 'expounde *the causes of thunder*, of wyndes, of eclipses, and suche other inexplicable thynges, nothying doubting, as if they had crepte into natures bosome, or were of counsaile with the Goddes' (*PF*, p. 77 [my emphasis]).[63]

Of course, the irony at work in this scene is that posing this hitherto theoretical question about the 'cause of thunder' is manifestly relevant to those stranded on the heath. The desire to make sense of the universe by causal logic and to control it by creating conceptual systems is of pressing importance to the play as a whole. At the close of Lear's mock trial of his daughters, playing the role of the judge, he rules: 'let them anatomize Regan; see what breeds about her heart. Is there any cause in nature that makes these hard hearts?' (III. 6. 73–75). Paradoxically, Lear's fantasy of scientific certainty through the vivisection of Regan to find out the 'cause' of her and Goneril's cruelty characterises him as insane. Such an inquiry is every bit as hardhearted as philosophies that exalt the rational at the expense of the passions. Even in his perverse fantasy of being imprisoned with his virtuous daughter, Lear envisages an impossible separation of thought from the body, aspiring to a god-like clear-sightedness. He tells Cordelia that 'we' will 'take upon's the mystery of things | As if we were God's spies. And we'll wear out | In a walled prison packs and sects of great ones' (V. 3. 16–19). His acceptance that they cannot aspire to absolute knowledge remains parasitical on the intentional forms of reason, premised on the kind of self-preservation that ultimately destroys the major characters of the play.

Cordelia's words of forgiveness are a denial of thinking in terms of cause and consequence. 'I know you do not love me, for your sisters | Have, as I remember, done me wrong. | You have some cause, they have not' (IV. 7. 72–74), says the semi-conscious King, to whom she 'lies beautifully and generously':[64] 'No cause, no cause' (75).[65] The implication is clear: what is remarkable in human nature is not icy reason's ability to fashion systems with which to gain imaginary mastery over things. Rather, it is the ability to go beyond this logic. What is remarkable in human nature is the ability to love inexplicably and stupidly. Indeed, Gloucester memorably deflates the mastery of intention, when he wryly observes of Poor Tom that 'He has some reason, else he could not beg' (IV. 1. 34).

6.7 The Excellent Foppery of Man

In *The Countesse of Pembrokes Arcadia*, from which Shakespeare drew the Gloucester plot, the virtuous Pamela inveighs against the seeming 'knowledge' of mankind, with which he 'puffeth' himself 'up' (*KJV*, I Corinthians 8. 1). She points to the paradox that 'while by pregancie of his imagination [man] strives for things supernaturall, [he] meanwhile loose[s] his own naturall felicitie' (*NDSS*, 7, p. 412). In *Lear*, the way in which man's faith in his own systems blinds him to the way things are is evidenced by Gloucester's bizarre response to Edgar's alleged plans for parricide. He immediately invokes the supernatural as a way of explaining what, of course, turns out to be Edmund's all too natural act of self-preservation:

> These late eclipses in the sun and moon portend no good to us. Though the wisdom of Nature can reason it thus and thus, yet nature finds itself scourged by sequent effects.
>
> (II. 2. 103–106)

Gloucester ascribes cosmic causality, a providential significance, to what is actually Edmund's manipulation of this tendency of thought: 'This is the excellent foppery of the world, that when we are sick in fortune, often the surfeits of our own behaviour, we make guilty of our disasters of the sun, the moon and the stars (118–21). Like the astronomer satirised in Sidney's *Apology for Poetry*, who falls into a 'ditch' because he is looking at the stars,[66] Gloucester's stargazing causes him to fall flat on his face. But what is really disarming about this is that Edmund's insights are eminently sensible. One of the main perpetrators of evil in the play offers an entirely rational self-justification.

It is perhaps surprising that the providential reading of *Lear* has had such mileage. Attempts in the play to ascribe divine purpose to this 'great stage of fools' (IV. 6. 179) are exposed as mere platitudes. When he reveals his identity to his brother, Edgar invokes the principle of an ordered universe:

> My name is Edgar and thy father's son.
> The gods are just and of our pleasant vices
> Make instruments to plague us:
> The dark and vicious place where thee he got
> Cost him his eyes.
>
> (V. 3. 167–71)

But, once again, he has got it entirely wrong. For Edgar, his father's blinding attests to the way in which human law ultimately reflects the will of the divine. Although his idea that the 'gods are just' is borne out by Goneril's and Regan's deaths moments later, this attempt to impose a theory on mere contingencies contributes to what Albany calls the 'Great thing of us forgot' (235): the pressing danger Lear and Cordelia are in. She is hanged partly because of bad timing and partly because of Albany and Edgar's protracted discussion, a consequence, perhaps, of their desire to foreclose a game in which all is still left to play for. After Cordelia's death, it is impossible to concur with his assessment that 'The gods are just'. It exemplifies, with savage irony, what Bates means when she writes: 'The fact that men wanted – even needed – to attribute meaning to the world didn't in the least make it meaningful'.[67] As Montaigne observes: 'Presumption is our naturall and originall infirmitie' (*E*, Book II, Chapter 7, p. 250).

6.8 A 0 Without a Figure

The primary way in which *homo economicus* has lent meaning to the universe is through quantification, numeration and calculation: although it is not possible to say what something is, numeration means that it is always possible to measure it and thus bring it within the compass of theory; Stultitia mocks natural philosophers that 'take vpon [themselves] to measure the sonne, the moon, the planets and theyr compasses, as it were by *ynchmeale, or drawne with a line*' (*PF*, p. 77). While quantification is necessary in the business of self-preservation, the action of the play is at pains to point out that when one attempts to quantify abstract factors in human relations – love, for instance – the consequences are disastrous. Demanding an objective measure of affection, Lear asks his daughters: 'Which of you shall we say doth love us most?' (I. 1. 51) and is blind to the fact that 'There's beggary in the love that can be reckoned' (*Anthony and Cleopatra*, I. 1. 15). This objectifying tendency of thought is made manifest when he refers to his youngest daughter as his 'best object' (I. 1. 215), a comment that, because of its blindness, exposes a pernicious ideology which falsely aligns love with possession.

Despite the way in which the two elder sisters use the same quantification against him, whittling down the number of his attendant knights, even when he is on the heath, delivering his vain incantation to the Fool and the thunder, Lear still figures affection in pecuniary terms:

> I tax not you, you elements, with unkindness.
> I never gave you kingdom, called you children;
> You owe me no subscription.
>
> (III. 2. 16–19)

This comment is ugly not only because of the sentiments it expresses, but also in the way in which it expresses them – 'Low and vulgar expressions extremely darken the beauty of *sublimity*'.[68] Cordelia's famous response to his test, 'nothing, my Lord', gives the lie to reckoning the love between parent and child, an absolute 'bond' (I. 4. 93).

Like Touchstone, Lear's Fool grasps the formal systems of the sensible world. He points out that the number zero is a cipher, requiring other numbers to signify: 'nothing will come of nothing' (I. 1. 90). Castigating the King's 'hideous rashness' (I. 4. 152), he comments: 'Now thou art a 0 without a figure; I am better than thou art now. I am a fool, thou art nothing' (I. 4. 182–84). He turns quantification against itself by mathematically *proving* that Lear has made a dire error in thinking of love as something that can be quantified. What the Fool formulates explicitly is implicit in Lear's demand that Goneril and Regan 'part betwixt' them his 'coronet' (I. 1. 140), since it is as physically impossible to split one 'coronet' into two and have it remain a usable crown as it is mathematically impossible to divide an '0 without a figure' and get a result of anything other than zero. The Fool reiterates this point moments later, suggesting that Lear is a 'shelled peascod' (190). This grotesque image both colloquially evokes the King's impotence, his physical vulnerability, and presages the important idea that 'Robes and furred gowns hide all' (IV. 6. 161) – there is always a frail body beneath the grandiose insignia of authority.

Lear's response to Cordelia's 'nothing' is proverbial: 'nothing will come of nothing', and this is emphasised when he reuses it in his terse dialogue with the Fool (see I. 4. 130). Rather than suggesting, as Erasmus does in the introduction to his *Adages*, that, owing to their ubiquity, there is some 'native power of truth' in 'proverbs' (*CWE*, 31, p. 17), *Lear*, like *The Winter's Tale*, implies that proverbial expressions can blind people to the particulars of their situation, providing a way of forcing the contingencies of experience into a predetermined formula. Instead of reflecting on what Cordelia means, he immediately resorts to the ossified wisdom of the ancients; far from being a folksy alternative to the grand theories of the intellectuals, proverbial wisdom is further attacked when, in an attempt to justify her treatment of her father, Goneril employs the Erasmian adage: 'Old fools are babes again' (I. 3. 20).[69]

Yet the repetition of the word 'nothing' not only gives the lie to proverbial wisdom, but also sets the play's dominant pattern of imagery, circularity, in motion, a pattern that plays a significant role in the play's exposure of the limitations of ratiocination. Noughts, crowns, wheels – not to mention, spectacles, eye-sockets, the 'operation of the orbs' (I. 1. 112) and female genitalia – are evocative of circles, a geometrical form that symbolises the whole and possess a formal coherence that is at odds with life. In the context of *Lear*, Booth contends that the 'image of the Wheel is, above all, finite' and it is, therefore, a 'deliberately inappropriate'[70] symbol in a play that conspicuously lacks the sense of an ending.

It is the Fool who first invokes Fortune's Wheel, advising Kent to 'Let go thy hold when a great wheel runs down a hill lest it break thy neck with following it; but the great one that goes up the hill, let him draw thee after'

(II. 2. 261–63), which is clearly echoed by Edmund's dying comment: 'The wheel is come full circle, I am here' (V. 3. 172). Because the Fool has already invoked this commonplace idea, it becomes unfixed and acquires the vital semantic indeterminacy characteristic of the discourse of folly. Moreover, his comment dialogises the providential account of history: to make sense of the senseless, Lear, Gloucester and Edgar all sincerely invoke a narrative that the Fool holds at a playful distance. Both Edmund's capitulation to the feeble determinism that he earlier ridicules and Lear's reflection on his tragic predicament – he is 'bound | Upon a wheel of fire that mine own tears | Do scald like moulten lead' (IV. 7. 46–49) – are subject to structural irony. Lear is denied the dignity that might make such an observation profound. And his moment of self-reflection cannot help but sound uncannily like a bombastic invocation of the Fool's insight.

6.9 This Prophecy Merlin Shall Make

The Fool's prophecy, like the Porter scene in *Macbeth* and the Graveyard Scene in *Hamlet*, displays an uncanny grasp of the themes, ideas and images present in the play's serious action; it 'pulls into focus the battle between utopian possibilities and dystopian realities that rages at the heart of the tragedy':[71]

> When priests are more in word than matter,
> When brewers mar their malt with water,
> When nobles are their tailors' tutors,
> No heretics burned but wenches' suitors:
> When every case in law is right
> No Squire in debt, nor no poor Knight;
> When slanders do not live in tongues,
> Nor cut-purses come not to throngs
> When usurers tell their Gold in the field,
> And bawds and whores do churches build,
> Then shall the realm of Albion
> Come to great confusion:
> Then comes the time, who lives to see't,
> That going shall be used with feet.
> This prophecy Merlin shall make, for I live before his time.
>
> (III. 2. 79–96)

The notion of being 'more in word than matter' recalls two central concerns of the play: first, the discrepancy between what Goneril and Regan 'profess' (I. 1. 72) and how they treat their father. Second, the King's folly, his desire to 'retain the name and all th'addition to a king' (I. 1. 136), which makes him recall the proverbial 'Tragedy King', an expression which Erasmus glosses as applying to 'a proud and pompous man, or to one who is a king in name alone but has little power' (*CWE*, 33, p. 26). Next, the image of inversion, 'when nobles are their tailors' tutors', reiterates the suggestions made by Poor Tom, Kent and Lear, which evoke the histrionic nature of the normal world, where everyday clothing is nothing but a costume or disguise.

When Kent insults Oswald by saying 'a tailor made thee' (II. 2. 53–54), what he means is that Oswald's authority is improvised – no less than the authority of the Justice Lear rails against, or the judicial clout of the Fool and Madman in the mock-trial in the hovel. The imagery of 'wenches' suitors' being 'burnt' by venereal disease prefigures both Lear's misogynistic description of female genitalia ('there is the sulphurous pit, burning, scalding, stench, consumption!' [IV. 6. 124–25]) and Edgar's comments about the 'vicious place' from whence his brother came.

In short, the Fool builds the concerns of the sensible world into his nonsense prophecy; crucially, this soliloquy, which, like the Chorus in *Henry V*, is found only in the Folio, ultimately subverts its ostensible function: it conspicuously fails to let the audience know what the Fool really thinks. Yet it does generate dialogism, for it offers an interlude that sets the play's ostensibly solid and serious ideas and identities spinning, dissolving their significance in comic indeterminacy. It philosophises through paradox; as Prentki observes: 'It is in the contradiction between what humanity is and what it has the capacity to imagine that the fool finds the space in which to play with the irony inherent in the human condition'.[72] This prophecy operates in a way not altogether different from Cordelia's, Kent's and Edgar's recurrent asides, which use the liberties of aesthetic semblance to comment upon the action in which they are embroiled. And it thereby holds the 'horror' (V. 3. 262) of the action at arm's length for a moment.

Allen R. Shickman convincingly shows that the Fool would originally have delivered this prophecy to a mirror, evoking the 'iconography of Prudence, who, in addition to bearing a glass, often wears the mask of an old man behind her head to signify the wisdom of the years with its ability to look both forward and backwards'.[73] While the irony of the Fool invoking the allegorical figure of Prudence is lost on Shickman, the way in which the prophecy looks both forwards and backwards warrants comment.

The prophecy avoids talking about the madness of the purposeful world in the systematic language of reason. Instead, it uses material from the world of reason, which the play exposes as dangerously irrational, to create a prophecy of a prophecy, a prophecy that remains impossible to grasp in today's terms; it is detached from the world but fashioned out of material drawn from its historical situation. In this respect it is realistic. It would be too reassuring to suggest that it is a consequence of the supra-rational 'metaphysical inspiration'[74] of Christian ecstasy, since the play operates by 'interpolat[ing] into a universe that's beyond man's control little worlds of his own devising, and it is this which confers on the play the power of a god'.[75]

This nonsense prophecy liberates the play from the argument that it exhibits the same drive for mastery over things as the intentional discourses to which *Lear* gives the lie. With caustic irony on the part of the playwright, murder is, after all, referred to as 'man's work' (V. 3. 40). The prophecy offers an enigmatic glimpse of a future in which life is not at the mercy of reason's dishonourable intentions, evoking a time of 'confusion' in which reason is reconciled with the senselessness of its compulsion to make sense of things. Despite being narrated by a spouter of nonsense, More's *Utopia* is clearly ordered and, like the Fool's prophecy, its constitutive contrast is between the world as it is and the world as it could be, although this realm of 'if' is, of course, a utopia or 'no-place'. Even this sort of conceptual coherence is absent from the Fool's prophecy. From a time in the distant past, he predicts a prophecy that 'Merlin shall make' in the mythological past of an equivocal future of 'great confusion', a future, in other words, that is different but not perfect. A few years after *Lear* was first performed, the *King James Bible* annotates Chapter 2 of Isaiah as depicting '*The great confusion which commeth by sin*'. In any case, the fool predicts his future utopia or dystopia in a performance. This prophecy of a prophecy actually happens in the present, and because it is voiced on stage, in the here and now, there is always the implicit suggestion that it will be reiterated in future performances.

Ultimately, this anachronistic jumbling of timescapes confounds the clock-time, upon which theoretical man's systems and the world of work depend, while simultaneously giving the lie to the cyclical account of time, with its emblems of Fortune's Wheel and its recurrent festivals, which Barber, Laroque and Bakhtin are wont to sentimentalise. Not least because it is 'dreaming on things to come' ('Sonnet 107', 2) in a play that otherwise implies that circumstances dictate characters' innermost desires – 'Men are as the time is' (V. 3. 31–32) – the Fool's prophecy is, like all great poetry, revolutionary nonsense. Far from being 'without hope',[76] the Fool, amidst the horrors of the heath, hopes for a radically new, absolutely unpredictable future, an enigmatic and tantalising future – or rather, future of a future – that is viewed as much through a darkened glass now as it was when it was first performed. Paradoxically, while the revolutionary and revelatory potential of his nonsense dies with him, this thwarting of the possibility that things could be different – that 'Humanity' may one day not 'perforce prey on itself | Like monsters of the deep' (IV. 2. 50–51) – is performed over and over again.

6.10 Let Us Deal Justly

The final aspect of this play's pervasive attack on systems and the assumptions they create is *King Lear*'s attack on the law. What Paul A. Cantor writes in his detailed consideration of the relationship between natural law and human law resonates with what I have argued about the dangers of trying to force things to make sense: 'In Lear's monumental self-assurance as a reigning monarch, he had always assumed that the political order is rooted in the natural, that nature supports human justice'.[77] For Nietzsche, as for Montaigne, the central misapprehension that underlies systematic knowledge is precisely this 'self-assurance':[78] the assumption that the way things are corresponds to the way that human theories order them; as Folly puts it: 'eche man is made a foole in his own wisdome' (*PF*, p. 107).

That 'the play is structured around four attempted acts of justice' is nothing new,[79] but the relation of folly to this structural and thematic trope has not been considered, despite the fact that the opening love-trial is pure folly. Not only does Lear stage 'an interlude with himself as the chief actor',[80] but this serious scenario also has a decidedly 'comic aspect'.[81] Lear's second trial of his daughters, found only in the Quarto, is full of bitterly ironic comic incongruity. To his mind, the naked and shivering Poor Tom is a 'robed man of justice' (III. 6. 36) and the Fool his 'yoke-fellow of equity' (37). They both play along with his second interlude:

EDGAR: Let us deal justly.
Sleepest or wakest thou, jolly shepherd?
Thy sheep be in the corn;
And for one blast of thy minikin mouth,
Thy sheep shall take no harm.
Pur, the cat is gray.
KING LEAR: Arraign her first; 'tis Goneril – I here take my oath before this honourable assembly – she kicked the poor King her father.
FOOL: Come hither, mistress: is your name Goneril?
KING LEAR: She cannot deny it.
FOOL: Cry you mercy, I took you for a joint-stool.
KING LEAR: And here's another, whose warped looks proclaim what store her heart is made on. Stop her there! Arms, arms, sword, fire! Corruption in the place! False justicer, why hast thou let her 'scape?
EDGAR: Bless thy five wits!

(III. 6. 40–56)

Only a madman could think it possible to impose order ('deal justly') in this situation. Perhaps this is why Poor Tom's pregnant nonsense is interspersed with the performative utterances – blessing, taking oaths and dealing impartially – of the rational world. Lear's ridiculous accusation that the mock-court is corrupt is later echoed in his encounter with Gloucester, in which he realises that the 'authority' he had thought to be innate is not the consequence of natural laws, but an expedient fiction perpetuated by those in power for purely self-serving ends: 'A dog's obeyed in office' (IV. 6. 150, 152–55). The time when human and natural law correspond, 'When every case in law is right' (III. 1. 85), must remain for the present an unlikely hope in a foolish tale. What is darkly comic is that Lear views the abject beggar, one wronged by the law, as one who has corrupted the ideal of law, abusing his power out of self-interest.

In this respect, the scene is a microcosm of the play as a whole. By staging a system *in extremis*, it exposes the fact that conceptual systems do not so much make sense of how things *are*, but rather how things can be *theorised*.

Nonetheless, the pragmatic argument that these systems are necessary fictions is evident; after his daughters have whittled the number of his knights down to nothing, Lear justifies their existence on purely theoretical grounds:

> O, reason not the need! Our basest beggars
> Are in the poorest thing superfluous;
> Allow not nature more than nature needs,
> Man's life is cheap as beast's.
>
> (II. 2. 452–56)

He implies that fictions of certainty constitute what is special about man, what makes him different from a 'beast'. Although Cantor argues that humans 'need to establish conventions in order to fulfil their natures',[82] the play implies that what is important is to retain a critical awareness of the holes in even the most watertight systems – to retain, in other words, something of the wise fool's dazzling detachment from explicit values.

Insofar as Lear substitutes inanimate objects for people and empty words for feeling, this trial is child's play – as the Fool's ironic apology to the 'joint-stall' implies. Goneril is tried for subjecting her father to slapstick indignity. He swears – quite contrary to what has been shown – that 'she kicked the poor King her father'. This actually denigrates his suffering, reimagining her callous indifference as a festive inversion gone too far – such carnival violence is present in the sources. Her greatest crime is that she has violated the rules of his earlier game, which allowed him to play at being a king. This is not the only place in the play where something of the comic violence of *The Comedy of Errors* resurfaces and frustrates any sort of tragic grandeur: Kent trips Oswald and then suffers the indignity of the stocks; Goneril plucks the defenceless Gloucester's beard, adding insult to the injury of the blinding that is about to take place. This is compounded by the cruel humour derived from Gloucester's blinding: Goneril quips, 'let him smell | His way to Dover' (III. 7. 92–93), while on Dover beach, her father quibbles: 'Your eyes are in a heavy case, your purse in a light, yet you see how this world goes' (IV. 6. 143–44).

6.11 Thy Life's a Miracle

The blinded Earl's pratfall is by far the most gleefully inappropriate moment of 'sudden glory'; any sort of dignity, gleaned from this paradoxically self-determining action of self-annihilation, is denied him. His attempted suicide, a demonic inversion of the idea of a leap of faith, is a piece of ill-timed slapstick, which Kott aptly describes as a 'pantomime'.[83] Assuming the persona of a peasant, Edgar insists to his father that he was tempted by a devil to jump. He describes it thus:

> As I stood here below methought his eyes
> Were two full moons. He had a thousand noses,

Horns welked and waved like the enraged sea.
It was some fiend.

(IV. 6. 69–71)

What Gloucester's fall and resurrection make clear is that actors are an author's automatons – as Bates argues, drama, like Freud's grandson, plays the '*fort*, *da*!' game. Characters are killed, their fictive existence obliterated, only to be resurrected and to take their final bows and do it all again in the next performance, a fact that is famously acknowledged in *Julius Caesar* when Brutus asks: 'How many times shall Caesar bleed in sport?' (III. 1. 115).

The 'fiend' to whom Edgar refers, a monster capable of creating and destroying, could be seen as a demonic double of the author; a far cry from the urbane haplessness of Chaucer's Sir Topas, Shakespeare's phantasmagorical alter ego is monstrously ugly, like something out of Revelations. The mirthless irony is, of course, that although Gloucester is convinced that his 'life's a miracle' (IV. 6. 55), his heart nonetheless 'Burst[s] smilingly' (V. 3. 198) when Edgar reveals his true identity to his father later in the act. Gloucester may have come to realise the error of his ways and the absurdity of the values that he had hitherto cherished, but this makes no difference. He dies.

It is, moreover, no 'miracle' that he is revived onstage, since, like Prospero, the playwright possesses the capacity to resurrect the dead. But this magic is a consequence of the dramatist's control over his materials, an absolute control over things that man can only ever have in that most artificial of things: art. Lear's response to what appears to be the cosmic injustice of it all, the brute fact that 'in this world there is no poetic justice', [84] underscores this fact:

And my poor fool is hanged. No, no, no life!
Why should a dog, a horse, a rat have life
And thou no breath at all? O thou'lt come no more,
Never, never, never, never.

(V. 3. 304–307)

Lear's dying hope – 'Look there, look there!' (309) – is an illusion. And for all his demands, injunctions and conjurations, he cannot bring his daughter back to life. Death, it transpires, can no more be straightened out than it can be given cosmic significance – as Aeschylus's Prometheus reflects, 'Craft [*technê*] is far weaker than necessity'.[85] What art can do, however, is express the dreadful consequences of theoretical, magical, instrumental and quantitative ways of thinking and how such ways of understanding help inculcate a 'Humanity' that 'must perforce pray upon itself, | Like monsters of the deep' (IV. 2. 50–51).

* * *

For Adorno, 'great artworks, as destructive works, have also retained the power to destroy the authority of their success. Their radiance is dark; the beautiful permeates the negativity, which appears to have mastered it'

(*AT*, p. 66). This remarkable idea is borne out by *Lear*, a tragedy that destroys the 'success' of an aesthetics based on mastery, decorum and correct proportion. Indeed, the common assumption that shaping experience into pleasing forms is an unequivocally positive thing is exposed as, at best, naïve and, at worst, deeply suspect.

The play's sceptical assault upon the systems of the reasonable world clearly belies the affirmative assumptions of Bradley's influential assessment of the play:

> The final and total result is one in which pity and terror, carried perhaps to the extreme limits of art, are so blended with a sense of law and beauty that we feel at last, not depression and much less despair, but a consciousness of greatness in pain, and of solemnity in the mystery we cannot fathom.[86]

The worst, it seems, is not the worst so long as the audience is charmingly affected by the horrors of the play. Yet *Lear* conspicuously fails to conform to the laws of aesthetic proportion and it lacks tragic seriousness – no 'solemnity' can be adduced from Gloucester's pratfall. The 'greatness in pain' that Bradley celebrates petrifies the abject realities of suffering and death – the shitting, bleeding agony of real life – into something aesthetically palatable, whereas *Lear* does not recoil – like Conrad's Kurtz – from the horrors perpetrated in the name of certainty. Rather, with a desperate and primal urgency, this tragedy's ugliness denounces the certainties that reason fashions. And herein lies *King Lear*'s disarming beauty, its terrible eloquence. If the play says anything clearly at all, it is that the all too human tendency to grasp for certainties is, more often than not, merely clutching at straws.

Notes

1. *Heiner Müller: Werke 4*, ed. by Frank Hörnigk (Frankfurt: Suhrkamp, 2001), pp. 551–554 (p. 553) [the irregular capitalisation is Müller's]; 'Shortly before the third cock's crow a clown will tear the fool's cap off the philosopher' (*Hamlet Machine and Other Texts for the Stage*, ed. and trans. by Carl Webber (New York: Performing Arts Journal Publications, 1984), p. 53.
2. *Shakespeare's Great Stage of Fools* (Basingstoke: Palgrave, 2011), p. 101.
3. James Calderwood and Frank Kermode provide extensive analyses of the use of oxymora and puns in *Hamlet* (see *To Be and Not To Be: Negation and Metadrama in Hamlet* (New York: Columbia University Press, 1983), pp. 64–80 and *Shakespeare's Language* (Harmondsworth: Penguin, 2000), pp. 101–108).
4. *Play in a Godless World: The Theory and Practice of Play in Shakespeare, Nietzsche and Freud* (London: Open Gate Press, 1999), p. 142; Kermode points out that it is an example of hendiadys, a figure of speech in which paired words denote a single idea that can 'take us to the heart of the play' (*Shakespeare's Language*, p. 101).
5. Jacques Lacan, 'Desire and the Interpretation of Desire in *Hamlet*', *YFS*, 55 (1977), 30–51 (p. 33).

6. A. D. Nuttall, *Shakespeare the Thinker* (London and New Haven: Yale University Press, 2007), p. 393.
7. *Free Will: Art and Power on Shakespeare's Stage* (Manchester: Manchester University Press, 2013), p. 207.
8. Terence Hawkes, *That Shakespeherian Rag: Essays on a Critical Process* (London: Methuen, 1986), p. 94.
9. *Dogg's Hamlet*, Tom Stoppard's truncated *Hamlet*, boils the play down to a 15-minute sequence, which, according to R. A. Foakes, 'reveals it to be a farce' (*Hamlet Versus Lear: Cultural Politics and Shakespeare's Art* (Cambridge: Cambridge University Press, 1993), p. 42); Heiner Müller's astonishing appropriation, 'Die Hamletmaschine', enlists ideas of absurdity and aporia latent in the original in order to deconstruct conservative ideas about *Hamlet*; Howard Barker's rewrite is attuned to the riddling ambiguities of the original and centres on Gertrude's phatic 'cry' (see 'Gertrude—The Cry' in *Gertrude—The Cry and Knowledge and a Girl* (London: Calder, 2002), pp. 9–93).
10. See Peter Davison, 'The Comedy of *Hamlet*', in *Hamlet: Contemporary Critical Essays*, ed. by Martin Coyle (Basingstoke: Palgrave, 1992), pp. 37–46; Ann Thompson, 'Infinite Jest: The Comedy of *Hamlet*, Prince of Denmark', *SS*, 56 (2003), 93–104; Phyllis Gorfain uses zoological theories of play and Bakhtin in her reading of *Hamlet* (see 'Towards a Theory of Play and the Carnivalesque in *Hamlet*', in *Shakespeare and Carnival: After Bakhtin*, ed. by Ronald Knowles (Basingstoke: Palgrave, 1998), pp. 152–76).
11. Despite the promising comparison, Ivan Turgenev's study of *Hamlet* and *Don Quixote* focuses on considering what universal 'types' each character represents and pays no direct attention to the nature of folly in these texts (see *Hamlet and Don Quixote*, trans. by Robert Nicholls (London: Hendersons, 1930), p. 8); Robert Weimann points out that Hamlet's madness 'attracts suspicion' and considers it in the light of theatrical traditions of staging madness (*Shakespeare and the Popular Tradition in the Theater*, trans. by Robert Schwartz (Baltimore, MD: Johns Hopkins University Press, 1979), p. 128; and Tim Prenki augments these arguments, adding philosophical insights (see *The Fool in European Theatre: Stages of Folly* (Basingstoke: Palgrave, 2012), pp. 96–110). Bell examines the Prince's engagement with folly (see *Great Stage*, pp. 100–110); Michael Groves argues along much the same lines, albeit in a more measured tone (see 'Hamlet as a Fool', *HamS*, 4 (1982), 72–88); see also Harry Levin, 'The Antic Disposition', in *Shakespeare: Hamlet*, ed. by John Jump, Casebook Series (London: Macmillan, 1968), pp. 122–136 and Dimiter Daphinoff, 'Shakespeares Narren' in *Der Narr: Beiträge zu einem Interdisziplinären Gespräch* (Freiburg: Universitätsverlag, 1991), pp. 57–71 [p. 68]).
12. *Shakespeare*, 3rd edn (Basingstoke: Palgrave, 2002), p. 169.
13. 'Desire and the Interpretation of Desire', p. 33.
14. Ghose, p. 1005.
15. In early modern English, 'engineer' could signify both 'a person who makes engines, structures and systems' and 'an author or designer of something; a plotter, a schemer' (*OED*., definitions, nos. 1 and 5a).
16. *Laughter: An Essay on the Meaning of the Comic*, trans. by Cloudesley Breton and Fred Rothwell (Rockville, MD: Manor, 2008), p. 8.
17. Prentki, p. 98, p. 99.
18. *Heiner Müller: Werke 4*, p. 542. Müller writes in capitals, does not punctuate, and starts writing in English as quoted; the full translation is: 'I'M LUGGING

MY HEAVY | BRAIN | LIKE A HUNCHBACKED CLOWN | NUMBER TWO IN THE SPRING OF COMMUNISM | SOMETHING IS ROTTEN IN THIS AGE OF HOPE' (Webber, p. 53 [translation modified]).

19. See Ghose, pp. 1004–1006.
20. *Ibid.*, pp. 1003–1018.
21. *Folly and Insanity in Renaissance Literature* (New York: Centre for Medieval and Early Renaissance Studies, 1986), p. 86.
22. 'Dissertation sur la trágedie ancienne et moderne', quoted in Ghose, p. 1003.
23. *The Arte of English Poesie,* ed. by Gladys Dodge Willcock and Alice Walker (Cambridge: Cambridge University Press, 1935), p. 141.
24. *Praisers of Folly: Erasmus, Rabelais, Shakespeare* (London: Victor Gollancz, 1964), p. 42.
25. Peter G. Bietenholz has speculated that this is a reference to Erasmus's *Praise of Folly*, which describes old age in comparable terms; see *Encounters with a Radical Erasmus: Erasmus' Work as a Source of Radical Thought in Early Modern Europe* (Buffalo: University of Toronto Press, 2009), p. 260.
26. Bell, p. 102.
27. *Shakespeare the Thinker*, p. 201.
28. *Shakespeare*, p. 175.
29. Bates, p. 171.
30. *The Gay Science with a Prelude in Rhymes and an Appendix of Songs*, trans. by Walter Kaufmann (New York: Vintage, 1974), p. 95.
31. For a thorough analysis of *Hamlet* and the iconographic and literary tradition of the *danse macrbre* in late medieval and early modern Europe, see Sophie Oosterwijk, '"Alas, poor Yorick": Death, the fool and the *danse macabre*' in Stefanie Knöll, ed., *Narren – Masken – Karneval: Meisterwerke von Dürer bis Kubin aus der Düsseldorfer Graphiksammlung: Mensch und Tod* (Regensburg: Schnell and Steiner, 2009), pp. 20–33.
32. Annabel Patterson, *Shakespeare and the Popular Voice* (Oxford: Blackwell, 1989), p. 103.
33. Ghose, p. 1004.
34. *Das Prinzip Hoffnung*, 3 vols (Frankfurt: Suhrkamp, 1959; repr, 1985), I, p. 3.
35. 'Here's fine revolution': Shakespeare's Philosophy of the Future', *Essays in Criticism*, 63 (2013), 105–126 (p. 124).
36. *OED*.
37. The syllogism is a figure of analytic reason that Stultitia finds distasteful; see *PF*, p. 48.
38. 'Jesting with Death', p. 1011.
39. Bates, p. 210.
40. Jan Kott's influential existentialist reading of the play ('*King Lear* or *Endgame*', in *Shakespeare: An Anthology of Criticism*, 1945–2000, ed. by Russ McDonald (London: Blackwell, 2004), pp. 174–191), along with the cold war productions of Grigori Kozintsev (*Korol Lir* 1971) and Peter Brook (1962), established the idea that Lear is an absurdist masterpiece *avant la lettre*; for an analysis of *Lear* in Jean Paul Sartre's criticism, see Hazel E. Barnes, 'Flaubert and Sartre on Madness in *King Lear*', *Philosophy and Literature*, 10 (1986), 211–221; and in light of the existentialist concept of an individual's self-determining "choice" see Jagannath Chakravorty, 'King Lear's 'Choice': An Existentialist Approach', *Poetica*, 4 (1976), 97–110. Stephen Booth emphasises the play's refusal to

'fulfil the generic promise inherent in a story' and argues that it implies that 'perception of pattern is folly' (*King Lear, Macbeth, Indefinition and Tragedy* (London: Yale University Press, 1983), pp. 14, 22), while R. A. Foakes argues that the increasing popularity of *Lear* in the second half of the twentieth century can be partly attributed to the bleak *Zeitgeist* of the Cold War era: see *Hamlet Versus Lear: Cultural Politics and Shakespeare's Art* (Cambridge: Cambridge University Press, 1993), esp. p. 42.

41. *Kritische Schriften und Briefe*, ed. by Edgar Lohner, 7 vols (Stuttgart: W. Kohlhammer, 1967–75), VI, p. 176.
42. Bradley famously writes: 'Should we not be at least as near the truth if we called this poem *The Redemption of King Lear*, and declared that the business of "the gods" with him was neither to torment him, nor to teach him a "noble anger", but to lead him to attain through apparently hopeless failure the very end and aim of life?' (*Shakespearean Tragedy*, 2nd edn (London: Macmillan, 1919 [1904]), p. 286); John Danby follows Bradley and reads the play in terms of a contrast between the Machiavellian idea of nature, invoked by Edmund, and a benevolent natural order (see *Shakespeare's Doctrine of Nature: A Study of King Lear* (London: Faber and Faber, 1948; repr. 1982)). Although Jonathan Bate's reading of *Lear's* anti-stoicism in the light of Montaigne goes some way to establishing the centrality of the 'wise fool' in Shakespeare's mature philosophical vision, it ultimately falls back on a redemptive reading, albeit a redemption though scepticism: 'it seems to me that in Shakespeare's strand of "wise fooling", a kind of divine history is smuggled back into the raw natural world of *Lear*' ('Shakespeare's Foolosophy', in *Shakespeare Performed: Essays in Honor of R. A. Foakes*, ed. by Grace Ioppolo (Newark: University of Delaware Press, 2000), pp. 17–33 [p. 26]); John X., Evans argues along comparable lines in 'Erasmus's Folly and Shakespeare's *King Lear*: A Study in Humanist Intertextuality', *Moreana*, 27 (1990), 3–23.
43. 'Hope and Despair in *King Lear*: The Gospel and the Crisis of Natural Law', in Jeffrey Kahan, ed., *King Lear: New Critical Essays*, Shakespeare Criticism, 33 (London: Routledge, 2008), pp. 253–277 (p. 253).
44. Kermode, p. 195.
45. Kott, p. 113.
46. Christopher Marlowe, *Dr Faustus* in *Christopher Marlowe:* The *Complete Plays*, ed. by Frank Romany and Robert Lindsey (Harmondsworth: Penguin, 2003), p. 356 [Scene 3, 78].
47. *The Demonic: Literature and Experience* (London: Routledge, 2013), p. 224.
48. The word 'cold' occurs more times in Lear than in any other play by Shakespeare; it and its variants appear 17 times in the *Conflated Text*.
49. Bate, p. 25.
50. Bradley, p. 248.
51. '*King Lear* or *Endgame*', p. 105.
52. *Treatise on Laughter*, trans. by Gregory David De Rocher (Tuscaloosa, AL: University of Alabama Press, 1980), p. 20.
53. *Treatise of Human Nature*, in *The English Works of Thomas Hobbes*, ed. by William Molesworth, 12 Vols (London: Bohn, 1839–1845; repr. Routledge, 1992), IV, p. 46.
54. *The Wheel of Fire*, p. 160.
55. Longinus [?],*An Essay upon the Sublime*, trans. by T. Leigh (Oxford: Leon. Lichfield, 1698), p. 3.

56. *Ibid.*, p. 179.
57. Kott, p. 104.
58. 'Shakespeare's Foolosophy', p. 27; '*King Lear* or *Endgame*', p. 104.
59. *Play in a Godless World*, p. iv.
60. Richard Strier, 'Against the Rule of Reason: Praise of Passion from Petrarch to Luther to Shakespeare to Herbert', in *Reading the Early Modern Passions: Essays in the Cultural Traditions of Emotion*, ed. by Gail Kern Paster, Katherine Rowe and Mary Floyd-Wilson (Philadelphia: University of Pennsylvania Press, 2004), pp. 23–42 (p. 23).
61. Fernie, p. 227.
62. Joubert, p. 17.
63. *Ibid.*, p. 17.
64. Bate, p. 29.
65. In *Leir*, Cordelia forgives him thus: 'O grieve not you, my Lord, you have no cause | Let not your passions move your mind a whit' (*NDSS*, 7, p. 367). Shakespeare amplifies the phrase 'No cause' and omits her advice to her father to retain his stoic fortitude.
66. *An Apology for Poetry*, p. 88.
67. *Play in a Godless World*, p. 49.
68. *An Essay on the Sublime*, p. 85.
69. The very same proverb is voiced by Erasmus's Stultitia and analysed in his *Adages* (see *PF*, p. 17; *CWE*, 31, p. 414). Furthermore, Lear's fool uses one of Erasmus's *Adages* in a particularly caustic put-down of his master at I. 4. 148–50; see Kermode, p. 187.
70. *Indefinition and Tragedy*, p. 13.
71. Ryan, 'Here's fine revolution', p. 108.
72. *The Fool in European Theatre*, p. 113.
73. 'The Fool's Mirror in *King Lear*', *ELR*, 21 (1991), 75–86 (p. 80).
74. Strier, p. 32.
75. Bates, p. 13.
76. Daphinoff, 'Shakespeares Narren', p. 66.
77. 'The Cause of Thunder: Nature and Justice in *King Lear*', in Jeffrey Kahan, ed. *King Lear: New Critical Essays*, pp. 231–252 (p. 231); strictly speaking, however, this assumption is also present in *Leir*:.

    Nay, if thou talke of reason, then be mute;
    For with good reason I can thee confute.
    If they, which first by nature's sacred law,
    Do owe me tribute of their lives;
    If they to whom I always have bin kinde,
    And bountiful beyond comparison;
    If they, for whom I have undone myself,
    And brought my age into extreme want,
    Do now reject, contemne, despise, abhor me,
    What reason moveth thee to sorrow for me?

    (NDSS, 7, p. 359)

78. See Bates, esp. pp. 42–83.
79. Cantor, p. 239.
80. Wilson Knight, p. 161.

81. *Ibid.*, p. 161.
82. 'The Cause of Thunder', p. 245.
83. '*King Lear* or *Endgame*', p. 113.
84. Enid Welsford, *The Fool: His Social and Literary History* (London: Faber and Faber, 1935; repr. 1968), p. 265.
85. Aeschylus, *Prometheus Bound*, in *Greek Tragedies 1: Aeschylus: Agamemnon, Prometheus Bound; Sophocles: Oedipus the King, Antigone; Euripides: Hippolytus*, ed. by Mark Griffith and others (Chicago: University of Chicago Press, 2013), pp. 65–113 (89) [L. 514].
86. Bradley, p. 279.

Epilogue

Sapere aude?

> Good sense affirms that in all things there is a determinable sense or direction (*sens*); but paradox is the affirmation of both senses or directions at the same time.[1]
>
> —Gilles Deleuze

A tension at the heart of this study has been how to provide a coherent account of the paradoxical wisdom of folly, without forcing such an essentially ephemeral phenomenon into the terms of good sense of which it is so devoutly critical. This is not least the case because Shakespeare's philosophy of folly, like Montaigne's *Essays*, proceeds without a methodology. In other words, this remarkable way of understanding lacks a predetermined formal structure. Indeed, the plays themselves make a mockery of the very footings upon which conventional, positivistic methodologies depend; the discourse of folly conspicuously lacks the rigorously delineated concepts, causal logic and clearly defined ends that one might associate with serious thought.

Shakespeare's 'true and lively knowledge'[2] consists of a sustained attack on – and estrangement of – philosophical and everyday certainties alike. It is primarily through folly's paradoxes and ironies that Shakespeare dissolves the crude dichotomies upon which received wisdom depends. Folly sets static identities, fixed categories and watertight concepts into play and exposes the inner contradictions in conventional ideas and traditional modes of understanding. Ultimately, it is through folly that Shakespeare stages the consequences of Nietzsche's Zarathustra's famous dictum, 'let that wisdom be false to us that brought no laughter with it', [3] for the philosophical potential of laughter lies in its ability to cut the pretentions of serious world down to size by exposing the hypocrisy and dogmatism of the purposeful world.

Although this study has sought to establish a sustained philosophy of folly in Shakespeare's works, it has not, of course, been possible to consider closely its role in every play. Nonetheless, the significance of folly in Shakespeare's collaborative plays, which have become a focal point of critical attention, is neither confined to Erasmus's walk-on role in *Sir Thomas More*, nor the fact that *Double Falsehood* is based on *Don Quixote*; rather, folly is closely bound to Shakespeare's disconcerting disavowal of authority and his famous capacity for Negative Capability. It is, moreover, not all that difficult to perceive how Mercutio's 'Queen Mab' speech presages the aesthetics of deformity discussed in Chapter Six or how a reading of *Troilus and Cressida* might corroborate my analysis of Shakespeare's self-critical historiography.

Shakespeare's critical attitude towards history, it transpires, is the cornerstone of his philosophical vision; it accounts not only for his deflation of the memorable deeds of medieval kings, but also for his mockery of worn out poetic tropes (and the ways of thinking that attend them) in the comedies and his interest in the tragic consequences of being hoodwinked by the past. In fact, the very notion of conventional wisdom is an oxymoron. Since it goes beyond the given and takes the audience *para doxa*, the discourse of folly is necessarily unconventional and unsure of itself. It retains a playful awareness that its peculiar wisdom might, after all, be mere nonsense. True philosophy inheres in playful estrangement. The paradoxical wisdom of folly in Shakespeare is neither limited to specific characters, nor is it simply a theme. Rather, mapping folly's erratic movement furnishes the reader with insight into at least four of the ways these plays understand the world and their place within it.

First, folly is keyed into the innately utopian inclination of cognition, the perennial tendency of 'imagination' to body 'forth | The forms of things unknown' (*Midsummer Night's Dream*, V. 1. 14–15), whereas philosophy has generally concerned itself with the interpretation of either the past or the present. Second, an awareness of folly fosters an appreciation of literature's affective power, a stubbornly pre-theoretical remainder that is close to the core of literature's appeal – Lear's distraught observation that Cordelia will 'come no more, | Never, never, never, never' (*King Lear*, V. 3. 306–307) expresses the desolation of immense personal loss with a primal eloquence and dramatic urgency that is impossible to match in a philosophical analysis of grief. Third, literature is comfortable with the fool's knowledge that even the grandest conceptual systems are transient: art, especially the temporal arts of drama and music, are best understood by fathoming their laws of motion, not by viewing them as allegories of the world in which they were conceived, which require decoding. Finally, an appreciation of Shakespeare's folly makes possible a fuller understanding of how irony provides a way of perceiving and engaging with the world.

'No epilogue, I pray you; for your play needs no excuse' (*A Midsummer Night's Dream*, V. 1. 340). To conclude anything too conclusive about Shakespeare's folly would be an act of folly, for it would gravely misconceive the vital indeterminacy of its paradoxical subject matter. Because it does not seek to sublate two discrete identities into one sense or 'direction', paradox is both a complex rhetorical figure and a sort of negative dialectics in miniature. Indeed, this study has examined a series of paradoxes. Quite apart from either the paradoxes associated with wise folly, considered in Chapters One and Three, or the rich contemporary context of thinking through paradox, examined in Chapter Two, my analysis of the plays in the final three chapters of this study revolves around three paradoxes. Shakespeare's paradoxical historiography retells historical events, even as it criticises the representation of history; the comedies imply that one should hope for a thoroughly unexpected and radically new future, whereas *Hamlet* and *King Lear* refuse to forget their separation from the brute facts of reality and create a profoundly anti-aesthetic aesthetics.

Instead of concluding with results and a clear-cut direction of study, I will draw to a close with a paradox, one that I think attests both to the way that paradoxes pull in two directions and how they beget other paradoxes. If one understands the process of Enlightenment to consist of 'the human being's emergence from his self-incurred minority',[4] Shakespeare enlightens his audience through the discourse of folly. It is primarily through this discourse that he frees his audience from their enthralment to conventional ideas and established modes of reasoning. Yet the paradoxical wisdom of folly lies, first and foremost, in its sceptical refusal to trust itself, to assert either that its implications are straightforwardly true or that its ways of perceiving the world are correct. Folly, therefore, does not teach one to trust one's own understanding. It does something far more important and, ultimately, more enlightening: the paradoxical wisdom of folly teaches us to distrust our own wisdom.

Notes

1. *The Logic of Sense*, ed. by Constantin V. Boundas, trans. by Mark Lester and Charles Stivale (London: Bloomsbury, 2013 [1969]), p. 3.
2. Philip Sidney, *An Apology for Poetry: or the Defence of Poetry*, ed. by R. W. Maslen (Manchester: Manchester University Press, 2002), p. 90.
3. *Thus Spoke Zarathustra*, trans. by R. J. Hollingdale (Harmondsworth: Penguin, 1961; repr. 2005), p. 228.
4. Immanuel Kant, 'An Answer to the Question: What is Enlightenment?" in Immanuel Kant, *Practical Philosophy*, trans. by Mary C. Gregor (Cambridge: Cambridge University Press, 1999), pp. 1–22 (p. 17).

Bibliography

As recommended by the *MHRA Style Guide*, frequently cited journal titles are abbreviated following the system of *The Year's Work in Modern Language Studies*.

Primary Sources

Agrippa, Heinrich Cornelius, *Henrie Cornelius Agrippa, of the Vanitie and Vncertaintie of Artes and Sciences, Englished by Ia. San. Gent* (London: Henry Wykes, [1530] 1569) (STC: 204).

Aristotle, *Generation of Animals*, trans. by A. L. Peck, LOEB Classical Library, 366 (Cambridge: Harvard University Press, 1963).

Armin, Robert, *A Shakespeare Jest Book: Robert Armin's Foole upon Foole (1600): A Critical Old Spelling Edition*, ed. by H. F. Lippincott (Salzburg: Institut für Englische Sprache und Literatur, 1973).

Bacon, Francis, *The Major Works*, ed. by Brian Vickers (Oxford: Oxford University Press, 2008).

Bate, Jonathan, and others eds., *Shakespeare and Others: Collaborative Plays*, (Basingstoke: Palgrave, 2013).

Biblia Sacra Vulgata: Holy Bible in Latin, ed. by Rodger Gryson and others, 4th rev. edn (Peabody, MA: Hendrickson, 1994).

The Bible: Authorized King James Version with Apocrypha, ed. by Robert Carroll and Stephen Prickett (Oxford: Oxford University Press, 1997).

Blake, William, *Complete Writings with Variant Readings*, ed. by Geoffrey Keynes (Oxford: Oxford University Press, 1969).

Brandt, Sebastian, *The Shyppe of Fooles*, trans. by Alexander Barclay (London: Wynky[n] de Worde, [1494] 1509) (STC: 13547).

Bright, Timothy, *A Treatise of Melancholie Containing the Causes Thereof, & Reasons of the Strange Effects It Worketh in our Minds and Bodies: With the Physicke Cure, and Spirituall Consolation for Such as Haue thereto Adioyned an Afflicted Conscience* (London: Thomas Vautrollier, 1586) (STC: 3747).

Bruce, Susan, *Three Early Modern Utopias: Utopia, The New Atlantis and The Isle of Pines* (Oxford: Oxford University Press, 1999; repr. 2008).

Bullough, Geoffrey, ed., *The Narrative and Dramatic Sources of Shakespeare*, 8 vols (London: Routledge, 1957–1975).

Burton, Robert, *The Anatomy of Melancholy and Commentary*, ed. by Thomas C. Faulkner, Nicholas K. Kiessling and Rhonda L. Blair, 5 vols (Oxford: Oxford University Press, 1989–1994).

The Byble That Is to Say All the Holy Scripture: In Whych Are Co[n]tayned the Olde and New Testamente, Truly [and] Purely Tra[n]slated into English, [and] Nowe Lately with Greate Industry [and] Dilige[n]ce Recognised, trans. by William Tyndale and others (London: S. Mierdman, 1549) (STC: 2077).

Castiglione, Baldesar, *The Book of the Courtier*, trans. by George Bull (Harmondsworth: Penguin, 2004).

Chaucer, Geoffrey, *The Riverside Chaucer*, ed. by Larry D. Benson and others (Oxford: Oxford University Press, 1987).

Cornwallis, William, *The Essays by Sir William Cornwallis the Younger*, ed. by D.C. Allen (Baltimore, MD: Johns Hopkins University Press, 1946).

Cusanus, *The Idiot in Four Books. The First and Second of Wisdome. The Third of the Minde. The Fourth of Statick Experiments, or Experiments of the Ballance. By the Famous and Learned C. Cusanus*, trans. by John Everard (London: William Leak, 1650).

Cusanus, *Of Learned Ignorance*, trans. by Germain Heron (Eugene, OR: Wipf & Stock, 2007; repr, Yale University Press, 1954).

Donne, John, *The Complete English Poems of John Donne*, ed. by A.J. Smith (Harmondsworth: Penguin, 1976).

Donne, John, *The Sermons of John Donne*, ed. by George R. Porter and Evelyn M. Simpson, 10 vols (Berkeley: University of California Press, 1953–1962).

Earle, Richard, *Microcosmography: or A Piece of the World Discovered in Essays and Characters*, ed. by Harold Osborne (London: University Tutorial Press, [n. d]).

Erasmus, *The Collected Works of Erasmus*, 86 vols (Toronto: University of Toronto Press, 1974–).

Erasmus, *Here Folowith a Scorneful Image or Monstrus Shape of a Maruelous Stra[n]ge Fygure Called, Sileni Alcibiadis*, trans. by anon (London: John Gough, 1543).

Erasmus, Opera Omnia Desiderii Erasmi, ed. by various, 9 vols (Amsterdam: E.J. Brill/London: Elsevier, 1964–2005).

Erasmus, The Praise of Folie, trans. by Sir Thomas Chaloner, ed. by Clarence H. Miller, Early English Text Society, 257 (London: Oxford University Press, 1965).

Erasmus, The Praise of Folly with Curious Cuts by Hans Holbein and an Epistle Dedication to Sir Thomas More (London: Reeves and Turner, 1876).

Estienne, Charles, *The Defence of Contraries Paradoxes against Common Opinion, Debated in Forme of Declamations in Place of Publike Censure: only to exercise Yong Wittes in Difficult Matters. Wherein Is No Offence to Gods Honour, the Estate of Princes, or Priuate Mens Honest Actions: but Pleasant Recreation to Beguile the Iniquity of Time. Translated out of French by A.M. one of the Messengers of her Maiesties Chamber*, trans. by Anthony Munday (London: John Windet, 1593) (STC: 6467).

Garzoni, Tomaso, *The Hospitall of Incurable Fooles: Erected in English, as Neer the First Italian Modell and Platforme, as the Vnskilfull Hand of an Ignorant architect Could Deuise*, Ipazzi, é li Prudenti, Fanno Giustissima Bilancia, trans. by anon (London: Edmund Bollifant, 1600) (STC: 11634).

Happé, Peter, ed. *English Mystery Plays: A Selection* (Harmondsworth: Penguin, 1975; repr. 1985).

Hodgson, Phyllis, *The Cloud of Unknowing and Related Treatises* (Exeter: Catholic Records Press, 1982).

Joubert, Laurent, *Treatise on Laughter*, trans. by Gregory David De Rocher (Tuscaloosa, AL: University of Alabama Press, 1980).

Lindow, Wolfgang, ed., *Ein kurtzweilig Lesen von Dil Ulenspiegel* (Stuttgart: Reclam, 2001).

Lucian, 'How to Write History', in *The Works of Lucian of Samosata*, trans. by H. W. and F. G. Fowler, 4 vols (Oxford: Clarendon Press, 1905), II, pp. 110–137.

Lucretius, *De rerum natura*, trans. by W. H. D. Rouse, rev. by Martin Ferguson Smith, LOEB Classical Library, 181 (Cambridge, MA: Harvard University Press, 1924; rev. edn. 1975).

Machiavelli, Niccolò, *The Prince*, ed. and trans. by Peter Bondanella and Mark Musa (Oxford: Oxford University Press, 1984).

Mann, Thomas, 'The Joker', in *Death in Venice and Other Stories*, ed. and trans. by David Luke (London: Vintage, 1998), pp. 29–61.

Marlowe, Christopher, *The Complete Plays*, ed. by Frank Romany and Robert Lindsey (Harmondsworth: Penguin, 2003).

Middleton, Thomas, *Five Plays*, ed. by Brian Loughrey and Neil Taylor (Harmondsworth: Penguin, 1988).

Mirandola, Giovanni Pico della, *On the Dignity of Man, On Being and the One and Heptaplus*, trans. by Charles Glenn Wallis et al. (Indianapolis: Hackette, 1998).

Montaigne, Michel de, *The Essays of Montaigne*, trans. by Donald A. Fame (London: Everyman, 2003).

Montaigne, Michel de, *Essays Written in French by Michael Lord of Montaigne, Knight of the Order of S. Michael, Gentleman of the French Kings Chamber: Done into English, According to the Last French Edition, by Iohn Florio Reader of the Italian Tongue Vnto the Soueraigne Maiestie of Anna, Queene of England, Scotland, France and Ireland, &c. And One of the Gentlemen of Hir Royall Priuie Chamber*, trans. by John Florio (London: Melch. Bradwood, 1613) (STC: 18042).

More, Thomas, *The Complete Works of St. Thomas More*, trans. and ed. by various, 15 vols (London: Yale University Press, 1976–1997).

More, Thomas, *The Latin Epigrams of Thomas More*, ed. and trans. by Leicester Bradner and Charles Arthur Lynch (Chicago: University of Chicago Press, 1953).

More, Thomas, *Utopia* ed. and trans. by Paul Turner (Harmondsworth: Penguin, 1961, repr. 1986).

More, Thomas, *Utopia: A Revised Translation, Backgrounds, Criticism*, ed. and trans. by Robert M. Adams (New York: Norton, 1992).

More, Thomas, *Utopia and the Sileni Alcibiades*, ed. and trans. by David Wootton (London: Hachette, 1999).

Müller, Heiner, 'Die Hamletmaschine', in *Heiner Müller: Werke 4*, ed. by Frank Hörnigk and others (Frankfurt: Suhrkamp, 2001), pp. 181–89.

Muller, Heiner, *Hamlet Machine and Other Texts for the Stage*, ed. and trans. by Carl Webber (New York: Performing Arts Journal Publications, 1984).

Munday, Anthony, [?] *A Second and Third Blast of Retrait from Plaies and Theaters the One Whereof Was Sounded by a Reuerend Byshop Dead Long Since; the Other by a Worshipful and Zealous Gentleman Now Aliue: One Showing the Filthines of Plaies in Times Past; the Other the Abhomination of Theaters in the Time Present: both Expresly Prouing that that Common-weale Is Nigh vnto the Cursse of God, wherein either Plaiers Be Made of, or Theaters Maintained. Set forth by Anglo-phile Eutheo* (London: Denham, 1580) (STC: 352:10).

Nashe, Thomas, *Nashe's Lenten Stuff, Containing the Description and First Procreation and Increase of the Town of Great Yarmouth in Norfolk, With a New Play Never Played before, of the Praise of the Red Herring* (London: Valentine Simmes, 1599) (STC: 18370).

Ovid, *Metamorphoses*, ed. by Madeleine Forey, trans. by Arthur Golding (Harmondsworth: Penguin, 2002 [1567]).

Puttenham, George, *The Arte of English Poesie*, ed. Gladys Doidge Willcock and Alice Walker (Cambridge: Cambridge University Press, 1935).

Prynne, William, *Histrio-mastix: The Players Scourge, or, Actors Tragaedie, Divided into Two Parts. Wherein It Is Largely Evidenced, by Divers Arguments, by the Concurring Authorities and Resolutions of Sundry Texts of Scripture ... That Popular Stage-Playes ... are Sinfull, Heathenish, Lewde, Ungodly Spectacles, and Most Pernicious Corruptions; Condemned in all Ages, as Intolerable Mischiefes to Churches, to Republickes, to the Manners, Mindes, and Soules of Men. And That the Profession of Play-poets, of Stage-players; Together with the Penning, Acting, and Frequenting of Stage-playes, are Unlawfull, Infamous and Misbeseeming Christians. All Pretences to the Contrary are Here Likewise fully Answered; and the Unlawfulnes of Acting, of Beholding Academicall Enterludes, Briefly Discussed; besides Sundry other Particulars Concerning Dancing, Dicing, Health-drinking, &c. of which the Table Will Informe You* (London: E.A. and W.I., 1633) (STC: 1285:15).

Rabelais, François, *Gargantua and Pantagruel*, trans. by Sir Thomas Urquhart and Pierre Le Motteux (London: Everyman, 1994).

Shakespeare, William, *Mr William Shakespeare's Comedies, Histories and Tragedies*, ed. by Helge Kökeritz (London: Oxford University Press, 1955).

Shakespeare, William, *Hamlet*, ed. by Ann Thompson and Neil Taylor, The Arden Shakespeare, third series (Walton-upon-Thames: Arden, 2006).

Shakespeare, William, *King Lear*, ed. by R. A. Foakes, The Arden Shakespeare, third series (Walton-upon-Thames: Arden, 1997).

Shakespeare, William, *Othello*, ed. by Michael Neill (Oxford: Oxford University Press, 2006).

Shakespeare, William, *Shakespeare's Plays in Quarto: A Facsimile Edition from the Henry E. Huntington Library*, ed. by Michael B. Allen and Kenneth Muir (Berkeley, CA: University of California Press, 1981).

Shakespeare, William, *The Norton Shakespeare*, ed. by Stephen Greenblatt and others (New York: Norton, 1997).

Shakespeare, William, and John Fletcher, *Double Falsehood or the Distressed Lovers*, ed. by Brean Hammond, The Arden Shakespeare, third series (London: Methuen, 2010).

Sidney, Philip, *An Apology for Poetry: or the Defence of Poesy*, ed. by R. W. Maslen (Manchester: Manchester University Press, 2002).

Spevack, Marvin, ed., *The Harvard Concordance to Shakespeare* (Hildesheim: Georg Olms, 1973).

Sterne, Thomas, *Tristram Shandy*, ed. by Howard Anderson (New York: Norton, 1980).

Stubbs, Phillip, *The Anatomie of Abuses Contayning a Discouerie, or Briefe Summarie of such Notable Vices and Imperfections, as Now Raigne in Many Christian Countreyes of the Worlde: but (Especiallie) in a Verie Famous Ilande Called Ailgna: Together, with Most Fearefull Examples of Gods Iudgementes,*

Executed Vpon the Wicked for the Same, aswell in Ailgna of Late, as in Other Places, Elsewhere. Verie Godly, to be Read of all True Christians, Euerie Here: but Most Needefull, to be Regarded in Englande. Made Dialogue-wise, by Phillip Stubbes. Seene and allowed, according to order (London: John Kingston, 1583) (STC: 23376).

Wagner, William, *A Very Merry and Pithy Comedy Called: The Longer Thou Livest The More Foole Thou Art and Enough is as Good as a Feast*, ed. by Mark Benbow (Lincoln: University of Nebraska Press, 1967).

Wright, Thomas, *Passions of the Minde in Generall* (London: Valintine Simmes, 1601) (STC: 26039).

Secondary Sources

Adorno, Theodor W., *Aesthetic Theory*, ed. by Gretel Adorno and Rolf Tiedemann, trans. by Robert Hullot-Kentor (London: Continum, 2004; repr. 2012).

Adorno, Theodor W., 'The Essay as Form', trans. by Bob Hullot-Kentor, *New German Critique*, 32 (1984), 151–171.

Adorno, Theodor W., *Gesammelte Schriften*, ed. by Rolf Tiedemann, 20 Vols (Frankfurt: Suhrkamp, 2003).

Adorno, Theodor W., *History and Freedom: Lectures 1964–5* ed. by Rolf Tiedemann, trans. by Rodney Livingstone (Maldon: Polity, 2008).

Adorno, Theodor W., *Lectures on Negative Dialectics*, ed. by Rolf Tiedemann, trans. by Rodney Livingstone (Cambridge: Polity, 2008).

Adorno, Theodor W., *Minima Moralia: Reflections on a Damaged Life*, trans. by Edmund Jephcott (London: Verso, 2005).

Adorno, Theodor W., *Negative Dialectics*, trans. by E. B. Ashton (London: Continuum, 1973; repr. 2007).

Adorno, Theodor W., *Notes to Literature*, ed. by Rolf Tiedemann, trans. by Shierry Weber Nicholson, 2 vols (Chichester: Columbia University Press, 1991).

Adorno, Theodor W., *Problems of Moral Philosophy*, ed. by Thomas Schroder, trans. by Rodney Livingstone (Cambridge: Polity, 2000).

Aers, David, 'A Whisper in the Ear of Early Modernists; or, Reflections on Literary Critics Writing "The History of the Subject"', in *Culture and History 1300–1600: Essays on English Communities, Identities and Writing*, ed. by David Aers (London: Harvester, 1992), pp. 184–204.

Anderson, Thomas, 'Class, Class Consciousness and Specters of Marx in Shakespeare's History Plays', *Literature Compass*, 1 (2004), 1–12.

Arab, Rona, 'Ruthless Power and Ambivalent Glory: The Rebel-Labourer in *2 Henry VI*', *Journal for Early Modern Cultural Studies*, 5 (2005), 5–36.

Auerbach, Erich, *Mimesis: The Representation of Reality in Western Literature*, trans. by Willard R. Task (Princeton, NJ: Princeton University Press, 1953; repr. 2003).

Augustijn, Cornelis, *Erasmus: His Life, Work and Influence*, trans. by J. C. Grayson (Toronto: University of Toronto Press, 1991).

Badiou, Alain, *Manifesto for Philosophy*, trans. by Norman Madrasz (New York: State University of New York, 1992).

Badiou, Alain, *Saint Paul: The Foundation of Universalism*, trans. by Ray Brassier (Stanford: Stanford University Press, 2003 [1997]).

Bakhtin, Mikhail, *The Dialogic Imagination: Four Essays*, ed. by Michael Holquist trans. by Caryl Emerson and Michael Holquist (Austin, TX: University of Texas Press, 1981).

Bakhtin, Mikhail, *Rabelais and His World*, trans. by Helene Iswolsky (Bloomington, IA: Indiana University Press, 1984).

Baldo, Jonathon, *Memory in Shakespeare's Histories: Stages of Forgetting in Early Modern England* (London: Routledge, 2012).

Baldo, Jonathon, 'The Historical Sublime in Shakespeare's *Richard II*' in *Forgetting Faith? Confessional Negotiations in Early Modern Europe*, ed. by Isabel Karremann, Cornel Zwierlein and Inga Mai Groote (Berlin: De Gruyter, 2012), pp. 81–98.

Baldwin, T. M., *William Shakespeare's Small Latine & Less Greke*, 2 vols (Urbana: University of Illinois Press, 1944).

Bainton, Roland, *Erasmus of Christendom* (London: Collins, 1969).

Barber, C. L., *Shakespeare's Festive Comedy: A Study of Dramatic Form and Its Relation to Social Custom* (Princeton, NJ: Princeton University Press, 1959; repr. 1990).

Barker, David, 'Topical Utopias: Radicalizing Humanism in Sixteenth-Century England', *SEL*, 36 (1996), 1–30.

Barnes, Hazel E., 'Flaubert and Sartre on Madness in *King Lear*', *Philosophy and Literature*, 10 (1986), 211–221.

Barton, Anne, 'Leontes and the Spider', in *Shakespeare: The Last Plays*, ed. by Kiernan Ryan (Basingstoke: Routledge, 1999), pp. 22–42.

Basu, Anupam, 'Identity, Performance, and Performed Identities: Folly and Madness in *King Lear*', *Journal of Drama Studies*, 5 (2011), 35–48.

Bate, Jonathan, 'Shakespeare's Foolosophy', in *Shakespeare Performed: Essays in Honor of R. A. Foakes*, ed. by Grace Ioppolo (Newark: University of Delaware Press, 2000), pp. 17–33.

Bates, Catherine, *Play in a Godless World: The Theory and Practice of Play in Shakespeare, Nietzsche and Freud* (London: Open Gate Press, 1999).

Bath, Michael, 'Weeping Stags and Melancholy Lovers: The Iconography of *As You Like It*, II, I', *Emblematica*, 1 (1986), 13–42.

Battenhouse, Roy, *Christian Irony in Shakespeare's Histories*, ed. by Peter Milward, 2 vols, Renaissance Monographs, 37–38 (Tokyo: Renaissance Institute Sophia University, 2009).

Battenhouse, Roy, 'Falstaff as Parodist and Perhaps Holy Fool', *PMLA*, 90 (1975), 32–52.

Battenhouse, Roy, '*Henry V* in the Light of Erasmus', *ShakS*, 17 (1985), 77–88.

Baumann, Uwe, ed., *William Shakespeare: Historien und Tragödien: Neue Wege der Forschung* (Darmstadt: Wissenschaftliche Buchgesellschaft, 2007).

Bell, Robert H., *Jocoserious Joyce: The Fate of Folly in Ulysses* (Ithaca, NY: Cornell University Press, 1991).

Bell, Robert H., *Shakespeare's Great Stage of Fools* (Basingstoke: Palgrave, 2011).

Belsey, Catherine, 'Shakespeare's Sad Tale for Winter: *Hamlet* and the Tradition of Fireside Ghost Stories', *SQ*, 61 (2010), 1–27.

Benjamin, Walter, *Illuminations*, trans. by Harry Zohn (New York: Schocken Books, 1969).

Benjamin, Walter, *The Origins of German Tragic Drama*, trans. by John Osborne (London: Verso, 1998; repr. 2009).

Bennett, Robert B., *Romance and Reformation: The Erasmian Spirit of Shakespeare's Measure for Measure* (London: Associated University Press, 2000).
Berger, Harry, Jr., 'The Prince's Dog: Falstaff and the Perils of Speech-Prefixity', *SQ*, 49 (1998), 40–73.
Bergson, Henri, *Laughter: An Essay on the Meaning of the Comic*, trans. by Cloudesley Breton and Fred Rothwell (Rockville, MA: Manor, 2008).
Bertram, Benjamin, *The Time Is out of Joint: Skepticism in Shakespeare's England* (Newark: University of Delaware Press, 2004).
Bezio, Kirstin, 'Politics and Play: The National Stage and the Player King in Shakespeare's *Henry V* and *Macbeth*', *Quidditas*, 31 (2010), 11–21.
Bietenholz, Peter, G., *Encounters with a Radical Erasmus: Erasmus' Work as a Source of Radical Thought in Early Modern Europe* (Buffalo: University of Toronto Press, 2009).
Billington, Sandra, *Mock Kings in Medieval Society and Renaissance Drama* (Oxford: Oxford University Press, 1991).
Birkinshaw, Catharine, "Past the wit of man': *A Midsummer Night's Dream's* Debt to *Praise of Folly*', *Shakespeare in Southern Africa*, 5 (1992), 43–58.
Bishop, T. G., *Shakespeare and the Theatre of Wonder* (Cambridge: Cambridge University Press, 1996).
Bloch, Ernst, *Das Prinzip Hoffnung*, 3 vols, Ernst Bloch Werkausgabe, 3 (Frankfurt: Suhrkamp, 1959; repr, 1985).
Bloch, Ernst, *Thomas Münzer als Theologe der Revolution*, Ernst Bloch Werkausgabe, 2 (Frankfurt: Suhrkamp, 1961 [1921]).
Bowie, Andrew, *Adorno and the Ends of Philosophy* (Cambridge: Polity, 2013).
Bowie, Andrew, *From Romanticism to Critical Theory: The Philosophy of German Literary Theory* (London: Routledge, 1997).
Bradley, A. C., *Shakespearean Tragedy*, 2nd edn (London: Macmillian, 1919 [1904]).
Bradshaw, Brendan, 'More on Utopia', *The Historical Journal*, 24 (1981), 1–27.
Bristol, Michael D., *Carnival and Theater: Plebeian Culture and the Structure of Authority in Renaissance England* (New York: Methuen, 1985).
Bristol, Michael D., 'Charivari and the Comedy of Abjection in *Othello*', in *True Rites and Maimed Rites: Ritual and Anti-Ritual in Shakespeare and his Age*, ed. byLinda Woodbridge and Edward Berry (Urbana: University of Illinois Press, 1992), pp. 207–224.
Bristol, Michael D., 'In Search of the Bear: Spatiotemporal Form and the Heterogeneity of Economies in *The Winter's Tale*', *SQ*, 42 (1991), 145–67.
Bristol, Michael D., 'Macbeth the Philosopher: Rethinking Context', *NLH*, 42 (2011), 641–662.
Bromwich, David, ed., *Romantic Critical Essays* (Cambridge: Cambridge University Press, 1987).
Budra, Paul, *A Mirror for Magistrates and the de Casibus Tradition* (Toronto and Buffalo: University of Toronto Press, 2000).
Bulger, Thomas, 'The Utopic Structure of the *Tempest*', *Utopian Studies*, 5 (1994), 38–47.
Bulman, Lois Helen, 'Concepts of Folly in English Renaissance Literature with Particular Reference to Shakespeare and Jonson' (unpublished doctoral thesis, University of St Andrews, 1990).
Calder, Ruth, 'From Grotesque to Silenus: Register and Satirical Self-Depiction in the *Essais* of Montaigne' (unpublished doctoral thesis, Royal Holloway, University of London, 1993).

Calderwood, James, *Macbeth and Tragic Action* (New York: University of Massachusetts Press, 1986).
Campion, Edmund J., *Montaigne, Rabelais and Marot as Readers of Erasmus* (Lewiston, NY: Edwin Mellen, 1995).
Cassirer, Ernst, *The Individual and the Cosmos in Renaissance Philosophy*, trans. by Mario Domandi (Philadelphia: University of Pennsylvania Press, 1972).
Cave, Terence, *How to Read Montaigne* (London: Grata, 2007).
Cave, Terence, *The Cornucopian Text: Problems of Writing in the French Renaissance* (Oxford: Oxford University Press, 1979; repr. 2002).
Cavell, Stanley, *Disowning Knowledge in Six Plays of Shakespeare* (Cambridge: Cambridge University Press, 1987).
Chakravarti, Paromita, "I have none other but a woman's reason': Folly, Femininity, and Sexuality in Renaissance Discourses and Shakespeare's Plays', *ShY*, 8 (2008), 136–161.
Chakravorty, Jagannath, 'King Lear's "Choice": An Existentialist Approach', *Poetica*, 4 (1976), 97–110.
Chesterton, G. K., *On Lying in Bed and Other Essays*, ed. by Alberto Manguel (Calgary: Bayeux Arts, 2000).
Christian, Lynda, 'The Metamorphosis of Erasmus' Folly', *Journal of the History of Ideas*, 32 (1971), 289–294.
Christian, Lynda, *Theatrum Mundi: The History of an Idea* (New York: Garland, 1987).
Claeys, Gregory, ed., *The Cambridge Companion to Utopian Literature* (Cambridge: Cambridge University Press, 2010).
Cockett, Peter, 'The Jests of Lean Leonard and the Touchstones of Robert Armin and David Tennant', *NTQ*, 22 (2006), 141–154.
Coetzee, J. M., 'Erasmus: Madness and Rivalry', in *Giving Offence: Essays on Censorship* (Chicago: University of Chicago Press, 1996), pp. 83–103.
Colie, R. L., *Paradoxia Epidemica: The Renaissance Tradition of Paradox* (Princeton: Princeton University Press, 1966).
Cook, Debora, 'Madness and the Cogito: Derrida's Critique of *Folie et déraison*', *Journal of the British Society for Phenomenology*, 21 (1990), 164–174.
Corti, Claudia, ed., *Silenos: Erasmus in Elizabethan Literature*, Studi di Letterature Moderne e Comparate, 1 (Pisa: Pancini, 1998).
Critchley, Simon, *On Humour* (Abingdon: Routledge, 2002).
Cutrofello, Andrew, 'It Takes a Village Idiot: And Other Lessons Cynthia Willett Teaches us', *The Journal of Speculative Philosophy*, 24 (2010), 85–95.
Daalder, Joost, 'Perspectives of Madness in *Twelfth Night*', *ES*, 78 (1997), 105–110.
Daphinoff, Dimiter, 'Shakespeares Narren', in *Der Narr: Beiträge zu einem Interdisziplinären Gespräch* (Freiburg: Universitätsverlag, 1991), pp. 57–71.
Dean, Paul, "Nothing that is so, is so': *Twelfth Night* and Transubstantiation', *Literature & Theology*, 17 (2003), 281–297.
Deleuze, Gilles, *The Logic of Sense*, ed. by Constanntin V. Boundas, trans. by Mark Lester and Charles Stivale (London: Bloomsbury, 2013 [1969]).
Derrida, Jacques, *Acts of Literature*, ed. by Derek Atteridge (London: Routledge, 1992).
Derrida, Jacques, *Specters of Marx: The State of Debt, The Work of Mourning and the New International*, trans. by Peggy Kamuf (Routledge: London, 1994).
Descartes, René, *Meditations, Objections, and Replies*, trans. and ed. by Roger Ariew and Donald Cress (Indianapolis, IA: Hackett, 2006).

Devereux, E. J., *Renaissance English Translations of Erasmus: A Bibliography* (Toronto: University of Toronto Press, 1983).
Dobin, Howard, *Merlin's Disciples: Prophecy, Poetry, and Power in Renaissance England* (Stanford: Stanford University Press, 1990).
Dollimore, Jonathan, *Radical Tragedy: Religion, Ideology and Power in the Drama of Shakespeare and his Contemporaries*, 2nd edn (Basingstoke: Palgrave, 2004 [1984]).
Döring, Tobias, '*Dinner for One*: Sir Toby und die kulturelle Arbeit am Vergessen', *Deutsche Shakespeare-Gesellschaft Jahrbuch*, 145 (2009), 124–140.
Drew, Anne, 'No Deposit, No Return: The Cap and Bells in *Hamlet* and *Endgame*', in *Past Crimson, Past Woe: The Shakespeare Beckett Connection*, ed. by Anne Drew (New York: Garland, 1993), pp. 79–89.
Eagleton, Terry, *William Shakespeare* (Oxford: Blackwell, 1986).
Eco, Umberto, and Marilyn Migiel, 'An Ars Oblivionalis? Forget It!', *PLMA*, 103 (1988), 254–261.
Edmunson, Mark, *Literature against Philosophy From Plato to Derrida* (Cambridge: Cambridge University Press, 1995).
Eisaman Maus, Katherine, *Being and Having in Shakespeare: Oxford Wells Shakespeare Lectures* (Oxford: Oxford University Press, 2013).
Eisenbichler, Konrad, and Wim Hüsken eds., *Carnival and the Carnivalesque: The Fool, The Reformer, The Wildman and Others in Early Modern Theatre* (Amsterdam: Rodolphi, 1999).
Elliot, T. S. *Selected Essays* (London: Faber and Faber, 1932; repr. 1999).
Ellis, David, 'Falstaff and the Problems of Comedy', *Cambridge Quarterly* 34 (2005), 95–108.
Empson, William, 'Fool in *Lear*', *SR*, 57 (1949), 177–214.
Evans, John X., 'Erasmus' Folly and Shakespeare's *King Lear*: A Study in Humanist Intertextuality', *Moreana*, 27 (1990), 3–23.
Fernie, Ewan, *The Demonic: Literature and Experience* (London: Routledge, 2013).
Fischer, Joshua, 'Digesting Falstaff: Food and Nation in *Shakespeare's Henry IV Plays*', *English Studies*, 2 (2009) <http://www.uta.edu/english/ees/pdf/fisher2.pdf>.
Fisher, Gerhard, and Bernhard Greiner, eds., *The Play within the Play: The Performance of Meta-theatre and Self-Reflection*, Internationale Forschungen zur Allegemeinen und Vergleichenden Literaturewissenschaft, 112 (Amsterdam: Rodopi, 2007).
Flögel, Karl Friedrich, *Geschichte des Grotesk-Komischen: ein Beitrag zur Geschichte der Menschheit*, ed. by Max Bauer, 2 vols (Munich: Georg Müller, 1914 [1788]).
Foakes, R. A., *Hamlet Versus Lear: Cultural Politics and Shakespeare's Art* (Cambridge: Cambridge University Press, 1993).
Foucault, Michel, *Abnormal: Lectures at the Collège de France*, ed. by Valerio Marchetti and Antonella Salomoni and trans. by Graham Burchell (London: Verso, 2003).
Foucault, Michel, *Discipline and Punish: The Birth of the Prison*, trans. by Alan Sheridan (Harmondsworth: Penguin, 1991).
Foucault, Michel, *The Government of Self and Others: Lectures at the Collège de France, 1982–3*, ed. by François Eward and Alessandro Fontana and trans. by Graham Burchell (Basingstoke: Palgrave, 2010).
Foucault, Michel, *The History of Madness*, ed. and trans., by Jean Khalfa and Jonathan Murphy (Basingstoke: Routledge, 2006).

Foucault, Michel, *The Order of Things: An Archaeology of the Human Sciences* (Basingstoke: Routledge, 2002; repr. 2012).

Foucault, Michel, *"Society Must be Defended": Lectures at the Collège de France, 1975–6*, ed. by Mauro Bertani and Alessandro Fontana, trans. by David Macey (London: Verso, 2003).

Frail, David, 'To the Point of Folly: Touchstone's Function in *As You Like It*', *MR*, 22 (1981), 695–717.

Freidrich, Hugo, *Montaigne* (Berkley: University of California Press, 1991).

Frenk, Joachim, 'Falstaff erzählen und zeigen', *Wissenschaftliches Seminar Online*, 3 (2005), 16–23 <http://<www.shakespearegesellschaft.de/publikationen/seminar?id=400>.

Freund, Elizabeth, '*Twelfth Night* and the Tyranny of Interpretation', *ELH*, 53 (1986), 471–489.

Gaedick, Walter, 'Der weise Narr in der englishchen Literatur von Erasmus bis Shakespeare' (unpublished inaugural dissertation, Friedrich Wilhelms Universität Berlin, 1928).

Garber, Marjorie, *Shakespeare's Ghost Writers: Literature as Uncanny Causality* (London: Routledge, 1987).

Garber, Marjorie, '"What's past is prologue": Temporality and Prophecy in Shakespeare's History Plays', in *Renaissance Genres: Essays on Theory, History and Interpretation*, ed. by Barbra Kiefer Lewalski, Harvard English Studies, 14 (London: Harvard University Press, 1986), pp. 301–332.

Ghose, Indira, 'Jesting with Death: Hamlet in the Graveyard', *TPr*, 24 (2010), 1003–1018.

Ghose, Indira, *Shakespeare and Laughter: A Cultural History* (Manchester: Manchester University Press, 2008).

Gibson, Andrew, *Beckett and Badiou: the Pathos of Intermittency* (Oxford: Oxford University Press, 2006).

Gil Harris, Jonathan, 'The New New Historicism's *Wunderkammer* of Objects', *European Journal of English Studies*, 4 (2000), 111–123.

Gil Harris, Jonathan, *Shakespeare and Literary Theory* (Oxford: Oxford University Press, 2010).

Ginsberg, Carlo, *Threads and Traces: True False Fictive*, trans. by Anne C. Tedeschi and John Tedeschi (Berkeley: University of California Press, 2012).

Goldsmith, Robert, *Wise Fools in Shakespeare* (Liverpool: Liverpool University Press, 1955; repr. 1977).

Gordon, Walter M., *Humanist Play and Belief: The Seriocomic Art of Desiderius Erasmus* (London: University of Toronto Press, 1990).

Grady, Hugh, 'Falstaff: Subjectivity between the Carnival and the Aesthetic', *MLR*, 96 (2001), 609–23.

Grady, Hugh, *Shakespeare and Impure Aesthetics* (Cambridge: Cambridge University Press, 2009).

Grady, Hugh ed., *Shakespeare and Modernity: Early Modern to Millennium* (London: Routledge, 2000).

Grady, Hugh, *Shakespeare, Machiavelli and Montaigne: Power and Subjectivity from* Richard III *to* Hamlet (Oxford: Oxford University Press, 2002).

Grassi, Ernesto, and Marisella Lorch, *Folly and Insanity in Renaissance Literature* (New York: Centre for Medieval and Early Renaissance Studies, 1986).

Grassi, Ernesto, and Marisella Lorch, *Rhetoric as Philosophy: The Humanist Tradition*, trans. by John Michael Krois and Azizeh Azodi (London: Pennsylvania State University Press, 1980).

Graves, Michael, 'Hamlet as a Fool', *HamS*, 4 (1982), 72–88.

De Grazia, Margreta, *Hamlet without Hamlet* (Cambridge: Cambridge University Press, 2007).

Greenblatt, Stephen, *Renaissance Self-Fashioning: From More to Shakespeare* (Chicago: University of Chicago Press, 1980; repr. 2005).

Greenblatt, Stephen, *Shakespeare's Freedom* (London: Chicago University Press, 2010).

Greenblatt, Stephen, *The Swerve: How the Renaissance Began* (London: Bodley Head, 2011).

Gurr, Andrew, '*Henry V* and the Bee's Commonwealth', *SS*, 30 (1977), 61–72.

Haarberg, Jon, *Parody and the Praise of Folly*, Acta Humaniora, 42 (Cambridge, MA: Scandinavian University Press, 1998).

Habermas, Jürgen, 'The Entwinement of Myth and Enlightenment: Re-reading *The Dialectic of Enlightenment*', *NGC*, 24 (2001), 13–30.

Hall, Sam Gilchrist, '"Civil Monsters": The Enlightened Dialectics of *Othello*', *The Postgraduate Journal of Aesthetics*, 9 (2012), 15–28.

Happé, Peter, "All mine own folly': The Function of Folly in *The Winter's Tale*', *Théâtre Tudor*, 10 (2011), 217–38.

Hardin, Richard F., *Civil Idolatry: Desacralizing and Monarchy in Spenser, Shakespeare and Milton* (London and Toronto: Associated University Presses, 1992).

Harris, Max, *Sacred Folly: A New History of the Feast of Fools* (Ithaca: Cornell University Press, 2011).

Hartle, Anne, *Michel de Montaigne: Accidental Philosopher* (Cambridge: Cambridge University Press, 2003).

Hassel, Chris, *Faith and Folly in Shakespeare's Romantic Comedies* (Athens, GA: University of Georgia Press, 1980; repr. 2000).

Hassel, Chris, "No Boasting like a Fool': *Macbeth* and Herod', *SP*, 98 (2001), 205–224.

Hawkes, David, *Idols of the Marketplace: Idolatry and Commodity Fetishism in English Literature, 1580–1680* (New York: Palgrave, 2001).

Hedlam-Wells, Robin, *Shakespeare's Humanism* (Cambridge: Cambridge University Press, 2005).

Hendrick, Don, 'Advantage, Affect, History, *Henry V*', *PLMA*, 118 (2003), 470–487.

Hendrick, Don, 'Male Surplus Value', *Renaissance Drama*, 31 (2002), 85–124.

Hillman, David, and Carla Mazzio, eds., *The Body in Parts: Fantasies of Corporeality in Early Modern Europe* (London: Routledge, 1997).

Holderness, Graham, *Shakespeare Recycled: The Making of Historical Drama* (Hemmel Hempstead: Harvester, 1992).

Honneth, Axel, *Reification: A New Look at an Old Idea with Judith Butler, Raymond Geuss and Jonathan Lear*, ed. by Martin Jay (Oxford: Oxford University Press, 2008).

Hopkins, Jasper, 'Nicholas of Cusa (1401–1464): First Modern Philosopher?', *Midwest Studies in Philosophy*, 26 (2002),12–29.

Horkheimer, Max, *Critical Theory: Selected Essays*, trans. by M. J. O'Connell and others (London: Continuum, 2002).

Horkheimer, Max, and Theodor W. Adorno, *Dialectic of Enlightenment: Philosophical Fragments*, ed. by Gunzelin Schmid Noerr, trans. by Edmund Jephcott (Stanford, CA: Stanford University Press, 2002).

Hornback, Robert, 'Blackfaced Fools, Black-Headed Birds, Fool Synonyms, and Shakespearean Allusions to Renaissance Blackface Folly', *NQ*, 55 (2008), 215–219.

Hornback, Robert, 'Black Shakespeareans vs. Minstrel Burlesques: 'Proper' English, Racist Blackface Dialect, and the Contest for Representing Blackness, 1821–1844', *ShakS*, 38 (2010), 125–160.

Hornback, Robert, 'Emblems of Folly in the First *Othello*: Renaissance Blackface, Moor's Coat, and Muckender', *CompD*, 35 (2001–2), 69–99.

Hornback, Robert, *The English Clown Tradition from the Middle Ages to Shakespeare*, Studies in Renaissance Literature, 26 (Cambridge: Brewer, 2009).

Hornback, Robert, 'Extravagant and Wheeling Strangers: Early Blackface Dancing Fools, Racial Representation, and the Limits of Identification', *Exemplaria*, 20 (2008), 197–223.

Hornback, Robert, 'Weimann and Shakespeare Among the Neoclassicals', *ShY* (2010), 183–204.

Huhn, Tom, ed., *The Cambridge Companion to Adorno* (Cambridge: Cambridge University Press, 2004).

Huizinga, Johannes, *Homo Lundens: A Study of the Play Element in Culture*, trans. by R. F. C. Hull (London: Routledge, 1949).

Hume, David, *A Treatise of Human Nature*, ed. by Ernest C. Mossner (Harmondsworth: Penguin, 1985).

Hunt, Maurice, *Shakespeare's Speculative Art* (Basingstoke: Palgrave, 2011).

Huston Wood, David, "He Something Seems Unsettled': Melancholy, Jealousy, and Subjective Temporality in *The Winter's Tale*', *Renaissance Drama*, 31 (2002), 185–213.

Iser, Wolfgang, *Prospecting: From Reader Response to Literary Anthropology* (Baltimore, MD: Johns Hopkins University Press, 1989).

Jackson, Ken, *Separate Theaters: Bethlem "Bedlam" Hospital and the Shakespearean Stage* (Newark: University of Delaware Press, 2005).

Jameson, Fredric, *Late Marxism: Adorno, or, the Persistence of the Dialectic* (London: Verso, 1990).

Jarvis, Simon, *Adorno: A Critical Introduction* (Cambridge: Blackwell, 1998).

Jenson, Pheobe, *Religion and Revelry in Shakespeare's Festive World* (Cambridge: Cambridge University Press, 2008; repr, 2010).

Johnson, Samuel, *Selected Writings*, ed. by Peter Martin (Cambridge: Harvard University Press, 2009).

Joughin, John, ed., *Philosophical Shakespeares*, Accents on Shakespeare (London: Routledge, 2000).

Kahan, Jeffrey, *King Lear: New Critical Essays*, Shakespeare Criticism, 33 (London: Routledge, 2008).

Kaiser, Walter, *Praisers of Folly: Erasmus, Rabelais, Shakespeare* (London: Victor Gollancz, 1964).

Kamps, Ivo, *Historiography and Ideology in Stuart Drama* (Cambridge: Cambridge University Press, 1996).

Kant, Immanuel, 'An Answer to the Question: "What is Enlightenment?"', in Immanuel Kant, *Practical Philosophy*, trans. by Mary C. Gregor (Cambridge: Cambridge University Press, 1999), pp. 1–22.

Kant, Immanuel, *Critique of Pure Reason*, ed. and trans., by Marcus Weigelt and Max Müller (Harmondsworth: Penguin, 2007).

Kazuo, Aoki, '*The Praise of Folly* and Shakespeare's Early and Middle Comedies', *ShStud*, 18 (1980), 1–27.

Kearney, Richard, *Strangers, Gods and Monsters* (London: Routledge, 2003).

Kendrick, Christopher, *Utopia, Carnival, and Commonwealth in Renaissance England* (Toronto: University of Toronto Press, 2004).

Kermode, Frank, *Shakespeare's Language* (Harmondsworth: Penguin, 2000).

Kerrigan, John, 'Oaths, Threats and *Henry V*', *RES*, 261 (2011), 551–571.

Kerrigan, John, 'Shakespeare, Oath's and Vows', *Proceedings From the British Academy 2009*, 167 (2010), 61–89.

Klene, Jean, 'The Fool, Folly, and the World Upside-Down in *Measure for Measure*', *Upstart Crow*, 3 (1980), 1–10.

Klibansky, Raymond, Erwin Panofsky, and Fritz Saxal, *Saturn and Melancholy: Studies in the History of Natural Philosophy, Religion, and Art* (London: Thomas Nelson, 1964).

Klooss, Wolfgang, 'Feasting with Falstaff: Luxus und Verschwendung im kulinarischen Diskurs von Shakespeares England' in *Texting Culture—Culturing Texts: Essays in Honour of Horst Breuer*, ed. by Anja Müller (Trier: Wissenschaftlicher Verlag, 2008), pp. 71–91.

Knapp, James A., *Image Ethics in Shakespeare and Spencer* (Basingstoke: Palgrave, 2011).

Knöll, Stefanie, ed., *Narren—Masken—Karneval: Meisterwerke von Dürer bis Kubin aus der Düsseldorfer Graphiksammlung Mensch und Tod* (Regensburg: Schnell and Steiner, 2009).

Knowles, Ronald ed., *Shakespeare and Carnival* (London: Macmillian, 1998).

Knowles, Ronald, *Shakespeare's Arguments with History* (Basingstoke: Palgrave, 2002).

Knutson, Roslyn, 'The History Play, Richard II, and Repertorial Commerce', in Jeremy Lopez, ed., *Richard II: New Critical Essays* (London: Routledge, 2012), pp. 74–94.

Kott, Jan, *The Bottom Translation: Marlowe, Shakespeare and the Carnival Tradition*, trans. by Daniela Miedzyrzecka (Evanston, IL: Northwestern University Press, 1987).

Lacan, Jacques, 'Desire and the Interpretation of Desire in *Hamlet*', *YFS*, 55 (1977), 30–51.

Lammers, Lukas, '"Eyed awry"—*Richard II* and the Shapes of History', *Shakespeare Jahrbuch*, 147 (2011), 145–154.

Langley, Eric, *Narcissism and Suicide in Shakespeare and his Contemporaries* (Oxford: Oxford University Press, 2009).

Langley, Eric, 'Postured Like a Whore?' Misreading Hermione's Statue', *RenStud*, 27 (2012), 318–340.

Laroque, François, *Shakespeare's Festive World: Elizabethan Seasonal Entertainment and the Professional Stage*, trans. by Janet Lloyd (Cambridge: Cambridge University Press, 1991 [1988]).

Levenson, Jill L., 'Shakespeare's Falstaff "The cause that wit is in other men"', *University of Toronto Quarterly*, 74 (2005), 722–28.

Levis, Frank Raymond, 'Diabolic Intellect and the Noble Hero', *Scrutiny*, 6 (1937), 259–283.

Lippincott, H. F., '*King Lear* and the Fools of Robert Armin', *SQ*, 26 (1975), 243–253.

Lott, Eric, *Love and Theft: Black-faced Minstrelsy and the American Working Class* (Oxford: Oxford University Press, 1993).

Luis-Martínez, Zenón, 'Shakespeare's Historical Drama as *Trauerspiel*: *Richard II*—and After', *ELH*, 75 (2008), 673–704.

Mack, Peter, 'Montaigne and Shakespeare: Source, Parallel or Comparison?', *Montaigne Studies*, XXXIII (2011), 151–181.

Mack, Peter, *Reading and Rhetoric in Erasmus, Montaigne and Shakespeare* (London: Bloomsbury, 2010).

Marrapodi, Michele, ed., *Shakespeare and Renaissance Literary Theories: Anglo-Italian Transactions* (Farnham: Ashgate, 2011).

Marx, Karl, *Capital: A Critique of Political Economy*, trans. by Ben Fowkes, 2 vols (Harmondsworth: Penguin, 1992).

Marx, Karl, *The Communist Manifesto*, ed. by Gareth Stedman Jones, trans. by Ben Fowkes (Harmondsworth: Penguin, 1972; repr, 2004).

McAlindon, Tom, *Shakespeare Minus 'Theory'* (Aldershot: Ashgate, 2004).

McCulloch, Andrew, '"Events Borrowed from History": the Real Life Drama of *Henry IV*', *The English Review*, 16 (2006), 2–5.

McCutcheon, Elizabeth, 'Denying the Contrary: More's use of Litotes in the *Utopia*', *Moreana*, 32 (1971), 107–122.

McLoughlin, Cathleen T., *Shakespeare, Rabelais, and the Comical Historical*, Currents in Comparative Romance Languages and Literatures, 80 (New York: Peter Lang, 2000).

Mousley, Andy, 'The New Literary Humanism: Towards a Critical Vocabulary', *TPr*, 24 (2010), 819–839.

Mousley, Andy, *Re-Humanising Shakespeare: Literary Humanism, Wisdom and Modernity* (Edinburgh: Edinburgh University Press, 2007).

Mout, M., H. Smolinsky and J. Trapman, eds., *Erasmianism: Idea and Reality* (Amsterdam: Royal Netherlands Academy of Arts and Sciences, 1997).

Muir, Kenneth, 'Shakespeare and Erasmus', *N&Q*, 10 (1956), 423–424.

Neely, Carol Thomas, *Distracted Subjects: Madness and Gender in Shakespeare and Early Modern Culture* (Ithaca, NY: Cornell University Press, 2004).

Nietzsche, Friedrich, *The Gay Science with a Prelude in Rhymes and an Appendix of Songs*, trans. by Walter Kaufmann (New York: Vintage, 1974).

Nietzsche, Friedrich, *Sämtliche Werke*, ed. by Giorgio Colli and Mazzino Montinari, Kritische Studienausgabe, 6 vols (Munich and Berlin: Deutscher Taschenbuch Verlag/de Gruyter, 1988), VI.

Nigg, Walter, *Der christliche Narr* (Zurich: Artimis, 1956).

Nuttall, A. D., *Shakespeare the Thinker* (London and New Haven: Yale University Press, 2007).

Olin, John, 'Erasmus' *Adagia* and More's *Utopia*', *Moreana*, 100 (1989), 127–136.

Oosterwijk, Sophie, "Alas, poor Yorick': Death, the fool and the *danse macabre*', in *Narren—Masken—Karneval: Meisterwerke von Dürer bis Kubin aus der Düsseldorfer Graphiksammlung Mensch und Tod*, ed. by Stefanie Knöll (Regensburg: Schnell and Steiner, 2009), pp. 20–33.

Otto, Beatrice K., *Fools Are Everywhere: The Court Jester around the World* (Chicago, IL: University of Chicago Press, 2001).

Owens, Anne, '*As You Like It*: Or, *The Anatomy of Melancholy*?', *QWERTY*, 7 (1997), 15–26.

Paster, Gail Kern, 'The Humor of It: Bodies, Fluids, and Social Discipline in Shakespearean Comedy', in *A Companion to Shakespeare's Works: The Comedies*, ed. by Richard Dutton and Jean E. Howard, 4 vols (Malden, MA: Blackwell, 2003), III, pp. 47–67.

Paster, Gail Kern, *Humoring the Body: Emotions and the Shakespearean Stage* (Chicago: The University of Chicago Press, 2004).

Patterson, Annabel, *Shakespeare and the Popular Voice* (Oxford: Blackwell, 1989).

Pfister, Manfred, 'Comic Subversion: A Bakhtinian View of the Comic in Shakespeare', *Deutsche Shakespeare Gesellschaft Jahrbuch* (1987), 27–43.

Pierce, Robert B., "I stumbled when I saw': Interpreting Gloucester's Blindness in *King Lear*', *Philosophy and Literature*, 36 (2012), 153–165.

Planic, Zdravko, 'Reading *The Merchant of Venice* Through Adorno', *Journal of Cultural and Religious Theory*, 8 (2007), 20–41.

Pollard, Warren, 'Outsiderness in Human Nature', *Psychoanalytic Quarterly*, 81 (2012), 931–953.

Poole, A. D., 'Laughter, Forgetting, and Shakespeare', in *English Comedy*, ed. by Michael Cordener, Peter Holland and John Kerrigan (Cambridge: Cambridge University Press, 1994), pp. 85–99.

Poole, A. D., and Richard Scholar, eds., *Comparative and Interdiciplinary Essays for A. D. Nuttall* (Oxford: Legenda, 2007).

Prenki, Tim, *The Fool in European Theatre: Stages of Folly* (Basingstoke: Palgrave, 2012).

Pugliatti, Paola, *Shakespeare the Historian* (Basingstoke: Palgrave, 1996).

Pyle, Sandra, *Mirth and Morality of Shakespeare's Holy Fools* (Lewiston, MA: Edward Mellen, 1998).

Rackin, Phyllis, *Stages of History: Shakespeare's English Chronicles* (Ithaca: Cornell University Press, 1990).

Rhodes, Neil, *Elizabethan Grotesque* (London: Routledge, 1980).

Robb, David, ed., *Clowns, Fools and Picaros: Popular Forms in Theatre, Fiction and Film*, Probing the Boundaries, 47 (Amsterdam: Rodopi, 2007).

Roberts, Preston Thomas, Jr., 'The Redemption of King Lear', *Renascence*, 26 (1974), 189–206.

Rose, Margaret, *Parody: Ancient, Modern and Post-Modern* (Cambridge: Cambridge University Press, 1993).

Rosencrantz, Karl, *Ästhetik des Haßlichen*, ed. by Dieter Kliche (Stuttgart: Reclam, 1990; repr. 2007 [1853]).

Rosenstein, Roy, 'Richard the Redless: Representations of Richard II from Boccaccio and Polydore to Hollingshed and Shakespeare', in *International Conference on Travels and Translations in the Sixteenth Century: Selected Papers from the Second International Conference of the Tudor Symposium*, ed. by Michael Pincombe (Aldershot: Ashgate, 2004), pp. 137–154.

Ruberry-Blanc, Pauline, 'Savage Madness Meets with Comic Folly: The Cases of Orlando and Philaster', *Théâtre Tudor*, 10 (2011), 191–202.

Rutter, David, *Shakespeare's Festive History: Feasting, Festivity, Fasting and Lent in the Second Henriad* (Aldershot: Ashgate, 2003).

Ryan, Kiernan, *Shakespeare*, 3rd edn (Basingstoke: Palgrave, 2002).

Ryan, Kiernan, *Shakespeare's Comedies* (Basingstoke: Palgrave, 2009).

Ryan, Kiernan, 'Shakespeare's Inhumanity', *ShakS*, 66 (2013), 220–231.

Ryan, Kiernan, *Shakespeare's Universality: Here's Fine Revolution* (London: Bloomsbury, 2015).
Shickman, Allen R., 'The Fool's Mirror in *King Lear*', *ELR*, 21 (1991), 75–86.
Schlegel, A. W., *Kritische Schriften und Briefe*, ed. by Edgar Lohner, 7 vols (Stuttgart: W. Kohlhammer, 1967–75), VI.
Schlegel, Friedrich, *Philosophical Fragments*, trans. by Peter Firchow (Minneapolis and London: University of Minnesota Press, 1991).
Schleiner, Winfried, *Melancholy, Genius, and Utopia in the Renaissance*, Wolfenbütteler Abhandlung zur Renaissanceforschung, 10 (Wisbaden: Otto Harrassowitz, 1991).
Schmitz, Heinz-Günter, *Das Hofnarrenwesen der frühen Neuzeit: Claus Narr von Torgau und seine Geschichten* (Münster: Lit, 2004).
Schweppenhäuser, Gerhard, 'Narrenschelte und Pathos der Vernunft. Zum Narrenmotiv bei Sebastian Brandt und Erasmus von Rotterdam', *Neophilologus*, 71 (1987), 559–574.
Schweppenhäuser, Gerhard, *Theodor W. Adorno: An Introduction*, trans. by James Rollenston (Durham, NC: Duke University Press, 2009).
Screech, M. A., *Ecstasy and the Praise of Folly* (London: Duckworth, 1980).
Screech, M. A., *Laughter at the Foot of the Cross* (London: Duckworth, 1998).
Screech, M. A., *Montaigne and Melancholy: The Wisdom of the Essays* (London: Duckworth, 1980; repr. 2000).
Screech, M. A., *Rabelais* (London: Duckworth, 1979).
Sherwood, Terry G., *The Self in Early Modern Literature: For the Common Good* (Pittsburgh: Duquesne University Press, 2007).
Somerset, J. A. B., 'Shakespeare's Great Stage of Fools, 1599–1607', in *A Mirror up to Shakespeare: Essays in Honour of G. R. Hibbard*, ed. by Jack Cooper Grey (Toronto: University of Toronto Press, 1984), pp. 68–92.
Somerset, J. A. B., 'Incongruity and Folly: Shakespeare's Jacobean Fools', *Trivium*, 20 (1985), 129–146.
Southworth, John, *Fools and Jesters at the English Court* (Stroud: Sutton, 1998).
Stallybrass, Peter, and Margretia De Gratzia, 'The Materiality of the Shakespearean Text', *SQ*, 44 (1993), 255–283.
Stenberg, Doug, "Tom's a-cold': Transformation and Redemption in *King Lear* and *The Fisher King*', *Literature/Film Quarterly*, 22 (1994), 160–169.
Stewart, Stanley, *Shakespeare and Philosophy* (Oxford: Routledge, 2010).
Stockard, Emily, E., 'Transposed to Form and Dignity: Christian Folly and the Subversion of Hierarchy in *A Midsummer Night's Dream*', *R&L*, 29 (1997), 1–20.
Strier, Richard, 'Against the Rule of Reason: Praise of Passion from Petrarch to Luther to Shakespeare to Herbert', in *Reading the Early Modern Passions: Essays in the Cultural Traditions of Emotion*, ed. by Gail Kern Paster, Katherine Rowe and Mary Floyd-Wilson (Philadelphia: University of Pennsylvania Press, 2004), pp. 23–42.
Stritmatter, Roger, and Lynne Kositsky, 'Pale as Death: The Fictionalizing Influence of Erasmus's *Naufragium* on the Renaissance Travel Narrative', in *Discovering Shakespeare: A Festschrift in Honour of Isobel Holden*, ed. by Daniel Wright (Portland, OR: The Shakespeare Authorship Research Centre, 2009), pp. 143–152.
Swain, Barbara, *Fools and Folly during the Middle Ages and the Renaissance* (New York: Columbia University Press, 1932).

Tambling, Jeremy, *Allegory and the Work of Melancholy: The Late Medieval and Shakespeare*, ed. by Alberto Martino, Internationale Forschungen zur Allgemeinen und Vergleichenden Literaturwissenschaft, 72 (Amsterdam: Rodopi, 2004).

Tiller, Kenneth J., 'The Fool as Physician in Shakespeare's Plays', in *Shakespeare's Theories of Blood, Character and Class: A Festschrift for David Shelley Berkeley*, ed. by Peter C. Rollins and Alan Smith (Bern: Peter Lang, 2001), pp. 43–60.

John Turner, *The Tragic Romances of Feudalism*, in Graham Holderness, Nick Potter and John Turner, *Shakespeare: The Play of History* (Houndsmills: Macmillan, 1987), pp. 85–150 (p. 92).

Van Dijkhuizen, Jan Frans, *Devil Theatre: Demonic Possession and Empiricism in English Renaissance Drama, 1558–1642*, Studies in Renaissance Literature 19 (Woodbridge: Brewer, 2007).

Vaught, Jennifer, C., *Carnival and Literature in Early Modern England* (Farnham: Ashgate, 2012).

Videbæk, Bente, *The Clown in Shakespeare's Theatre*, Contributions in Drama and Theatre Studies, 69 (London: Greenwood Press, 1996).

Waldron, Jennifer, 'Gaping upon Plays: Shakespeare, Gosson, and the Reformation of Vision', *Critical Matrix*, 12 (2001), 48–77.

Wai-fong, Cheang, 'Laughter, Play, and Irony: Re-reading the Comic Space in Shakespeare's Second Tetralogy', *NTU Studies in Language and Literature*, 10 (2001), 51–74.

Walker, Lewis, '*Timon of Athens* and the Morality Tradition', *ShakS*, 12 (1979), 159–177.

Wehrs, Donald, 'Moral Physiology, Ethical Prototypes, and the Denaturing of Sense in Shakespearean Tragedy', *College Literature*, 33 (2006), 76–92.

Wehrs, Donald, 'Touching Words: Embodying Ethics in Erasmus, Shakespearean Comedy, and Contemporary Theory', *MP*, 104 (2006), 1–33.

Weil, Herbert, 'Montaigne and Falstaff' *Shakespeare Newsletter*, 58 (2008), 49–70.

Weimann, Robert, *Shakespeare and the Popular Tradition in the Theatre*, trans. by Robert Schwartz (Baltimore, MD: Johns Hopkins University Press, 1979).

Wellmer, Albrecht, 'Adorno and the Difficulties of a Critical Reconstruction of the Historical Present', trans. by Frederik van Gelder, <www.amsterdam-adorno.net/T_wellmer_twa.pdf> [accessed 3 November 2011].

Welsford, Enid, *The Fool: His Social and Literary History* (London: Faber and Faber, 1935; repr. 1968).

Wells, Stanley, 'Lear in the Fool's Shadow' *TLS*, July 16, 1982; p. 764; Issue 4137.

Wells, Stanley, *Shakespeare and Love* (Oxford: Oxford University Press, 2010).

Wilcox, Helen, 'Needy Nothing Trimmed in Jollity', in *Renaissance Historicisms: Essays in Honour of Arthur F. Kinney*, ed. by James M. Dutcher and Anne Lake Prescott (Newark: University of Delaware Press, 2008), pp. 313–329.

Wiles, David, *Shakespeare's Clown: The Actor and Text in Elizabethan Playhouse* (Cambridge: Cambridge University Press, 1987).

Willeford, William, *The Fool and His Sceptre: A Study in Clowns and Jesters and Their Audience* (London: Edward Arnold, 1969).

Williams, Paul, V. A., ed., *The Fool and the Trickster* (Cambridge: Brewer, 1979).

Wilson, Richard, *Free Will: Art and Power on Shakespeare's Stage* (Manchester: Manchester University Press, 2013).

Wilson, Richard, *Secret Shakespeare: Studies in Theatre, Religion and Resistance* (Manchester: Manchester University Press, 2004).

Wilson, Richard, *Shakespeare and French Theory: King of Shadows* (London: Routledge, 2007).

Woodbridge, Linda, ed., *Money in the Age of Shakespeare: Essays in New Economic Criticism* (New York: Palgrave, 2003).

Zijderveld, Anton C., *Reality in a Looking Glass: Rationality through and Analysis of Traditional Folly* (Basingstoke: Palgrave, 1982).

Žižek, Slavoj, *The Fragile Absolute—or, why is the Christian Legacy Worth Fighting for?* (London: Verso, 2000).

Index

Printed in Dunstable, United Kingdom

74167959R00123